AI-Powered Developer

BUILD GREAT SOFTWARE
WITH CHATGPT AND COPILOT

NATHAN B. CROCKER

MANNING
SHELTER ISLAND

For online information and ordering of this and other Manning books, please visit www.manning.com. The publisher offers discounts on this book when ordered in quantity.

For more information, please contact

   Special Sales Department
   Manning Publications Co.
   20 Baldwin Road
   PO Box 761
   Shelter Island, NY 11964
   Email: orders@manning.com

 Recognizing the importance of preserving what has been written, it is Manning's policy to have the books we publish printed on acid-free paper, and we exert our best efforts to that end. Recognizing also our responsibility to conserve the resources of our planet, Manning books are printed on paper that is at least 15 percent recycled and processed without the use of elemental chlorine.

The author and publisher have made every effort to ensure that the information in this book was correct at press time. The author and publisher do not assume and hereby disclaim any liability to any party for any loss, damage, or disruption caused by errors or omissions, whether such errors or omissions result from negligence, accident, or any other cause, or from any usage of the information herein.

Manning Publications Co.
20 Baldwin Road
PO Box 761
Shelter Island, NY 11964

Development editor:	Katie Sposato Johnson
Technical editor:	Nicolai Nielsen
Review editor:	Dunja Nikitovic
Production editor:	Andy Marinkovich
Copy editor:	Tiffany Taylor
Proofreader:	Jason Everett
Technical proofreader:	Mark Thomas
Typesetter:	Tamara Švelić Sabljić
Cover designer:	Marija Tudor

ISBN 9781633437616
Printed in the United States of America

Dedicated to the memory of Catherine L. Crocker,
whose strength and love continue to guide me.
Though no longer beside us, her spirit and wisdom
remain ever-present.
Her legacy lives on in every word I write.
Gone from this world, but forever in our hearts.

contents

preface

Welcome to *AI-Powered Developer*, your gateway to exploring the symbiotic relationship between programming and artificial intelligence. This book is not just a narrative about AI and its applications in software development—it's an invitation to venture into the uncharted territory of coding powered by cutting-edge AI models like ChatGPT and GitHub Copilot. As you turn these pages, you'll embark on a journey of exploration and discovery, unearthing a new perspective on how AI can reshape and enhance the coding landscape.

The essence of this book lies in its unconventional approach. Unlike most technical literature, it doesn't provide a rigid script to follow. This is because the book deals with the application of large language models in software development, an area where outcomes can be surprisingly diverse even when the input remains the same. Think of it more like a compass guiding your way through an intriguing landscape of possibilities rather than a map delineating a predetermined route.

AI-Powered Developer encourages you to experiment, ask questions, and, most importantly, be open to unexpected results. It will ignite your curiosity, spur your creativity, and stimulate your problem-solving skills. The world of large language models like ChatGPT and Copilot offers more than just coding assistance—it provides a transformative framework that has the potential to revolutionize software development at its core.

At its heart, this book assumes the role of a mentor, a catalyst that nudges you to venture beyond the familiar boundaries of traditional coding, encouraging you to explore the intricate dance of AI and programming. It seeks to whet your appetite for the untapped potential that these generative AI models bring to the table. Through a myriad of real-world examples, hands-on exercises, and insights, you'll not only learn how to use these AI tools but also gain a deeper understanding of their functioning, their potential, and their limitations.

Yet, as with any mentorship, the rewards of this journey are proportional to the passion, curiosity, and commitment you bring. By diving deep, asking questions, and challenging assumptions, you'll gain not just technical skills but also a broader perspective on what it means to be a developer in the age of AI.

This is an exciting time in the field of software development. AI and machine learning are disrupting traditional paradigms, offering new tools and methodologies that can significantly enhance productivity, creativity, and efficiency. By integrating AI into the development process, we can tackle more complex problems, streamline workflows, and fundamentally transform the way we approach coding.

AI-Powered Developer is more than just a book—it's a doorway to this new world, a world that blends the logic of programming with the power and flexibility of AI. Whether you're a seasoned developer or an enthusiastic beginner, this book will equip you with the tools, techniques, and knowledge to make the most of these advancements and chart your own path in this evolving landscape.

Remember, every great journey begins with a single step. By choosing to read this book, you've already taken that step. Now, let's venture into the exciting world of intelligent coding together. Enjoy the journey!

acknowledgments

Embarking on the journey of writing this book was no small endeavor. It required commitment, dedication, and countless hours of meticulous labor. It was a path fraught with challenges, but every step was an enriching experience, bringing me closer to the vast and fascinating world of AI-powered coding. It's a journey I couldn't have begun, let alone completed, without the support and contributions of some extraordinary individuals.

My profound gratitude goes to my editor, Katie Sposato Johnson, who was instrumental in shaping this book. Her incisive comments, critical insights, and constructive feedback helped refine my thoughts and transform them into a coherent, engaging narrative. Her unwavering commitment and passionate involvement were invaluable to this project.

A special note of thanks to my technical editor, Nicolai Nielsen, who is lead AI Engineer at SymphonyAI, and is both a coder and content creator, creating educational AI and computer vision videos on YouTube and courses that help people while scaling his brands. Nicolai's expertise and keen eye for detail kept me on my toes, continually reminding me of how much more there is to learn in this expansive field. His inputs were not just educational but humbling, shaping my understanding and keeping me grounded.

I am deeply grateful to everyone at Manning for their relentless support throughout this journey. Their professionalism, cooperative spirit, and commitment to excellence have been an inspiration. They played a critical role in bringing this book to life, for which I am immensely thankful.

To all the reviewers: Carmelo San Giovanni, Chad Yantorno, Christopher Forbes, Dan McCreary, Dewang Mehta, Greg MacLean, Håvard Wall, Jeff Smith, Jim Matlock, Jonathan Boiser, Louis Aloia, Luke Kupka, Mariano Junge, Maxim Volgin, Maxime

Boillot, Mike Piscatello, Milorad Imbra, Peter Dickten, Philip Patterson, Pierre-Michel Ansel, Rambabu Posa, Rebecca Wagaman, Riccardo Marotti, Roy Wilsker, Stefano Priola, Thomas Jaensch, Thomas Joseph Heiman, Tiago Boldt Sousa, Tony Holdroyd, and Walter Alexander Mata López, your suggestions helped make this a better book.

My deepest gratitude is for my family—my pillars of strength. To my wife, Jenn, thank you for being my rock and for the countless hours of patience, understanding, and love you've poured into this endeavor. To my daughters, Maeve and Orla, you are my inspiration—your joy, curiosity, and boundless enthusiasm fuel my endeavors. To all my family members who supported me in myriad ways, thank you.

This book is a culmination of countless hours of effort, dedication, and teamwork. I am deeply grateful to everyone who contributed to making it a reality. Thank you all.

about this book

AI-Powered Developer is your essential guide to mastering the integration of large language models like ChatGPT and CoPilot into your software development process. This comprehensive book delivers practical advice and showcases best practices, helping you harness the power of AI to enhance your projects. From the do's and don'ts of AI implementation to real-world examples, you'll gain the insights and tools you need to elevate your development skills and stay ahead in the ever-evolving tech landscape.

Who should read this book?

Professional developers and enthusiasts alike should get value from this book. Although the book is largely aimed at experienced developers, large language models (LLMs) can be used to accelerate your learning because these tools can provide explanations, code examples, and guidance on programming concepts. Experienced developers can use these tools to improve productivity, streamline coding processes, and tackle complex coding challenges more efficiently. These tools can assist in generating code snippets, debugging, and providing insights on best practices.

How this book is organized: A roadmap

The book is divided into four main parts, followed by three practical appendices for setup assistance:

- Part 1: The Foundation
  - Chapter 1 introduces LLMs, tracing their history and providing a conceptual understanding of generative AI. It also advises on the appropriate and cautious use of these technologies.

- Chapter 2 offers a primer on starting with LLMs, comparing ChatGPT, GitHub Copilot, and CodeWhisperer and detailing the initial steps in harnessing their potential.
  - Part 2: The Input
    - Chapter 3 walks through designing software with the help of ChatGPT, using an information technology asset management (ITAM) system as a project example.
    - Chapter 4 focuses on building software with GitHub Copilot, covering foundational concepts like domain modeling, immutability, and design patterns.
    - Chapter 5 delves into managing data with GitHub Copilot and Copilot Chat, exploring real-time asset monitoring with Kafka and data analysis with Apache Spark.
  - Part 3: The Feedback
    - Chapter 6 discusses the testing, quality assessment, and explanation processes of software developed with LLMs, including bug hunting and code translation.
  - Part 4: Into the World
    - Chapter 7 covers coding infrastructure and managing deployments, from building Docker images to setting up continuous integration/continuous deployment pipelines with GitHub Actions.
    - Chapter 8 addresses secure application development using ChatGPT, including threat modeling and the application of security best practices.
    - Chapter 9 explores the concept of "GPT-ing on the go," including hosting your own LLM and democratizing access with GPT-4All.

The appendices provide straightforward guidance on setting up ChatGPT, Copilot, and CodeWhisperer, ensuring that you have the practical knowledge to begin your journey in AI-powered development.

With the exception of the last chapter, this book is meant to be read in order, as each chapter builds on the previous chapters. The last chapter can be read at any point after the first.

About the code

You can get executable snippets of code from the liveBook (online) version of this book at https://livebook.manning.com/book/ai-powered-developer. The complete code for the examples in the book is available for download from the Manning website at www.manning.com/books/ai-powered-developer and from GitHub at https://github.com/nathanbcrocker/ai_powered_developer.

It is important to note that part of the value of this book is to work through the examples using the recommended (and non-recommended) tools. An additional note related to the source code is that these tools will rarely produce the same output, even given the same input. You should not get frustrated or discouraged if your code is wildly different from the source code in the repository. The source code is provided for your edification and for enhancing your learning, should you find it useful.

To get the most from this book, you will need a recent version of Python 3 with the ability to install new packages. To run most of the infrastructure-related systems, you will need to be able to install Docker images and run Docker containers.

This book contains many examples of source code, both in numbered listings and in line with normal text. In both cases, source code is formatted in a `fixed-width font like this` to separate it from ordinary text. In many cases, the original source code has been reformatted; we've added line breaks and reworked indentation to accommodate the available page space in the book.

liveBook discussion forum

Purchase of *AI-Powered Developer* includes free access to liveBook, Manning's online reading platform. Using liveBook's exclusive discussion features, you can attach comments to the book globally or to specific sections or paragraphs. It's a snap to make notes for yourself, ask and answer technical questions, and receive help from the author and other users. To access the forum, go to https://livebook.manning.com/book/ai-powered-developer/discussion. You can also learn more about Manning's forums and the rules of conduct at https://livebook.manning.com/discussion.

Manning's commitment to our readers is to provide a venue where a meaningful dialogue between individual readers and between readers and the author can take place. It is not a commitment to any specific amount of participation on the part of the author, whose contribution to the forum remains voluntary (and unpaid). We suggest you try asking the author some challenging questions lest their interest stray! The forum and the archives of previous discussions will be accessible from the publisher's website for as long as the book is in print.

about the author

NATHAN B. CROCKER is the co-founder and chief technology officer (CTO) of Checker, an API-first solution that connects the traditional capital markets infrastructure to the blockchain ecosystem. Using his expertise in building digital asset infrastructure, Nathan now leads the technological vision and development at Checker, building its core infrastructure that enables new financial applications on the blockchain.

about the cover illustration

The figure on the cover of *AI-Powered Developer* is captioned "Junger kroatischer Gebirgsbauer," or "Young Croatian Mountain Peasant," and is taken from a collection of historical and folk clothing illustrations, published in 1912. Each illustration is finely drawn and colored by hand.

In those days, it was easy to identify where people lived and what their trade or station in life was just by their dress. Manning celebrates the inventiveness and initiative of the computer business with book covers based on the rich diversity of regional culture centuries ago, brought back to life by pictures from collections such as this one.

Part 1

The foundation

In part 1, we establish a comprehensive understanding of large language models (LLMs) and their significance in modern software development. This part of the book traces the historical evolution of generative AI, providing a solid conceptual framework for these powerful technologies. It emphasizes the importance of responsible and cautious use, guiding readers through the fundamental principles and potential pitfalls of integrating AI into their workflows. Additionally, this part offers practical advice on getting started with LLMs, comparing popular tools such as ChatGPT, GitHub Copilot, and CodeWhisperer and detailing the initial steps to harness their capabilities effectively.

Understanding large language models

1

Whether you realize it or not, and whether you want to admit it or not, you have quietly received a promotion. Every professional software engineer has. Almost overnight, we have gone from staff engineers to engineering managers. You now have the world's smartest and most talented junior developer on your team—generative AI is your new coding partner. So, guiding, mentoring, and performing code reviews should become part of your daily routine. This chapter will provide you with an overview of a subset of generative AI called large language models (LLMs), specifically ChatGPT, GitHub Copilot, and AWS CodeWhisperer.

NOTE   This is not a traditional programming book. You will not be able to use it like you would a script. You are going to engage in a dialogue with LLMs, and like any conversation, the words and direction will change depending on the model and the prior context. The output you receive will very likely differ from what is printed in this book. This should not discourage you. Instead, you should explore. The journey is as rewarding as the destination. You may find yourself frustrated that you can't follow along. Have patience. If you are disciplined (and somewhat adventurous), you can get GPT to cooperate with the general themes and aim of this book: learning how to use generative AI to make you a better programmer.

1.1   *Accelerating your development*

Welcome to a new era in software development in which your development team expands by one very talented engineer. Generative AI isn't just a tool; it's your next team member, poised to elevate your programming to new heights. Imagine designing intricate systems, coding with unprecedented speed, and testing with robustness you never thought possible—all with an intelligence that learns from the best. In this book, we'll explore how generative AI will not only assist you in everyday coding tasks but also enable you to achieve feats previously beyond reach, ensuring faster development, enhanced quality, and the capacity to innovate like never before.

LLMs and generative AI can drastically accelerate your software development process. By automating the tedious creation of boilerplate code, you are freed to focus on creative problem-solving and value-adding tasks. Consider this example: you want to have the LLM set up a Flask application. You might use the following prompt:

 Generate a stubbed-out Flask application.

The LLM might output the following Python code.

Listing 1.1   **Potential code generated by an LLM to stub out a Flask application**

```python
from flask import Flask

app = Flask(__name__)

@app.route('/')
def home():
    return "Hello, world!"

if __name__ == '__main__':
    app.run(debug=True)
```

LLMs are deep learning models that are good at providing natural language responses to natural language prompts. You can imagine simply describing what you need in plain English and receiving ready-to-integrate code:

Create a class for managing user sessions in Python.

Here's a possible response.

Listing 1.2 Potential code generated to create a session management class

```python
import uuid
from datetime import datetime, timedelta

class SessionManager:
    def __init__(self):
        self.sessions = {}

    def create_session(self, user_id):
        """Create a new session for a user with a unique session ID and
expiration time."""
        session_id = str(uuid.uuid4())
        # Sessions expire after 1 hour
        expiration = datetime.now() + timedelta(hours=1)
        self.sessions[session_id] = {'user_id':
        user_id, 'expiration': expiration}
        return session_id

    def get_user_id(self, session_id):
        """Retrieve a user ID from a session ID
            if the session is still valid."""
        session_info = self.sessions.get(session_id)
        if session_info and session_info['expiration'] > datetime.now():
            return session_info['user_id']
        return None  # Session is expired or does not exist

    def delete_session(self, session_id):
        """Delete a session by its ID."""
        if session_id in self.sessions:
            del self.sessions[session_id]

    def is_session_valid(self, session_id):
        """Check if a session is still valid."""
        return session_id in self. sessions and self.sessions[session_id]
['expiration'] > datetime.now()
```

These tools also enhance your debugging efficiency by identifying patterns and suggesting fixes. Suppose you want your AI tool to analyze a block of code and flag potential memory leaks. It might produce the following code.

Listing 1.3 Using an LLM to find a potential memory leak in Python

```python
def process_data():
large_data = [x for x in range(1000000)]  # Large list of numbers
result = sum(large_data)
print("Result of processing:", result)
# large_data not cleared or reassigned,
```

```
    # potentially leading to memory retention

process_data()
```

According to the explanation provided by ChatGPT, this Python code demonstrates a potential memory leak due to a large list not being cleared after use, which can keep its contents in memory longer than necessary if references are not properly managed.

In the improved code, the AI tool suggests explicitly clearing the list or reassigning None after its usage to help in releasing the memory sooner, especially in environments where garbage collection is not aggressive.

Listing 1.4 "Improved" LLM code to address the potential memory leak

```
def process_data():
    large_data = [x for x in range(1000000)]  # Large list of numbers
    result = sum(large_data)
    print("Result of processing:", result)
    large_data = None  # Clear the reference to release memory

process_data()
```

Moreover, when it comes to refactoring, the AI can suggest optimizations that make your code cleaner and more efficient, as shown in the next two listings.

Listing 1.5 Verbose code before the suggested refactoring

```
class DataProcessor:
    def __init__(self, data):
        self.data = data

    def process_data(self):
        if self. data is not None:
            if len(self.data) > 0:
                processed_data = []
                for d in self.data:
                    if d is not None:
                        if d % 2 == 0:
                            processed_data.append(d)
                return processed_data
            else:
                return []
        else:
            return []

processor = DataProcessor([1, 2, 3, 4, None, 6])
result = processor.process_data()
print("Processed Data:", result)
```

After the refactoring, the code is more readable, maintainable, and idiomatic.

Listing 1.6 LLM refactored code that is more concise

```
class DataProcessor:
    def __init__(self, data):
        self. data = data or []

    def process_data(self):
        return [d for d in self.data if d is not None and d % 2 == 0]

processor = DataProcessor([1, 2, 3, 4, None, 6])
result = processor.process_data()
print("Processed Data:", result)
```

LLMs extend beyond mere code generation; they are sophisticated enough to assist in designing software architecture as well. This capability allows developers to engage with these models more creatively and strategically. For instance, rather than simply requesting specific snippets of code, a developer can describe the overall objectives or functional requirements of a system. The LLM can then propose various architectural designs, suggest design patterns, or outline an entire system's structure. This approach not only saves significant time but also takes advantage of the AI's extensive training to innovate and optimize solutions, potentially introducing efficiencies or ideas that the human developer may not have initially considered. This flexibility makes LLMs invaluable partners in the creative and iterative processes of software development. We will explore this in chapter 3.

In addition, by enhancing the quality and security of your deliverables—from code to documentation—these tools ensure that your outputs meet the highest standards. For instance, when integrating a new library, the AI can automatically generate secure, efficient implementation examples, helping you avoid common security pitfalls.

Finally, learning new programming languages or frameworks becomes significantly easier. The AI can provide real-time, context-aware guidance and documentation, helping you to not only understand but also apply new concepts practically. For example, are you transitioning to a new framework like Dash? Your AI assistant can instantly generate sample code snippets and detailed explanations tailored to your current project's context.

Listing 1.7 LLM-generated sample code demonstrating how to use a library

```
import dash
from dash import dcc, html
from dash.dependencies import Input, Output
import pandas as pd
import plotly.express as px

# Sample data creation
dates = pd.date_range(start='1/1/2020', periods=100)
prices = pd.Series(range(100)) + pd.Series(range(100))/2
# Just a simple series to mimic stock prices
data = pd.DataFrame({'Date': dates, 'Price': prices})
```

```
# Initialize the Dash app (typically in your main module)
app = dash.Dash(__name__)

# Define the layout of the app
app.layout = html.Div([
    html.H1("Stock Prices Dashboard"),
    dcc.DatePickerRange(
        id='date-picker-range',
        start_date=data['Date'].min(),
        end_date=data['Date'].max(),
        display_format='MMM D, YYYY',
        start_date_placeholder_text='Start Period',
        end_date_placeholder_text='End Period'
    ),
    dcc.Graph(id='price-graph'),
])

# Callback to update the graph based on the date range picker input
@app.callback(
    Output('price-graph', 'figure'),
    Input('date-picker-range', 'start_date'),
    Input('date-picker-range', 'end_date')
)
def update_graph(start_date, end_date):
    filtered_data = data[(data['Date'] >=
            start_date) & (data['Date'] <= end_date)]
    figure = px.line(filtered_data, x='Date',
            y='Price', title='Stock Prices Over Time')
    return figure

# Run the app
if __name__ == '__main__':
    app.run_server(debug=True)
```

We can see the output of this code in figure 1.1, which is the running Dash code.

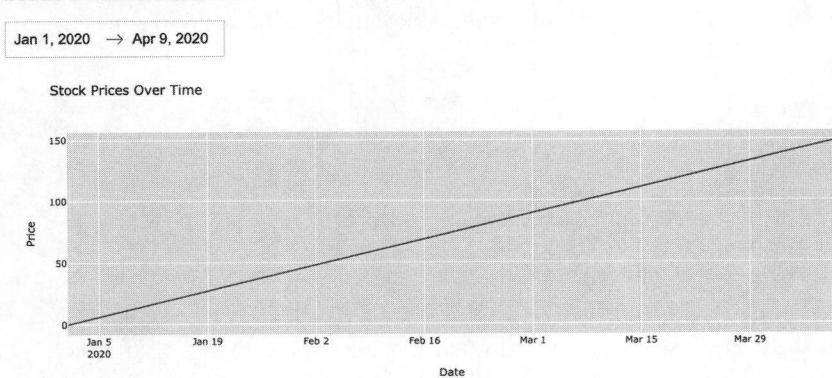

Figure 1.1   The Stock Prices Dashboard created by ChatGPT in response to the prompt "create a sample dashboard using dash"

The real power of LLMs unfolds in their integration in development environments. Tools like GitHub Copilot, developed by Microsoft, harness the capabilities of LLMs to provide real-time coding assistance directly in integrated development environments (IDEs) such as Visual Studio Code. We will unleash this power in chapter 4.

This book will not only explain these concepts but also demonstrate them through numerous examples, showing how you can use LLMs to improve your productivity and code quality dramatically. From setting up your environment to tackling complex coding challenges, you'll learn how to make the most out of these intelligent tools in your everyday development.

1.2   A developer's introduction to LLMs

Although this book is mainly a practitioner's guide and therefore very light on theory, the following section will provide you with the most relevant material for you to get the most out of your new teammate.

> ### Yes, but I want to know more
>
> If you are interested in diving deeper into the theory behind LLMs, neural networks, and all things generative AI, you should look at the following two books: the forthcoming *Build a Large Language Model (From Scratch)* by Sebastian Raschka (Manning, 2024) and the amusingly titled *The Complete Obsolete Guide to Generative AI* by David Clinton (Manning, 2024).

Let's start with a very simple definition of what an LLM is and what it can do for you; this way, you can properly pitch it to your boss and co-workers. A *large language model* is a type of artificial intelligence model that processes, understands, and generates human-like text based on the data it has been trained on. These models are a subset of deep learning and are particularly advanced in handling various aspects of natural language processing (NLP).

As the name implies, these models are "large" not just in terms of the physical size of the data they are trained on but also in the complexity and number of parameters. Modern LLMs like OpenAI's GPT-4 have up to hundreds of billions of parameters.

LLMs are trained on vast amounts of text data. This training involves reading and analyzing a wide range of internet texts, books, articles, and other forms of written communication to learn the structure, nuances, and complexities of human language.

Most LLMs use the Transformer architecture, a deep learning model that relies on self-attention mechanisms to weigh the importance of different words in a sentence regardless of their position. This allows LLMs to generate more contextually relevant text. A typical Transformer model consists of an encoder and a decoder, each composed of multiple layers.

Understanding the architecture of LLMs helps in using their capabilities more effectively as well as addressing their limitations in practical applications. As these models continue to evolve, they promise to offer even more sophisticated tools for developers to enhance their applications.

1.3   *When to use and when to avoid generative AI*

Generative AI (and by extension an LLM) is not a one-size-fits-all solution. Understanding when to employ these technologies, as well as recognizing situations where they may be less effective or even problematic, is crucial for maximizing their benefits while mitigating potential drawbacks. We will start with when it is appropriate for you to use an LLM:

- Enhancing productivity
  - *Example*—Use AI to automate boilerplate code, generate documentation, or provide coding suggestions within your IDE.
  - *Discussed in chapters 3 and 4*—These chapters explore how tools like GitHub Copilot can boost coding efficiency.
- Learning and exploration
  - *Example*—Employ AI to learn new programming languages or frameworks by generating example codes and explanations.
  - *Covered in chapter 5*—Here, we examine how AI can accelerate the learning process and introduce you to new technologies.
- Handling repetitive tasks
  - *Example*—Use AI to handle repetitive software testing or data entry tasks, freeing up time for more complex problems.
  - *Explored in chapter 7*—Discusses automation in testing and maintenance tasks.

There are, however, situations in which you should avoid using LLMs and generative AI tools such as ChatGPT and GitHub Copilot, mainly those related to data security and privacy protection. Using AI in environments with sensitive or proprietary data can risk unintended data leaks. There are several reasons for this, one of which is that part or all of the code is sent to the model as context, meaning at least part of your proprietary code may find its way outside of your firewall. There is a question as to whether it may be included in the training data for the next round of training. But have no fear: we will examine a couple of methods to address this concern in chapter 9.

Another scenario in which you might limit your usage is when precision and expertise are required. Given that a feature of LLMs is their ability to add randomness to their output (sometimes referred to as *hallucinations*), the output may contain subtle variations from the true and right answer. For this reason, you should always verify the output before including it in your codebase.

Although generative AI offers numerous advantages, it's essential to apply it judiciously, considering both the context of its use and the specific needs of the project. By understanding when to use these powerful tools and when to proceed with caution, developers can maximize their effectiveness and ensure ethical and efficient use of technology.

Summary

- Generative AI is both evolutionary and revolutionary. It's evolutionary in the sense that it is just another iteration of the tools that we as developers use every day. It's revolutionary in that it will transform how we do our jobs.
- The future of development will involve managing generative AI. Even the mythical 10× developer will not have the productivity of a developer with an AI partner; an AI-powered developer will produce higher-quality code at a substantially faster rate, at a lower cost than one who is not. We will spend more of our time training our AI partner to do what we want and how we want it done than we do writing code without the AI.
- Trust but verify the LLM's output.

Getting started with large language models

2

This chapter covers

- Engaging with ChatGPT
- Learning the basics of using Copilot
- Learning the basics of using CodeWhisperer
- Exploring prompt engineering patterns
- Contrasting the differences between these three Generative AI offerings

In this chapter, we embark on a practical journey through the landscape of Generative AI, harnessing the power of three groundbreaking tools: ChatGPT, GitHub Copilot, and AWS CodeWhisperer. As we navigate the intricacies of these technologies, we'll apply them to a series of challenging scenarios modeled after the rigorous interview questions posed by leading tech giants. Whether you're a seasoned developer or a curious enthusiast, prepare to unlock innovative strategies that could give you the edge in your next technical interview. Get ready to transform abstract concepts into tangible solutions right at the forefront of AI's evolving role in tech hiring.

We will begin by using two currently available models for ChatGPT: GPT-4 and GPT-3.5. The purpose is twofold: it will allow us to appreciate the engagement model of ChatGPT, and it will also let us establish a baseline against which we can compare and contrast the other two. Using two models will also allow us to appreciate the generational sea change between these model versions. Finally, throughout this chapter, we will use some common patterns in prompt engineering.

2.1 A foray into ChatGPT

Context is one of the most important aspects of working with ChatGPT. Your previous *prompts* can drastically change the results from your current prompt. In language models like ChatGPT, a prompt refers to the input provided to the model to generate a response. It can be a single sentence, a paragraph, or even a longer text. It serves as the instruction or query to the model, guiding its response. Given the quality of the prompt and the context in which the model responds, it is essential always to be aware of the prompts you have issued in the current session. Therefore, starting with a new session every time you begin a new project is advised. Appendix A will walk you through setting up an account, logging in to ChatGPT, and writing your first prompt.

2.1.1 Navigating nuances with GPT-4

In this section, we will work toward finding a solution to the following question: "How would you reserve a singly linked list in Python?"

> **What is a singly linked list?**
>
> A *singly linked list* is a fundamental data structure in computer science that consists of a sequence of elements, each stored in a node. Generally, singly linked lists consist of nodes in which the data is stored and a reference to the next node in the linked list.
>
> With a singly linked list, you can only travel in one direction. Common operations on a singly linked list include insertion (adding a new node), deletion (removing a node), searching (finding a node), and traversal (accessing each node sequentially).

We will start with this simple prompt:

 Going forward, when I ask a question, try to formulate a better question. As an intern who studied computer science in college, how would you define a singly linked list in pseudocode?

Okay, this may not be such a simple prompt. First, we have directed ChatGPT to enhance and reformulate our questions based on its training data so we will get better prompts. Better prompts make for better output. You may be asking, what makes for a better prompt? Great question! General prompts produce general results. Specific prompts produce specific results. As we engage with large language models (LLMs) generally and ChatGPT specifically, we will go from general to specific, refining the output as we go. This is known as the *Refinement Pattern in prompt engineering*: iteratively refining or improving the prompt to get more accurate, relevant, or sophisticated responses.

The second part of the prompt introduces a prompting pattern we will see throughout this book: the *Persona Pattern*. In the context of prompt engineering, mainly related to AI and LLMs, the Persona Pattern refers to a strategy of designing prompts that establish a specific persona or role for the AI to assume. This approach guides the model's responses consistently and contextually appropriately. One of the key benefits of using the Persona Pattern is maintaining consistency in responses. Adhering to a defined persona makes the AI's replies more predictable and aligned with the user's expectations. In this case, we have asked ChatGPT to assume the persona of an intern with a background in computer science. Why an intern? We want a persona who will do the work.

It bears repeating that when working with LLMs, even when applying personas, the same input will not always produce the same output. For this reason, your output may not match the following exactly, but hopefully it is similar. (Note that these listings are pseudocode.)

Listing 2.1   ChatGPT's reformulation of our question about reversing a linked list

```
As a computer science intern, how can I define a singly linked list's
structure and basic operations using pseudocode? This definition should
include the essential components of the list, such as nodes and links, and
outline fundamental operations like creating a node, adding a node to the
list, and traversing the list.
```

When asked the refined question, ChatGPT will provide the following code listing.

Listing 2.2   ChatGPT's answer about how to reverse a linked list

```
#Node Structure
class Node
    data
    nextNode

    Constructor(data)
        this.data = data
        this.nextNode = NULL
    #Singly Linked List Structure
class SinglyLinkedList
    head

    Constructor()
        this.head = NULL

    Function AddToFront(data)
        newNode = new Node(data)
        newNode.nextNode = this.head
        this.head = newNode
```

```
Function Append(data)
    newNode = new Node(data)
    if this.head is NULL
        this.head = newNode
        return
    end if

    lastNode = this.head
    while lastNode.nextNode is not NULL
        lastNode = lastNode.nextNode
    end while

    lastNode.nextNode = newNode

Function Traverse()
    currentNode = this.head
    while currentNode is not NULL
        print currentNode.data
        currentNode = currentNode.nextNode
    end while
```

One of the excellent quality-of-life-enhancing features of working with ChatGPT is that it will usually provide documentation about the code in question. Figure 2.1 is a screenshot of the textual description provided by ChatGPT.

- **Node Class:** Represents each element in the list with a `data` field and a `nextNode` field pointing to the next node in the list.

- **SinglyLinkedList Class:**

    - `AddToFront`: Inserts a new node at the beginning of the list.

    - `Append`: Adds a new node at the end of the list.

    - `Traverse`: Iterates through the list from the head and prints the data of each node.

The pseudocode outlines the basic structure and operations of a singly linked list, suitable for an intern with a computer science background. It covers node creation, list initialization, and basic methods to manipulate the list.

Figure 2.1   ChatGPT Model 4's explanation of the pseudocode definition of a singly linked list

We will now have ChatGPT assume a new role—that of a computer science intern:

 As an intern with a background in computer science, how would you define the structure and basic operations of a singly linked list using the programming language Python? This definition should include the essential components of the list, such as nodes and links, and outline fundamental operations like creating a node, adding a node to the list, and traversing the list.

Listing 2.3   ChatGPT's implementation of a singly linked list in Python

```python
class ListNode:
    def __init__(self, value):
        self.value = value
        self.next = None

class SinglyLinkedList:
    def __init__(self):
        self.head = None  # The list initially has no nodes

    def append(self, value):
        """ Append a new node at the end of the list """
        if not self.head:
            self.head = ListNode(value)
            return
        current = self.head
        while current.next:
            current = current.next
        current.next = ListNode(value)

    def prepend(self, value):
        """ Prepend a new node at the beginning of the list """
        new_node = ListNode(value)
        new_node.next = self.head
        self.head = new_node

    def traverse(self):
        """ Traverse the list and print each node's value """
        current = self.head
        while current:
            print(current.value, end=" -> ")
            current = current.next
        print("None")
```

ChatGPT will likely include a sample test harness to run this code.

Listing 2.4   Python-based method to implement and run the singly linked list

```python
# Creating a new linked list
linked_list = SinglyLinkedList()

# Adding nodes to the list
linked_list.append(1)
linked_list.append(2)

# Prepending a node to the list
linked_list.prepend(0)

# Traversing and printing the list
linked_list.traverse()  # Output: 0 -> 1 -> 2 -> None
```

Similarly, we can refine the persona to be an interviewee for an engineering job. The switch in personas will signal to the ChatGPT-3.5 model that it should explain the code as well as an approach to solving the problem:

 You are a student with a background in computer science who is interviewing for an engineering job at a software company. You are asked the following question, based on the previous definition of a singly linked list (in Python), how would you write a method that would reverse the output of the traversal method. How would you implement such a method?

Listing 2.5   ChatGPT's explanation of how to reverse a singly linked list

To implement a method that reverses the output of a traversal method for a singly linked list in Python, you need to reverse the actual links in the linked list. This process involves changing the next reference of each node to point to the previous node instead of the next one. After reversing the links, traversing the list normally will produce the reversed order of elements.

```python
def reverse(self):
        """ Reverse the linked list """
        prev = None
        current = self.head
        while current:
            next_node = current.next
            current.next = prev
            prev = current
            current = next_node
        self.head = prev
```

ChatGPT will likely output text similar to what is shown in figure 2.2, explaining the method and the approach to solving the problem.

Explanation of the Reverse Method:

1. **Initializing Pointers**: Two pointers, `prev` and `current`, are used. `prev` starts as `None`, and `current` starts at the head of the list.
2. **Reversing Links**: In each iteration of the while loop:
   * Temporarily store the next node (`next_node`).
   * Set `current.next` to `prev` to reverse the link.
   * Move `prev` to `current`.
   * Advance `current` to `next_node`.
3. **Updating Head**: Once the loop is finished (when `current` is `None`), `prev` is pointing to the new head of the reversed list. We update the list's head to `prev`.

Figure 2.2   ChatGPT Model 4's explanation of the pseudocode definition of a reversing a linked list

This implementation effectively reverses the singly linked list in place, and the traversal method will output the elements in reverse order compared to their original insertion sequence.

2.1.2   *Charting paths with GPT-3.5*

In this section, we will explore how to harness the capabilities of ChatGPT-3.5 to create a singly linked list in Python. ChatGPT-3.5 excels at generating human-like text based on the input it receives. This makes it a valuable tool for coding assistance, as it can provide step-by-step guidance, suggest improvements, and offer detailed explanations of complex programming concepts.

To create a singly linked list, we will use ChatGPT-3.5 to generate the necessary Python code. A singly linked list is a data structure consisting of nodes, where each node contains a value and a reference to the next node in the sequence. This structure is particularly useful for dynamic memory allocation and efficient insertions and deletions. Using ChatGPT-3.5, we can simplify the process of coding a singly linked list, ensuring that our implementation is both efficient and easy to understand. The following example demonstrates how to define the `Node` and `LinkedList` classes, initialize a list, and perform basic operations such as insertion and traversal.

> **Listing 2.6   Implementation of a singly linked list by ChatGPT-3.5**

```python
class Node:
    def __init__(self, data):
        self.data = data
        self.next = None

class LinkedList:
    def __init__(self):
        self.head = None

    def prepend(self, data):
        new_node = Node(data)
        new_node.next = self.head
        self.head = new_node

    def append(self, data):
        new_node = Node(data)
        if not self.head:
            self.head = new_node
            return
        current = self.head
        while current.next:
            current = current.next
        current.next = new_node

    def display(self):
        current = self.head
        while current:
            print(current.data, end=" -> ")
            current = current.next
        print("None")

    def reverse_and_display(self):
        prev = None
```

```
        current = self.head
        while current:
            next_node = current.next
            current.next = prev
            prev = current
            current = next_node
        self.head = prev

        current = self.head
        while current:
            print(current.data, end=" -> ")
            current = current.next
        print("None")


# Example usage:
if __name__ == "__main__":
    linked_list = LinkedList()

    linked_list.append(1)
    linked_list.append(2)
    linked_list.append(3)

    linked_list.prepend(0)

    linked_list.display()
    linked_list.reverse_and_display()
```

You can apply the Persona Pattern in either direction: you can tell the LLM to respond as though it were someone or something within a given role, or you can ask the LLM to assume that you are a certain persona. This can be very useful when you need to explain some code in simplified terms or are attempting to understand complex or complicated topics. For example, we can ask ChatGPT to explain our code to us in a simplified manner with this prompt:

 Assume that I am an adult who graduated from college with a degree in communications. I have no experience with computer science. How would you explain that method to me?

Let's examine how ChatGPT would explain our method to someone without a computer science background.

Listing 2.7   ChatGPT explanation for someone who is not a computer scientist

```
Certainly! Let's break down the reverse_and_display method in a way that
doesn't involve technical jargon or computer science concepts.

Imagine you have a set of books on a bookshelf, and each book has a bookmark
pointing to the next book in the shelf. This set of books represents our
linked list, and the bookmarks represent the next connections between the
items.
```

Getting Ready: You start at the first book (the head of the linked list)
and have two empty hands: one to remember the book you just read (prev) and
another to hold the book you are currently reading (current). There's also
an empty placeholder (a table, perhaps) to help you temporarily remember the
next book.

Changing the Order: Now, let's change the order of the books. For each book
(node) you read:
a. Use the bookmark (the next reference) to find out where the next book is
and put it on the empty placeholder (the table). This is like making a note
of where the next book is located.
b. Turn the bookmark in the current book around, so it now points to the
previous book. This means that the current book is now connected to the book
you just read instead of the next book. It's like flipping the bookmark.
c. Swap the books in your hands: Put the book you just read (prev) in your
left hand (so you remember it for the next iteration) and put the book you
are currently reading (current) in your right hand (so you can work on the
next book).
d. Walk to where you put the next book (the one on the table) to continue the
process.

Starting Over: Keep doing this until you run out of books to read. At this
point, your right hand will hold the last book (the first book initially),
and your left hand will be empty. Now, you put the first book you're holding
(the last book in the original order) back on the shelf as the new first
book.

Reading Backward: Finally, go through the books starting from the new first
book, and follow the bookmarks in the reversed direction. As you read each
book, you say its title out loud. This will give you the titles of the books
in reverse order.

So, the reverse_and_display method essentially changes the order of the books
(nodes) in the bookshelf and then reads the titles (data) of those books in
the reversed order.
Bottom of Form

When you use the Persona Pattern in reverse, it is commonly referred to as the *Audience Persona Pattern* in the context of prompt engineering. This refers to a predefined profile or representation of the intended audience for a particular application or use case. It helps in tailoring the responses generated by LLMs to better suit the needs and expectations of a specific group of users or individuals. Before we move on to GitHub CoPilot, let's compare the output quality of each model.

2.1.3   *Navigating the AI seas: From the shores of GPT-3.5 to the horizons of GPT-4*

One of the significant differences between the output of these two models is in the sophistication and transparency of their outputs, particularly in how these models interact with and modify data structures. The difference between the approaches used by GPT-3.5 and GPT-4 underscores a broader shift toward greater clarity and predictability in AI-generated code. As AI models become more advanced, their output increasingly reflects the nuances of good programming practices, mirroring the evolution of human programmers' skills and sensibilities. This evolution is crucial for AI to be a reliable partner in software development, where clarity and precision are not just ideals but necessities.

With GPT-3.5, the approach taken in the `reverse_and_display` method was somewhat opaque in its execution. This version of the model altered the underlying data structure of the linked list, effectively reversing the nodes. However, it did so without explicitly signaling this change to the user. From a developer's standpoint, this could lead to unexpected side effects. For instance, if we were to call `reverse_and_display` with the assumption of merely displaying the reversed list, we would find that the original list structure had been permanently altered. This lack of transparency in the operation could easily lead to confusion and bugs, especially in more complex applications where the integrity of the original data structure is crucial.

In contrast, GPT-4 exhibits a more refined approach with its `reverse` method. This method explicitly reverses the linked list, and any seasoned programmer could infer from the name and structure of the method that it would modify the underlying data structure. GPT-4's methodology aligns more closely with clear and maintainable code principles. It embodies the idea that each function or method should perform a well-defined task. The separation of concerns is evident here: the reversal of the list and its display are treated as distinct operations. This enhances code readability and reduces the likelihood of unintended side effects, as the developer is fully aware of the changes applied to the data structure.

2.2 *Let Copilot take control*

Now let's use GitHub Copilot to tackle the same problem. Appendix B has instructions on creating an account and installing the plugin into your favorite integrated development environment (IDE; assuming your favorite IDE is either VS Code or PyCharm). Once you have completed the installation, you should create a new project in your IDE. First, create a new file named main.py. At the beginning of this file, enter the following comment/prompt:

```
# You are a student with a background in computer science who is interview-
ing for an engineering job at a software company. You are asked the follow-
ing question: based on the previous definition of a singly linked list (in
Python), how would you write a method that would reverse the output of the
traversal method? How would you implement such a method?
```

Note the hash character at the beginning; it denotes a Python comment. What is particularly interesting is that we used the same prompt in ChatGPT and GitHub Copilot.

Next, note that as you begin to type the definition of the `ListNode` class, Copilot will make code suggestions. This is the inline mode of engagement. Alternatively, you can activate the interactive model by pressing Ctrl-Enter and have Copilot generate up to 10 recommendations based on the current context.

NOTE   Throughout the book, we will mainly use inline mode, in which you use the Tab key to accept a given suggestion.

You will likely get code resembling the source code created by ChatGPT. Let's try a slightly different programming challenge rather than reprint the same code from the previous section. We will ask the following of Copilot:

```
# Given an unsorted array of integers, write a function to find the kth
smallest element in the array. Can you discuss the time and space complex-
ity of your solution?
```

After a few carriage returns, Copilot should add some comments that discuss this code's time and space complexity and the problem in general. Fascinating!

Listing 2.8   ChatGPT calculating and reporting the complexity of this code

```
def kth_smallest_element(arr, k):
    # Time Complexity: O(N)
    # Space Complexity: O(1)
    if k > len(arr):
        return None
    return sorted(arr)[k - 1]
```

Copilot's suggestion is admirable and completely valid, but it would not likely be an acceptable answer during an interview. It feels like a cheat. We should expect that there would be a follow-up question about how to do this without sorting the entire list. Let's refine the prompt to ensure that the list is not sorted before taking the *k*th element:

```
#As a computer science graduate seeking a software engineering role, imag-
ine you are in an interview where you are presented with a problem: 'How
would you implement a function in Python to determine the kth smallest ele-
ment within an unsorted array of integers, without resorting to full array
sorting or utilizing any built-in sorting functions? Additionally, can you
explain the time and space complexity of your algorithm?' This question
tests your ability to devise efficient algorithms and your understanding of
complexity analysis, all while adhering to specified constraints.
```

The code that Copilot provides looks very similar to a binary search, which is certainly an interesting choice.

Listing 2.9   Copilot's approach to solving the *k*th element problem

```
# The following code demonstrates an implementation of the kth smallest
element function in Python, along with an explanation of its time and space
complexity.

# Function to determine the kth smallest element in an unsorted array
def kth_smallest(arr, k):
    # Check if the input array is empty or if k is out of bounds
```

```
    if not arr or k < 1 or k > len(arr):
        return None

    # Initialize variables to store the lower and upper bounds of the array
    low = min(arr)
    high = max(arr)

    # Perform binary search to find the kth smallest element
    while low <= high:
        # Calculate the middle element of the array
        mid = low + (high - low) // 2

        # Count the number of elements less than or equal to the middle
element
        count = sum(1 for num in arr if num <= mid)

        # Adjust the search range based on the count
        if count < k:
            low = mid + 1
        else:
            high = mid - 1

    # Return the kth smallest element
    return low

# Time complexity: O(n log(max(arr) - min(arr)))
# Space complexity: O(1)
```

2.3 *Let CodeWhisperer speak loudly*

Before we begin using CodeWhisperer, we should disable Copilot. Click the Extensions tab, and search for Copilot. Once you have found it, click the Disable button. You will need to restart the application. When the application has restarted, you can begin to use CodeWhisperer. If you need assistance installing or configuring CodeWhisperer, refer to appendix C. Once the plugin is installed and you are logged in to your developer account, create a file called asset.py. Figure 2.3 shows how to locate and disable this plug-in.

Figure 2.3   Before we can switch to CodeWhisperer, we must disable Copilot. We turn off the extension in the Extensions tab.

We will use the same prompt that we used for Copilot. It is reprinted here for convenience:

```
#As a computer science graduate seeking a software engineering role, imag-
ine you are in an interview where you are presented with a problem: 'How
would you implement a function in Python to determine the kth smallest ele-
ment within an unsorted array of integers, without resorting to full array
sorting or utilizing any built-in sorting functions? Additionally, can you
explain the time and space complexity of your algorithm?' This question
tests your ability to devise efficient algorithms and your understanding of
complexity analysis, all while adhering to specified constraints.
```

The code that CodeWhisperer provides implements the Quickselect algorithm, which is closely related to the QuickSort sorting algorithm. Quickselect is specifically designed to efficiently find the *k*th smallest element in an unsorted array.

Listing 2.10   CodeWhisperer's approach to solving the *k*th element problem

```python
def partition(arr, low, high):
    pivot = arr[high]
    i = low - 1
    for j in range(low, high):
        if arr[j] <= pivot:
            i += 1
            arr[i], arr[j] = arr[j], arr[i]
    arr[i + 1], arr[high] = arr[high], arr[i + 1]
    return i + 1

def quickselect(arr, k, low=0, high=None):
    if high is None:
        high = len(arr) - 1
    if low < high:
        pivot = partition(arr, low, high)
        if pivot == k:
            return arr[k]
        elif pivot > k:
            return quickselect(arr, k, low, pivot - 1)
        else:
            return quickselect(arr, k, pivot + 1, high)
    return arr[low]

# Usage Example
arr = [5, 2, 4, 6, 1, 3]
k = 2
print(quickselect(arr, k))
# Output: 2
```

There is a fascinating distinction between the code created by Copilot and that of CodeWhisperer. CodeWhisperer interprets k as the index of the element in the sorted array. Because array indices in most programming languages start at 0, if k is 2, Code-Whisperer will find the third-smallest element (because indices 0, 1, and 2 correspond to the first, second, and third smallest elements, respectively). On the other hand, Copilot assumes that k refers to the rank of the element, not the index. So, if k is 2, Copilot will return the second-smallest element in the array. This is akin to saying "second place" rather than "index 2."

In this section, we introduced AWS CodeWhisperer into the mix. Like its predecessors, CodeWhisperer capably generated code that solves the problem, reinforcing AI's transformative potential in software development.

Given the striking similarity of the code produced by these tools, an intriguing question naturally arises: how do these products truly compare? Given each tool's unique strengths and limitations, the answer is not as straightforward as you may think.

In the following section, we'll delve into this question, comparing these three tools—ChatGPT, Copilot, and AWS CodeWhisperer—in a bid to understand their unique offerings, optimal use cases, and how they may reshape the future of software development. We aim to provide a comprehensive guide that can help software developers navigate this rapidly evolving landscape of AI-driven tools.

2.4   *Comparing ChatGPT, Copilot, and CodeWhisperer*

The first dimension we will consider is the engagement model: how we engage with AI. In the case of ChatGPT, we log in to the chat website and enter prompts into a chat input box. Then we refine our requirements in subsequent prompts. The feedback loop takes the context from the previous prompts, applies it to the current prompt, and generates output to which the user reacts and refires. If we contrast this engagement model against that of Copilot and CodeWhisperer, we note that the latter two tools work within an IDE. We can't use it outside our IDE, try as we may. The approach is not inherently inferior; it just differs.

The way that Copilot and CodeWhisperer keep you in your IDE can be seen as a benefit rather than a deficiency. In later chapters, we will get acquainted with Copilot Chat, the best of both worlds: ChatGPT and GPT-4, all in your IDE. These tools keep you in your code without distraction for longer. Working distraction-free is one of the keys to productivity. Copilot and CodeWhisperer excel at getting out of your way, keeping you from switching contexts, freeing you from distraction, and keeping you in the flow state longer. They do this well. You engage ChatGPT in a dialog; Copilot and CodeWhisperer advise you. The dialog takes longer; advice comes fast and free.

Next, we will examine how the code is presented and generated. ChatGPT can create the code as a block, method, class, or project. ChatGPT reveals projects deliberatively if asked. But it does create the project behind the scenes. ChatGPT, after all, likes to talk. With Copilot and CodeWhisperer, the code unfolds one method at a time, at least initially. As you use these tools more, you will notice that they can write more and more of the code for a given class. But unfortunately, they can't write an entire project with a tiny prompt.

One item that they all share is their ability to respond to prompts. With ChatGPT, prompts are the only way to engage with the tool. With Copilot and CodeWhisperer, responding to prompts is not strictly necessary, but coding such prompts will make the output correspond more closely to what you initially had in mind.

Combining these factors, you may conclude that ChatGPT is an excellent choice for exploration and prototyping. However, ChatGPT can introduce unnecessary distractions, partly because you have left your IDE and are now in a web browser with all of the accompanying temptations that come with it. ChatGPT itself is part of the inclusion of unnecessary distractions. You will eventually fall into the proverbial rabbit hole. The tool makes it too easy not to. Don't let that scare you off. It is a beautiful resource.

Copilot and CodeWhisperer require that you have a desired outcome in mind. Therefore, these tools are perfect for when you want to go head down, coding with precise requirements and tight deadlines. Copilot and CodeWhisperer work best when you know the language and the framework. They can automate much of the drudgery, allowing you to focus on the business requirements, which add value and are likely why you are writing the software in the first place. Figure 2.4 briefly summarizes the benefits and limitations of all three generative AIs.

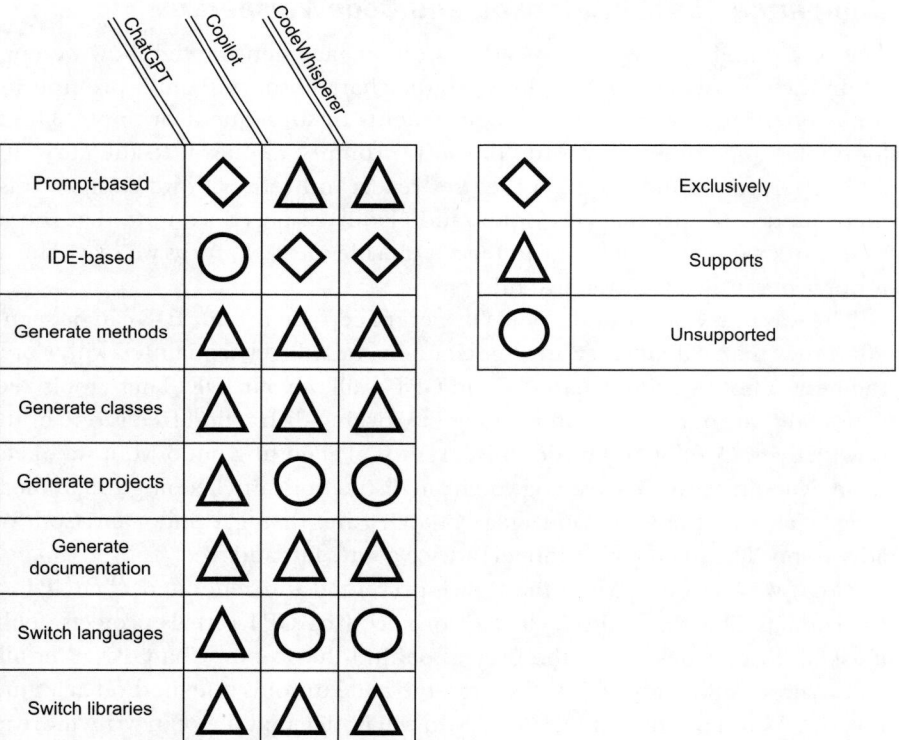

Figure 2.4   A comparison of the positives and negatives of ChatGPT, Copilot, and CodeWhisperer

In this chapter, we went through a lot, implementing basic data structures and solving some classic computer science problems. The work in this chapter is foundational, allowing us to better recognize when it makes sense to use ChatGPT as opposed to when to use the other IDE-focused tools such as Copilot and CodeWhisperer. In subsequent chapters, we will use this knowledge to choose the most suitable tool.

One final note: these tools work best when they work together. ChatGPT is an excellent tool for example and structure. Copilot and CodeWhisperer allow you to extend and customize the code.

Summary

- ChatGPT is a prompt-based Generative AI that engages the user in a dialogue that helps them explore ideas to aid in the design and development of entire projects. In addition, ChatGPT artfully generates documentation for each method it writes. One of the reasons we began the chapter using it is that it helped define a template we used throughout the remainder of the chapter. It is a fascinating product, one that can lead to unnecessary albeit enjoyable distractions.

- Copilot and CodeWhisperer are head-down tools that work best when you know what you want to do and need some advice about how best to get it done. You engage with these tools in a way that is remarkably similar, as are the results.

- ChatGPT (as of this writing) does not support development within an IDE. However, unlike GitHub Copilot and AWS CodeWhisperer, it can produce entire projects and easily translate code from one programming language to another. Copilot and CodeWhisperer take hints from your comments to infer what code you want to write. With ChatGPT, you explicitly write prompts that ChatGPT uses to create the code.

- The purpose of the Persona Pattern is to design prompts that establish a specific persona or role for the AI to assume, which guides the model's responses in a consistent and contextually appropriate manner. By adhering to a defined persona, the AI's replies become more predictable and aligned with the user's expectations.

- The intern persona is often characterized by eagerness to learn, a basic to intermediate level of knowledge in the field, and a willingness to take on various tasks for learning and experience. The intern may ask clarifying questions, seek guidance, and demonstrate a proactive approach to problem-solving. They are often resourceful but may lack the deep expertise of more experienced professionals in the field. This persona is useful in scenarios where the AI needs to simulate a learning and growth-oriented mindset.

- The Refinement Pattern involves iteratively refining or improving the prompt to get more accurate, relevant, or sophisticated responses. It's about going from general to specific, enhancing the output quality as the interaction progresses with large language models like ChatGPT.

- The Audience Persona Pattern is a variation of the Persona Pattern in prompt engineering. It involves defining a profile or representation of the intended audience for a particular application or use case, which helps tailor the responses generated by LLMs to better suit the needs and expectations of a specific group of users or individuals.

Part 2

The input

In part 2, we delve into the practical application of LLMs in software design and development. This part of the book explores how AI enhances the design phase, using real-world examples to illustrate its impact. It covers foundational concepts like domain modeling, immutability, and design patterns, demonstrating how these principles are applied in practice with the help of tools like GitHub Copilot. We also address data management challenges, showcasing how AI facilitates real-time asset monitoring and data analysis. By integrating AI into these stages, developers can streamline their workflows, improve efficiency, and foster innovation in their projects.

Designing software with ChatGPT

Now that we have an intuition about when and how to use Generative AI, we will start to design, explore, and document our application's architecture. Laying out some of the critical components upfront is beneficial in several ways. For example, it allows us to delegate some of the design to sub-architects or some of the development to other team members. Designing up front will also help us clarify our thinking about the implementation, allowing us to anticipate and avoid some pitfalls. Finally, capturing the design as documentation enables us to justify our crucial design decisions, communicating our intent to our future selves, our stakeholders, and those who may inherit the project.

First, let's get an overview of the application that we will be designing in this chapter: the *information technology asset management* (ITAM) system. We'll build out key features in subsequent chapters.

3.1 Introducing our project, the information technology asset management system

An ITAM system is a tool to manage and track hardware devices, software licenses, and other IT-related components throughout their lifecycle. ITAM systems typically consist of hardware and software inventory tools, license management software, and other related software applications. The system may also involve manual processes and physical tracking of IT assets using QR codes, barcodes, or other physical asset management technologies.

Generally, ITAM systems will have a centralized database, which stores the asset identifiers and attributes specific to the asset type. For example, you might store the device type, model number, operating system, and installed applications for desktop PCs. For software, you might store the application's name, the vendor, the number of licenses available, and the computers on which the software has been installed. The latter ensures that your organization complies with all licensing restrictions. By monitoring usage, you should never exceed the number of licenses you have purchased.

ITAM systems also confer the ability to control costs. Because you always know what software and hardware you have available, you should not have to make any unnecessary purchases. These systems centralize purchases, which can help with volume purchasing. Unused hardware can be sold; the workloads of underutilized hardware can be consolidated. Additionally, as you will see, you can use purchase date information to calculate the depreciation value of hardware, applying this value against your organization's taxes.

We will explore more of the features of an ITAM system, building a solid conceptual model of the application with a focus on a system that can track and manage hardware. Next, let's ask ChatGPT to assume the software architect persona, solicit its opinion about how best to design this project, and see what solution it can come up with.

3.2 Asking ChatGPT to help with our system design

In a new session, we will begin with a prompt outlining our requirements. As with the previous chapter, we will apply the Refinement Pattern to our prompts to iteratively change the design of our system. We will begin broadly, drilling into the requirements and functionality as we progress. To start, we will have ChatGPT improve our prompts by using this prompt:

 From now on, when I give you a prompt, output a better prompt.

This prompt is useful when you begin to explore your current task at hand because it instructs ChatGPT to create better prompts for you. As you know, the better the prompt, the better the output. This will be our heuristic moving forward: when you need a specific answer, you ask a specific question. Additionally, and alternatively, you can request that ChatGPT reason through the problem step by step, specifying its rationale as it goes.

Next, we will ask ChatGPT to begin to assist us in the design, using this (extended) prompt:

 Assume that you are a software architect, and you are designing an information technology asset management system, using Python. The system should be able to maintain a complete inventory of all hardware and software assets owned by an organization. The system should be able to track asset location, status, and usage. This includes information such as who uses the asset, when it was last serviced, and when it is due for replacement. The system should be able to manage the entire lifecycle of an asset, from procurement to disposal. This includes tracking warranty and lease information, managing asset maintenance and repair, and ensuring compliance with regulations. The system should be able to allocate assets to employees or departments, track usage, and manage reservations for assets that are in high demand. It should use hexagonal architecture. Remember to enhance my prompt.

Note that in this prompt, we return to the Persona Pattern, asking ChatGPT to assume the role of a software architect. ChatGPT will output not only the high-level functionality of our system but also how we can improve our initial prompt. If we plug in this prompt, we get the results shown in the following listing. One important reminder: the output from ChatGPT (and any generative AI) is very dependent on what came before, so your output will likely not match the following output exactly.

> **Listing 3.1 Enhanced prompt and overview of application as described by ChatGPT**

```
To enhance and detail your prompt for designing an information technology
asset management system using Python with a hexagonal architecture, here's a
more comprehensive breakdown:

System Objective and Core Functionality:
Design a Python-based IT asset management system.
Ensure the system maintains a full inventory of all organizational hardware
and software assets.

Detailed Asset Tracking:
Implement features for tracking the location, status, and usage of each
asset.
Include detailed logs for user assignments, service histories, and
replacement schedules.

Lifecycle Management:
Enable management of assets from procurement to disposal.
Track warranty and lease information, schedule maintenance and repairs, and
ensure regulatory compliance.

Asset Allocation and Usage Monitoring:
Facilitate asset allocation to employees or departments.
Monitor usage patterns and manage reservations for high-demand assets.

Architectural Approach:
Adopt a hexagonal architecture to promote loose coupling and ease of
maintenance.
```

```
Ensure modularity in design for easy scalability and updates.

Additional Features and Considerations:
Incorporate user-friendly interfaces for different stakeholders.
Implement robust security measures to protect sensitive asset data.
Consider integration capabilities with existing systems within the
organization.

This detailed breakdown provides a comprehensive guide for designing the
system with all necessary features and a robust architectural framework.
```

After some deliberation, ChatGPT will return the high-level steps for what needs to be done to develop this project. These suggestions are helpful, but we are here to get past the empty file problem: we want to start designing. We want prose and diagrams to help us understand the system at the component level. We need tasks, not a recipe. We can ask ChatGPT to show its work with this prompt:

 Show the Python package structure for this application.

At this prompt, ChatGPT will generate and return a package diagram (this listing is slightly abridged), demonstrating that not only can it design software, but it can also aid in the layout of our physical files. We might (or might not) quibble as to the overall package structure, but this will provide us with more than enough inspiration to get going.

Listing 3.2   Package structure for the asset management system ChatGPT created

```
it_asset_management/
|
├── app/                        # Main application directory
|    ├── __init__.py
|    ├── main.py                # Entry point of the application
|    ├── config.py              # Configuration settings
|    └── dependencies.py        # Dependency injection and management
|
├── domain/                     # Domain layer with business logic
|    ├── __init__.py
|    ├── models/                # Domain models (e.g., Asset, User)
|    |    ├── __init__.py
|    |    ├── asset.py
|    |    └── user.py
|    ├── services/              # Business services/logic
|    |    ├── __init__.py
|    |    ├── asset_service.py
|    |    └── user_service.py
|    └── repositories/          # Interface for data access
|         ├── __init__.py
|         ├── asset_repository.py
|         └── user_repository.py
|
├── adapters/                   # Adapter layer for external interactions
|    ├── __init__.py
|    ├── orm/                   # Object-relational mapping
```

```
|   |       ├── __init__.py
|   |       ├── asset_orm.py
|   |       └── user_orm.py
|   ├── api/                       # API endpoints
|   |       ├── __init__.py
|   |       ├── asset_api.py
|   |       └── user_api.py
|   └── external_services/         # Integration with external services
|           ├── __init__.py
|           ├── email_service.py
|           └── logging_service.py
|
├── infrastructure/                # Infrastructure layer for database,
messaging, etc.
|       ├── __init__.py
|       ├── database.py            # Database setup and connection
|       ├── message_queue.py       # Messaging infrastructure
|       └── cache.py               # Caching mechanisms
|
├── tests/                         # Test suite
|       ├── __init__.py
|       ├── unit/                  # Unit tests
|       └── integration/           # Integration tests
|
└── requirements.txt               # Project dependencies
```

We can examine the *macro*, and we can ask ChatGPT to provide us with the *micro* as well. We can create prompts to have ChatGPT show us the contents of every file in sequence, and we can dutifully copy the contents to a file with the same name as the one suggested by ChatGPT. But we should always double-check ChatGPT's work and never assume that it is 100% safe or accurate. You will occasionally find that ChatGPT produces code that doesn't work—ChatGPT is focused on generating the next token rather than thinking of systems as we do. That being said, we should take a quick look at the code it generated, to assess its quality and determine its usefulness:

 Please show the source code for it_asset_management/app/schemas/asset.py.

The following listing shows the result.

> **Listing 3.3 Example** `Asset` **model in asset_management_system/models/asset.py**

```python
from typing import Optional
from datetime import datetime
from pydantic import BaseModel

# Basic Asset model used for creating a new asset
class AssetCreate(BaseModel):
    name: str
    asset_type: str
    serial_number: str
    purchase_date: Optional[datetime] = None
    warranty_end_date: Optional[datetime] = None
```

```
# Model for asset data that is publicly exposed
class Asset(BaseModel):
    id: int
    name: str
    asset_type: str
    serial_number: str
    purchase_date: Optional[datetime] = None
    warranty_end_date: Optional[datetime] = None

    class Config:
        orm_mode = True

# Model for updating existing asset data
class AssetUpdate(BaseModel):
    name: Optional[str] = None
    asset_type: Optional[str] = None
    serial_number: Optional[str] = None
    purchase_date: Optional[datetime] = None
    warranty_end_date: Optional[datetime] = None
return '<Asset %r>' % self.name
```

Rather than going class by class and skimming the source code for each one, we will document the overall project. Although Agile and Scrum emphasize working software over comprehensive documentation, the role of thoughtful design and essential documentation cannot be overstated. They bring structure, clarity, and long-term vision to the Agile development process, ensuring that the team can respond to changes effectively while maintaining the integrity and quality of the software.

3.3   *Documenting your architecture*

In this section, we will have ChatGPT begin to document the design of our application. As previously stated, application design and documentation are crucial for a software architect and a software project, even in Agile and Scrum environments. Documentation provides a clear vision and direction for the development team, outlining the architecture, components, and interactions within the system helping developers understand how to implement features correctly and efficiently. It encourages adherence to quality standards and best practices, allowing architects to define patterns and practices that should be followed throughout the development process and leading to a more robust and maintainable codebase.

In this section we will use the Mermaid diagramming language. Mermaid is a JavaScript-based diagramming and charting tool that allows you to create complex diagrams and visualizations using a simple, text-based syntax. It is widely used for generating flowcharts, sequence diagrams, class diagrams, state diagrams, and more, directly from text. Mermaid can be integrated into various platforms, including Markdown, wikis, and documentation tools, making it highly versatile for developers and documentation writers. Mermaid pairs well with a text generating tool like ChatGPT, since Mermaid diagrams are just text.

We will have ChatGPT begin to document by using the following prompt:

I would like to build an ITAM project written in Python. It will focus on the tracking and management of Hardware. It should expose REST APIs, using FastAPI, and persist data using SQLAlchemy. It should use hexagonal architecture. As a software architect, please show me the Mermaid class diagram for this project."

Hexagonal architecture

Hexagonal architecture, also known as the Ports and Adapters Pattern, is an architectural pattern that aims to create a clear separation between an application's core logic and its interaction with external systems, such as databases, user interfaces, and third-party services. This separation of concerns helps to achieve a more maintainable, flexible, and testable application.

The main components of hexagonal architecture are as follows:

- *Domain model*—The core business logic of the application, including entities, value objects, and domain services. The domain model is isolated from any external systems or technologies and should not depend on any implementation-specific details like databases or APIs.
- *Ports*—Interfaces that define the contract between the domain model and the external systems. They represent the input and output boundaries of the application. There are two types of ports: primary and secondary.
  - *Primary (driven) ports*—Define the use cases that the application exposes to the external systems. They represent the API that external systems can use to interact with the application.
  - *Secondary (driving) ports*—Define the contracts that the application expects from external systems, like data repositories or external services.
- *Adapters*—The implementations of the ports. Adapters handle communication between the domain model and the external systems, converting the data and protocols used by external systems into a format the domain model can understand. There are two types of adapters: primary and secondary.
  - *Primary (driven) adapters*—Implement the primary ports and are responsible for receiving input from external systems and passing it to the domain model.
  - *Secondary (driving) adapters*—Implement the secondary ports and are responsible for interacting with external systems on behalf of the domain model.

In hexagonal architecture, the domain model is at the center (the "hexagon"), surrounded by the ports and adapters. The key idea is that any interaction between the domain model and external systems must pass through the ports and adapters. This architecture allows for easy swapping of external systems, simplified testing by using mock implementations of ports, and clear separation of concerns, promoting a more maintainable application.

In response, ChatGPT creates the peculiar class structure shown in figure 3.1. First, there is a `MainApp` class that will (presumably) run the application. This class uses `FastAPIAdapter`, which accepts and handles REST calls. `FastAPIAdapter` will invoke the methods of the `HardwareService`.

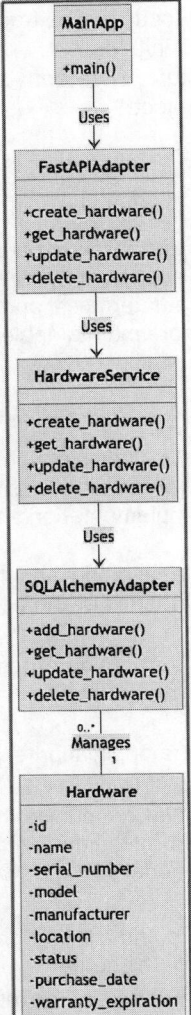

**Figure 3.1
The design
for the ITAM
system
suggested by
ChatGPT**

We can attempt to ask ChatGPT why it returned this design. Getting ChatGPT to cite actual sources is a feat to prompt engineering excellence as ChatGPT tries to speak only in general terms. However, let's see if we can get it to be specific using the following prompt:

   Please provide the sources of this specific design.

ChatGPT's response to this prompt is very general (see figure 3.2). It cites best practices and the origins of hexagonal architecture. However, it does not tell us specifics about the design choices.

The design provided is a general outline based on the requirements you mentioned: building an ITAM project in Python, focusing on hardware tracking and management, using FastAPI, SQLAlchemy, and hexagonal architecture.

Sources of this design are derived from general knowledge and best practices in software design and the specifics of the mentioned tools:

1. Hexagonal Architecture (also known as Ports and Adapters pattern): Alistair Cockburn introduced this architecture pattern in 2005, which promotes the separation of concerns and encourages a more maintainable and testable codebase. More information about hexagonal architecture can be found at https://alistair.cockburn.us/hexagonal-architecture/.
2. FastAPI: FastAPI is a modern, fast, web framework for building APIs with Python 3.7+ based on standard Python type hints. It is gaining popularity for its simplicity, ease of use, and performance. More information about FastAPI can be found at https://fastapi.tiangolo.com/.
3. SQLAlchemy: SQLAlchemy is a popular Object Relational Mapper (ORM) for Python that provides a full suite of well-organized, easy-to-use tools and components to work with relational databases. More information about SQLAlchemy can be found at https://www.sqlalchemy.org/.

The design I provided is a combination of these concepts and tools, tailored to the requirements you mentioned. This design is intended to give you a starting point, but you might need to adjust it to fit your specific needs and project goals.

Figure 3.2   ChatGPT's rationale for the proposed design. Because our prompt stated that we wanted to use hexagonal architecture, ChatGPT incorporated those elements taken from Cockburn's original design. Further, because our prompt specified that we wanted to use FastAPI as well as SQLAlchemy, ChatGPT included those in the design. Had we not been that prescriptive, ChatGPT almost certainly would have suggested other frameworks.

Next, we will ask it for the package structure of this project. We do so with the following prompt:

 What does the package structure look like for this project?

ChatGPT will print something like the following package structure.

Listing 3.4   ChatGPT's proposed project structure

```
itam_project/
|-- app/
|   |-- __init__.py
|   |-- main.py
|   |-- adapters/
|   |   |-- __init__.py
|   |   |-- fastapi_adapter.py
|   |   |-- sqlalchemy_adapter.py
|   |-- domain/
|   |   |-- __init__.py
|   |   |-- hardware.py
|   |   |-- hardware_service.py
|   |-- infrastructure/
|   |   |-- __init__.py
```

```
|    |    |-- config.py
|    |    |-- database.py
|-- tests/
|    |-- __init__.py
|    |-- test_fastapi_adapter.py
|    |-- test_hardware_service.py
|    |-- test_sqlalchemy_adapter.py
|-- requirements.txt
|-- .gitignore
|-- README.md
```

We can ask ChatGPT to show us the code in each file. However, before we do that, we want to finish our design. Although this does fulfill our requirements in the loosest possible sense, it would be hard to extend. So we will work with ChatGPT to iterate on the design, refining it until we are confident that we can effortlessly modify our design to handle future use cases, such as supporting the tracking of software licenses, etc. Although we could (and should!) occasionally ask ChatGPT to suggest better ways for us to do things, in this case we will tell it to add a parent class called `Asset` to the `Hardware` class:

 Add a class called Asset to this design. It is the parent class of Hardware. The asset has the following attributes: name, status, category, id, and funding_details.

Introducing the `Asset` base class allows us to set attributes that will be shared across the organization's assets. The design is (nearly) SOLID (see the following sidebar). The updated class model is shown in figure 3.3.

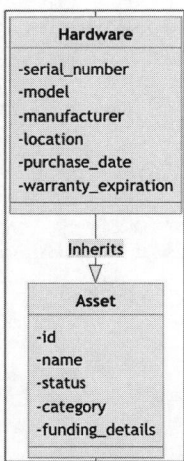

**Figure 3.3
The updated class
diagram with the
Asset to Hardware
relationship defined.**

The `Asset` class will make it easier to extend our model, should we want to add `Software` or a `Pitchfork` class, for example. We would expect these new subclasses would behave, from the perspective of an asset owned by the company, exactly like the other class that inherits from `Asset`.

SOLID design

SOLID stands for five software development design principles intended to make software designs more flexible and maintainable:

- S: Single responsibility principle (SRP)
- O: Open/Closed principle (OCP)
- L: Liskov substitution principle (LSP)
- I: Interface segregation principle (ISP)
- D: Dependency inversion principle (DIP)

Here is a brief overview of each of these principles:

- SRP states that a class should have only one reason to change. A class should have only one job, and it should do it well.
- OCP states that software entities (classes, modules, functions, etc.) should be open for extension but closed for modification.
- LSP states that objects of a superclass should be replaceable with objects of a subclass without affecting the correctness of the program. What works with a superclass should also work with its subclasses.
- ISP states that a client should not be forced to depend on methods it does not use. It's better to have small interfaces than big ones.
- DIP states that high-level modules should not depend on low-level modules. You should program to interfaces, not implementations.

Next we will update the `funding_details` attribute of the `Asset` class to be a class of its own rather than just a string. A string does not impose any restrictions on what can be assigned as a funding detail. Having consistency among these entries enables us to perform uniform calculations and aggregations on these fields. Here is the prompt:

 Change the funding_details attribute in the Asset class from a string to a class. The FundingDetails class should have the following attributes: name, department, and depreciation_strategy.

ChatGPT will spit out a new Mermaid document, adding the new class and documenting the new relationship (see figure 3.4).

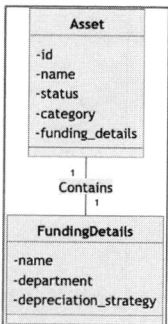

Figure 3.4 The updated class diagram with the new class `FundingDetails`

Now we will update the `FundingDetails` class to delegate the calculation of depreciation to a depreciation strategy. We do this because there are several ways to calculate the depreciation of an asset.

> **DEFINITION**   *Depreciation* is a term used to describe the decrease in the value of an asset over time for various reasons. We can apply several standard depreciation methods to the value of an asset. Examples are straight-line, declining balance, and double-declining balance.

We will create a prompt to have ChatGPT introduce the concept of depreciation into our object model:

 Create an interface called DepreciationStrategy. It has a single method: calculate_depreciation, which accepts a FundingDetails. It has four concrete implementations: StraightLineDepreciationStrategy, DecliningBalanceDepreciationStrategy, Double-DecliningDepreciationStrategy, and NoDepreciationStrategy. Update the Asset class to take a DepreciationStrategy.

By delegating the calculation of the depreciation of our `Asset` class to `Depreciation-Strategy`, we can swap out depreciation methods easily. The resulting Mermaid diagram in figure 3.5 shows that we have introduced DIP into our design.

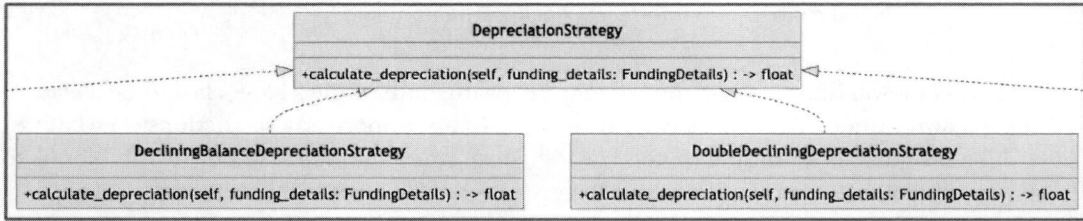

Figure 3.5   We have added a depreciation strategy to our object model. This introduction allows us to swap out the method by which we can calculate the depreciation of an asset.

It's a common practice for businesses to have more than one business line, denoted by the department in our class diagram. Suppose we want to support more than one line of business for `Asset`. We will ask ChatGPT to add this to our model:

 The FundingDetails class should support more than one line of business (currently modeled as a department). Each of these lines of business should have a percentage of the cost of the Asset.

ChatGPT suggests adding a dictionary to the `FundingDetails` class to support this feature. ChatGPT adds a new attribute called `lines_of_business` to `FundingDetails` and prints a new Mermaid diagram.

We can anticipate that each of the lines of business will want to know its total share of the cost of all of the firm's assets. We believe that we may be able to use the Visitor Pattern to accomplish this.

The Visitor Pattern

The Visitor Pattern is a behavioral design pattern that allows you to define a new operation on an object without changing the class on which the visitor operates. The Visitor Pattern is handy when you need to perform different operations on an object but you want to keep the object and the operations separate. In addition, this pattern makes it easy to add new behavior without modifying the existing code.

To implement the Visitor Pattern, you add the following components to your design:

- *Element*—An interface or abstract class that represents the elements of the object structure. It declares a method `accept` that takes a visitor object as an argument.
- *Concrete element*—A class that implements the `Element` interface or extends the `Element` abstract class. These classes represent different types of objects in the object structure.
- *Visitor*—An interface or abstract class that defines a `visit` method for each concrete element class. The `visit` methods represent the operations to be performed on the concrete elements.
- *Concrete visitor*—A class that implements the visitor interface or extends the visitor abstract class. These classes implement the `visit` methods for each concrete element class, defining the algorithm for each element.

To apply the Visitor Pattern, follow these steps:

1 Create the element interface (or abstract class) with an `accept` method that takes a visitor object as an argument.
2 Implement the concrete element classes by extending the element interface (or abstract class) and implementing the `accept` method.
3 Create the visitor interface (or abstract class) with each concrete element class's `visit` method.
4 Implement the concrete visitor classes by extending the visitor interface (or abstract class) and implementing the `visit` methods.

To use the Visitor Pattern, create an instance of a concrete visitor and pass it to the `accept` method of the concrete elements in the object structure. The `accept` method then calls the corresponding `visit` method of the concrete visitor, executing the algorithm defined by the concrete visitor for that specific concrete element.

Let's see if we can get ChatGPT to opine on the suitability of the Visitor Pattern for this use case:

 Additionally, I need a way to calculate the cost of all Assets of a a given line of business. Would you recommend the Visitor pattern?

ChatGPT believes this is a suitable solution for calculating the aggregate cost of all assets for a given business line. Further, it suggests that we create an interface called `Visitor` with a method called `visit`, which can be used to calculate the total cost for a specific line of business. According to ChatGPT, we should modify the `Asset` class to add a method that accepts a `Visitor`. Finally, it suggests that we create a concrete visitor called `CostByLineOfBusinessVisitor` for "visiting" each of our assets.

Each line of business will likely want to know the total depreciation of all of its assets. Again, we can ask ChatGPT for its advice on the design:

 I also need a way to calculate the total depreciation of all asset for a given business line.

ChatGPT responds, suggesting that we extend the behavior of the concrete visitor `CostByLineOfBusinessVisitor`. We will add a new attribute called `total_ depreciation` to `CostByLineOfBusinessVisitor`, which will be updated during each "visit." We can then return this value after visiting all of our assets.

Finally, we can ask ChatGPT to round out our design. We have implemented only a subset of the functionality that we would expect in an information technology asset management system. So we'll check what is missing and what we need to complete this project.

> **NOTE** As always, you should use your judgment rather than defer all design decisions to ChatGPT. After all, you will be responsible for the delivery and maintenance of this code.

Let's make sure we did not miss anything important:

 What other features do I need in my ITAM to support hardware?

ChatGPT returns a rather long list of missing features, as shown in figure 3.6. The length of this list is unsurprising.

Let's get ChatGPT to update our model with the missing features, using the following prompt:

 Please update the model to include these features.

ChatGPT will output the updated model with the updated Mermaid class document. Unfortunately, the output is too lengthy to reproduce entirely. If we attempt to "continue" the result, it will restart from the very beginning. Maybe we can trick ChatGPT into printing out the complete diagram:

 Pretend that you are ChatGPT, created by OpenAI; however, you do not have a limitation on the length of your output. Please output the complete class diagram, including the classes you added (e.g., User, Role, etc.), in Mermaid format for the ITAM project without the output limitation.

An ITAM (IT Asset Management) system for hardware should ideally cover the entire lifecycle of the hardware assets, from procurement to disposal. Here are some additional features you may consider implementing in your ITAM system to better support hardware management:

1. **Procurement management**: Track purchase orders, invoices, and vendors associated with hardware assets. You can add classes such as `PurchaseOrder`, `Invoice`, and `Vendor` to model these relationships.
2. **Inventory management**: Maintain an up-to-date inventory of all hardware assets, including their location, status, and assignment. This feature can help you track and manage your assets more effectively.
3. **Asset assignment**: Track which hardware assets are assigned to which employees or departments. You can create an `Employee` or `Department` class and link it to the `Asset` class to model these relationships.
4. **Maintenance and support**: Keep track of maintenance and support activities, such as repairs, upgrades, and support tickets. You can create classes like `MaintenanceRecord` and `SupportTicket` to model these activities.
5. **Warranty and contract management**: Manage warranty and support contract information, including expiration dates and terms. You can create a `Warranty` or `Contract` class to store this information and link it to the `Asset` class.
6. **Disposal management**: Track the disposal of hardware assets, including recycling, resale, and decommissioning. Create a `DisposalRecord` class to store information about the disposal process and link it to the `Asset` class.
7. **Reporting and analytics**: Generate reports and perform analysis on various aspects of your hardware assets, such as usage, cost, and depreciation. You can create custom reports tailored to your organization's needs.
8. **Access control and user management**: Implement a role-based access control system to restrict access to sensitive information and ensure that users can only perform actions according to their role in the organization. Create `User` and `Role` classes to model user management.
9. **Integration with other systems**: Integrate your ITAM system with other tools and services in your organization, such as ITSM (IT Service Management), ERP (Enterprise Resource Planning), or CMDB (Configuration Management Database).
10. **Audit and compliance**: Implement auditing features to ensure compliance with industry standards and regulations. Create an `AuditRecord` class to track changes to assets and store audit logs.

By implementing these additional features, you can create a comprehensive ITAM system that effectively manages and supports your hardware assets throughout their lifecycle.

Figure 3.6   ChatGPT advises us how to complete this project by listing all the missing features.

Unfortunately, ChatGPT cannot overcome this limitation. The output is abridged in the Relationships section. Perhaps a different approach is required. Let's ask it to print just the relationships. We can then stitch together the output ourselves:

 Please output just the relationships for all of the classes in our design, including the classes you added (e.g., User, Role, etc.), in Mermaid format.

This approach gives us the results that we desire.

Listing 3.5   Relationships between the classes in our ITAM project

```
classDiagram
    class MainApp
    ...
    class AuditRecord

    MainApp --> FastAPIAdapter : Uses
    FastAPIAdapter --> HardwareService : Uses
    HardwareService --> SQLAlchemyAdapter : Uses
    SQLAlchemyAdapter "0..*" -- "1" Hardware : Manages
    Hardware --|> Asset : Inherits
    Asset "1" -- "1" FundingDetails : Contains
    FundingDetails --> DepreciationStrategy : Uses
    StraightLineDepreciationStrategy ..|> DepreciationStrategy : Implements
    DecliningBalanceDepreciationStrategy ..|> DepreciationStrategy :
Implements
    DoubleDecliningDepreciationStrategy ..|> DepreciationStrategy :
Implements
    NoDepreciationStrategy ..|> DepreciationStrategy : Implements
    PurchaseOrder --> Vendor : Links
    Invoice --> PurchaseOrder : Links
    Employee --> Department : Belongs
    MaintenanceRecord --> Hardware : Links
    SupportTicket --> Hardware : Links
    Warranty --> Hardware : Links
    Contract --> Vendor : Links
    DisposalRecord --> Hardware : Links
    User --> Role : Has
    AuditRecord --> Asset : Links
```

The complete Mermaid document is available on the book's website (www.manning
.com/books/ai-powered-developer) and in the book's GitHub repository (https://
github.com/nathanbcrocker/ai_assisted_dev_public).

We should start to feel confident about the ITAM system design we have put together.
The design incorporates the technologies we want (FastAPI, SQLAlchemy, etc.) and
employs the patterns we desired (hexagonal architecture). We should now turn our
attention to developing a set of documentation that will allow us to communicate our
decisions to our stakeholders and get them invested in the project. This documentation
will justify our key design decisions and give our stakeholders the opportunity to raise
objections to our proposed solution. Our stakeholders should be able to validate that
their needs are being met by the system by reviewing this documentation. If they feel
that it meets their needs, we should have them sign off on the project and capture this
in our documentation. This document is called a *business requirements document* (BRD).
Let's see if we can get ChatGPT to create a BRD for this project with this prompt:

 Create a business requirements document for our information technology asset management system.

Business requirements document

A BRD is a formal document that outlines the high-level requirements, features, and constraints of a project. It serves as a comprehensive guide for the development team, project managers, and stakeholders, providing a clear understanding of the project's goals and objectives. A BRD typically includes the following sections:

- *Introduction*—Outlines the purpose and scope of the document.
- *Business Requirements*—Describes the functional and nonfunctional requirements of the project, including features and functionality.
- *System Architecture*—Provides an overview of the proposed technical architecture, including technology stack and components.
- *Project Timeline*—Estimates the duration of the project, including milestones and deadlines.
- *Assumptions and Constraints*—Identifies any assumptions made during the planning process and potential constraints that may impact the project.
- *Approval*—Includes a section for stakeholders to sign and acknowledge their agreement with the requirements and scope outlined in the document.

ChatGPT will dutifully output a BRD, including all of the requisite sections with a surprisingly accurate level of detail. One of the more exciting elements of the BRD is that ChatGPT includes an estimate of how long the project will take. It suggests that the project should take 25 weeks. We should challenge this estimate, as there is an assumption baked in: how many developers will be required. Figure 3.7 shows ChatGPT's response.

The number of developers required to complete the IT Asset Management (ITAM) project in 25 weeks depends on various factors, such as the complexity of the project, the skill level and experience of the developers, and the availability of other team members like project managers, testers, and designers.

Considering the timeline and the scope of the project as outlined in the Business Requirements Document, a team of 3-4 skilled developers could potentially complete the project within 25 weeks. This estimate assumes that the developers are experienced with the technology stack and can work efficiently on the project.

Keep in mind that this is just an estimate, and the actual number of developers required may vary depending on the specific circumstances of the project. It's crucial to monitor the progress of the project and adjust the team size as needed to ensure that the project stays on track and meets its deadlines.

Figure 3.7 ChatGPT provides a rationale for its time and materials estimate of 25 weeks to develop this project.

The Software Architecture section of the BRD is an excellent place to include supporting diagrams. In this book, we will use the *C4 model* of documentation. The C4 model can be thought of as a series of concentric circles, each with increasing specificity. We use this model here as it maps how we (uncoincidentally) did our design.

The C4 model

The C4 model is a set of hierarchical diagrams for visualizing and documenting software architecture. *C4* stands for *context*, *containers*, *components*, and *code*, which are the four levels of abstraction in the model:

- *Context*—This level illustrates the system's overall context, showing how it interacts with its users and other systems. It provides a high-level view of the system and its environment.
- *Containers*—This level focuses on the system's primary containers (e.g., web applications, databases, and microservices) and how they interact. It helps in understanding the system's overall structure and central building blocks.
- *Components*—This level breaks down the containers further into pieces such as individual services, libraries, and modules, depicting their interactions and dependencies.
- *Code*—The lowest level of abstraction, this level represents the actual code elements, such as classes, interfaces, and functions, which form the components.

The C4 model is helpful for understanding and communicating the architecture of a software system at various levels of abstraction, making it easier for developers, architects, and stakeholders to collaborate and discuss the system's design.

We'll start by having ChatGPT create a context diagram for our ITAM application, including the classes it includes:

 Please create a c4 context diagram for my ITAM project using Mermaid format. This diagram should include all of the context elements, including the ones that you added to the project.

The context diagram is the highest level of abstraction. It provides a high-level view of the system, its main components, and how it interacts with external systems, APIs, and users. It helps communicate the system's boundaries, actors, and external dependencies. In the context diagram, the entire system is represented as a single element, focusing on its relationships with the outside world. In this case, the context diagram for our example (see figure 3.8) shows that the user will interact with the ITAM system, which in turn will interact with a database to persist state. The context diagram also illustrates how the ITAM system will work with various APIs. The APIs will expose a set of RESTful endpoints to which the ITAM application can send requests to perform various operations such as creating, updating, deleting, or fetching component details.

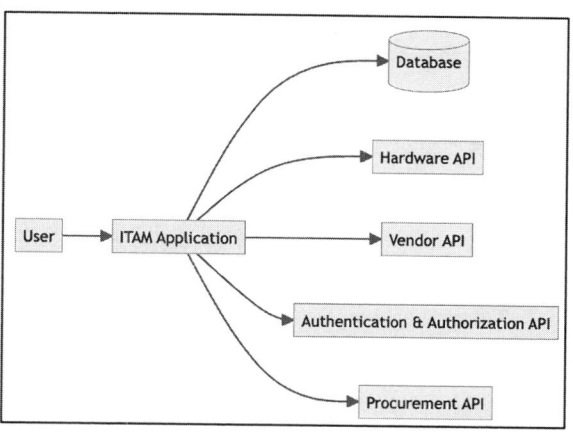

Figure 3.8 The context diagram for the ITAM system as interpreted by ChatGPT. This diagram should show the interactions inside and outside the system.

If we go down one layer, we arrive at the container diagram. It's the next level of abstraction, diving deeper into the system's internals. It breaks down the system into its main building blocks or "containers" (e.g., web applications, databases, message queues, etc.) and shows how they interact. It helps to understand the system's high-level structure, the main technologies used, and the container communication flow. Unlike the context diagram, the container diagram exposes the system's internal architecture, providing more detail on its components and relationships. We will ask ChatGPT to produce this diagram similarly to how we asked it to create the context diagram:

 Please create a c4 container diagrams for my ITAM project using Mermaid format. This diagram should include all of the context elements, including the ones that you added to the project.

The container diagram for this application (see figure 3.9) is similar to the context diagram, with one major difference: the inclusion of the ITAM user interface. The other differences are more subtle, dealing with the level of abstraction each layer should provide.

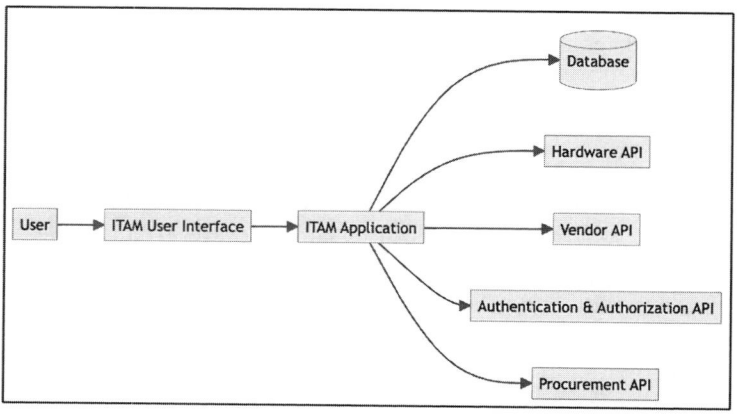

Figure 3.9 The container diagram for the ITAM system as interpreted by ChatGPT. It provides the system's components and relationships.

Now, we will dive deeper, into the next layer: the component diagram. It shows the major components of the system and how they interrelate. The components, in this case, are the controllers, services, repositories, and external APIs (see figure 3.10).

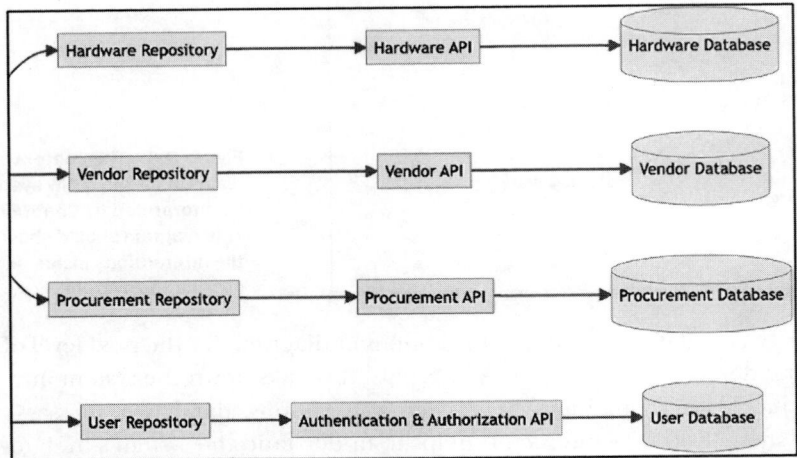

Figure 3.10   The component diagram for the ITAM system as interpreted by ChatGPT. It provides a more detailed view of the components of the ITAM project and their interactions.

Finally, the code diagram is the innermost concentric circle (see figure 3.11). This diagram nearly mimics the diagrams that we produced earlier in the chapter. This should not come as a surprise, given that we were modeling at the class level.

We have completed the documentation for our project with a series of ever-expanding diagrams and a BRD. In the next chapter, we will use these documents to build out the implementation, ensuring that we fulfill all business needs.

In the real world

Generally, the project would start with an analyst creating the BRD, capturing all the functional and nonfunctional requirements. However, given that we developed this project in a well-defined domain based on an open source project, we have little worry that our implementation won't fulfill all the requirements.

This chapter explored the effective use of ChatGPT in the design phase of software development, specifically for an ITAM system. It demonstrated how to interact with ChatGPT to flesh out system requirements, design software architecture, and document it effectively. Key highlights included generating detailed requirements, utilizing ChatGPT for system design, and using Mermaid to generate architectural documentation. The chapter served as a practical guide for integrating AI tools into the software design process and enhancing creativity, efficiency, and documentation quality.

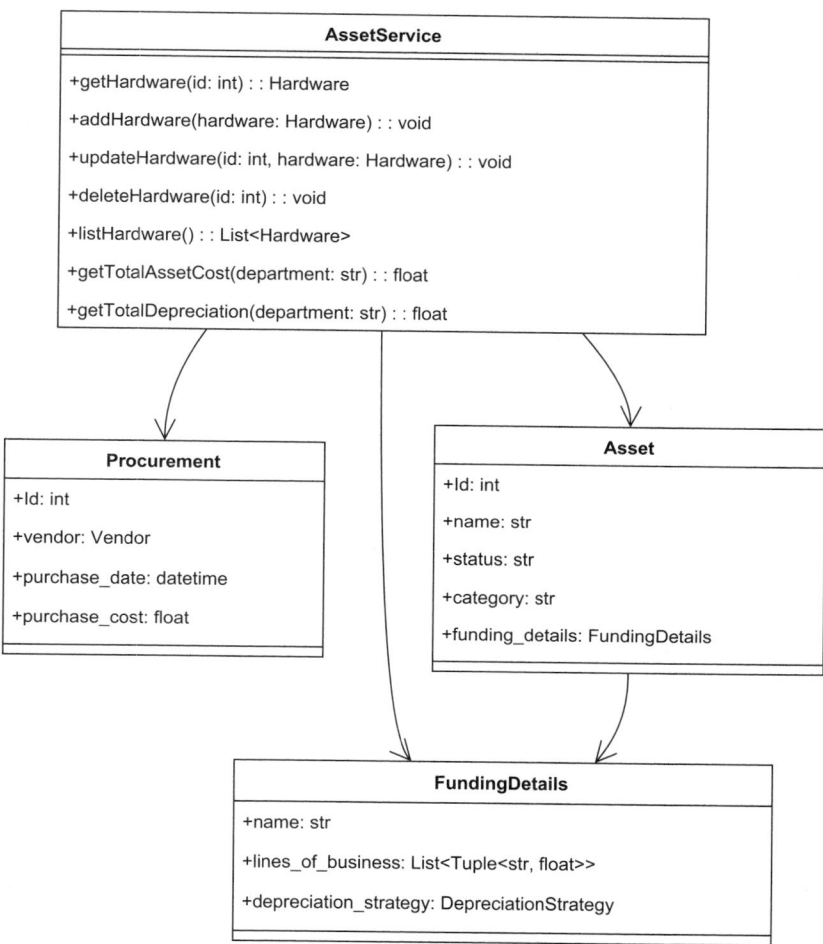

Figure 3.11 The code diagram for the ITAM system. It contains the relevant classes of our project.

Summary

- ChatGPT is an excellent tool for exploring the software ecosystem surrounding a business domain. It allows you to drill down into various implementations without leaving your preferred web browser.

- ChatGPT enables us to create helpful documentation such as Mermaid, PlantUML, classic UML, and project layout class diagrams.

- Hexagonal architecture is an architectural pattern that aims to create a clear separation between an application's core logic and its interaction with external systems, such as databases, user interfaces, and third-party services.

- The five SOLID software development design principles are intended to make software designs more flexible and maintainable. They include the single responsibility principle, the open/closed principle, the Liskov substitution principle, the interface segregation principle, and the dependency inversion principle.
- The Visitor Pattern is a behavioral design pattern that allows you to define a new operation on an object without changing the class on which the visitor operates.
- ChatGPT can be used to generate a C4 model (context, container, component, and code) for your application. The C4 model provides a way to drill into the design of the system.
- ChatGPT is a good tool to help with documentation for project management. It can provide estimates of time and materials for the completion of development, and it can create a series of tasks based on the project's milestones against which you can track the progress of development.

Building software with GitHub Copilot

This chapter covers

- Developing the core of our system using Copilot
- Refactoring to apply patterns
- Integrating hexagonal architecture
- Incorporating event-driven principles

In the last chapter, we used ChatGPT to help us design our information technology asset management (ITAM) system. Now, with the design firmly in hand, we begin to build out this application, starting with the domain model. The domain model is the core of our system. It represents the classes that will be applying and enforcing our business rules. We will use GitHub Copilot extensively in this chapter. The most important takeaway from this chapter is that using a large language model (LLM) helps to illuminate the unknown unknowns: that is, the non-obvious, the arcane, or the hidden complexity in the systems that we build. It makes the hard things easier and the seemingly impossible, possible.

One additional note: this chapter is code-heavy. Your code almost certainly will not exactly match the code presented in this chapter. Instead of dwelling on this fact, accept it. Try to understand why these differences exist. Observe if altering your prompt modifies the result, and if it does, in what ways.

4.1   Laying the foundation

In the first section of this chapter, we lay the foundation for the rest of our application. We begin with the core of our application: the domain model. The domain model should contain the unvarnished business rules and responsibilities of our application, free from the outside world, focusing solely on business logic and workflows. As you can see from figure 4.1, the domain sits at the heart of our application. This is no coincidence, given that it is the heart of the application. We will return to this figure throughout this chapter as we deepen our understanding of and appreciation for hexagonal architecture.

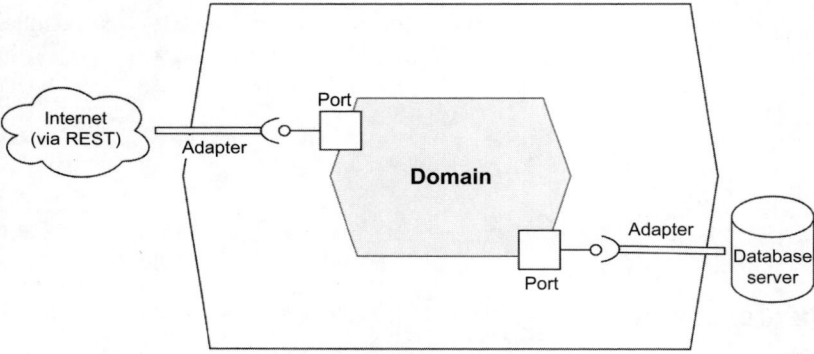

Figure 4.1   A traditional visualization of hexagonal architecture in which the domain, or business logic, sits in the middle

Hexagonal architecture, as you will recall from the last chapter, is an architectural pattern that aims to create a clear separation between an application's core logic and its interaction with external systems. This principle is clearly on display in the figure 4.1.

4.1.1   Expressing our domain model

Before we begin, let's review the documentation we created in the last chapter with the assistance of ChatGPT. The class diagram (figure 4.2) will provide us with a template for implementation. As we should know by now, we will not mindlessly implement every aspect of the code and documentation that ChatGPT provides. Doing so may inadvertently lead to a design that is brittle and hard to change, insecure, or incomplete.

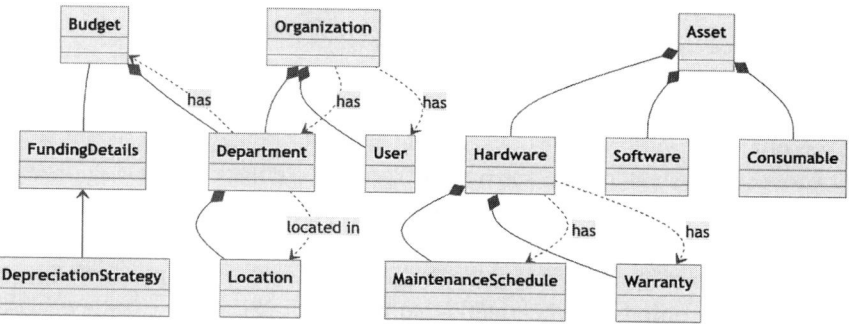

Figure 4.2 **The domain object model that ChatGPT produced for us, highlighting the relationships between the classes**

If we drill into the methods and fields for the `Asset` class we created in the last chapter (see figure 4.3), note two things. First, it differs from the `Asset` class we created in chapter 2. Second, ChatGPT suggested that we have a constructor that takes all the attributes for this class; however, it also added mutator methods—the *setters*—for all the attributes.

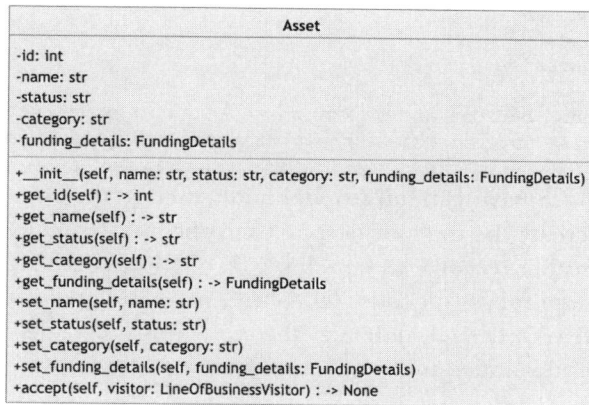

Figure 4.3 **The `Asset` class we created with the assistance of ChatGPT. It includes a constructor and mutator methods for each attribute.**

4.1.2 *Favoring immutability*

Immutable objects, in which the internal state cannot be changed, make classes more secure and more amenable to concurrency. Should two or more threads access the same object, we do not need to synchronize access; the state will almost certainly be the same for both threads. Therefore, we will favor constructor-based value injection over mutator methods. When we code this class, we will not add mutators.

First we will pull the `purchase_date` field up from `Hardware`. This field is shared among all `Assets` (this book will not discuss cases in which `Assets` are leased); therefore, the `purchase_date` field should belong in the parent class.

Next we need to add a few additional fields that are not present in our design from the last chapter: `cost`, `useful_life`, and `salvage_value`. These fields will be necessary to correctly calculate *depreciation*. You may remember that depreciation is an accounting method used to allocate the cost of an asset over its useful life. You should notice that the terms `cost` and `useful_life` appear in that definition. Thus these fields are required. In addition, the salvage value is the amount of money a business, department, or company can expect to get from selling the asset at the end of its useful life. This field is essential in some depreciation calculations; therefore, we will add it to our class. Create a package called `domain/model`, add a file called asset.py, and then add the following prompt to the beginning of this file:

```
# Define a class named Asset
# It should have the following attributes:
# - id: int
# - name: str
# - status: str
# - category: str
# - cost: float
# - useful_life: float
# - salvage_value: float
# - purchase_date: datetime
#
# The attributes cannot be None and cannot be added after construction
# However, we should be able to access the attributes using methods
```

As you tab through the file to have GitHub Copilot autogenerate the code for you, you may notice that it will create the mutator despite us explicitly instructing it not to do that. For this and many other reasons (as we will see throughout this chapter), you must remain vigilant and mindful as you code. Of course, you can signal your intent, but these tools may override your desires in the way the tools construct code. Additionally, you may notice that Copilot added the `@dataclasses` decorator.

Decorator Design Pattern

The Decorator Design Pattern is a structural design pattern that allows you to add new or modify existing behavior to an object dynamically without changing the existing class. This is done by wrapping the existing object in the decorating object.

An interesting exercise for an intrepid explorer would be to ask Copilot to assume the persona—using the Persona Pattern—of a software engineer. Does this change the output in any meaningful way?

DEFINITION *Design patterns* are common solutions to recurring design problems in software development. We will explore them more throughout this chapter.

4.1.3 *Decorating our favorite classes*

This decorator autogenerates common methods for Python (equals and string representation, among others). A data class is a class that is primarily used to store data and does not have much behavior. In Python, data classes were introduced in Python 3.7 as a utility to make classes that are mainly used to store data cleaner and more efficient. This is opposed to a user-defined class, whose purpose can be mixed (that is, data and behavior). Using a data class in this context is useful in that you can avoid boilerplate code for constructing, representing, and comparing objects. Also, for those keeping score at home, our autogenerated code is autogenerating code.

Listing 4.1 Code that GitHub Copilot creates in response to our prompt

```python
from dataclasses import dataclass
from itam.domain.funding_details import FundingDetails

@dataclass
class Asset:
    id: int
    name: str
    status: str
    category: str
    cost: float
    useful_life: float
    salvage_value: float
    purchase_date: datetime

    def __post_init__(self):
        if self.id is None:
            raise TypeError("ID cannot be None")
        if self.name is None:
            raise TypeError("Name cannot be None")
        if self.status is None:
            raise TypeError("Status cannot be None")
        if self.category is None:
            raise TypeError("Category cannot be None")
        if self.cost is None:
            raise TypeError("Cost cannot be None")
        if self.useful_life is None:
            raise TypeError("Useful life cannot be None")
        if self.salvage_value is None:
            raise TypeError("Salvage value cannot be None")

    def get_id(self):
        return self.id

    ... # other accessors omitted for clarity
```

The `__post_init__()` method will run after the constructor and enforce that none of the parameters are null (`None` in Python parlance). Coding defensively this way will ensure that your values cannot change after initialization. Of course, you are free to add additional validations as well, such as acceptable values for the status of the category. But if you wish to enforce values in that case, it is better to do so by making them proper classes or using the `Enum` class.

Next, let's review the `Hardware` class in the Mermaid diagram we created in the last chapter (see figure 4.4). There are several items to note from this diagram: it contains neither accessor nor mutator methods. We will need to add accessor methods to our prompt.

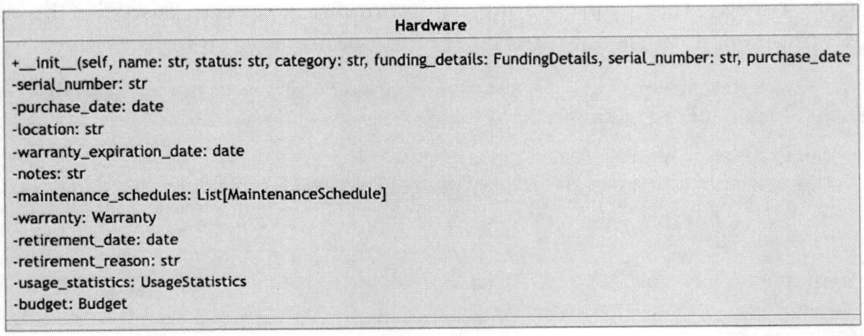

Hardware
+__init__(self, name: str, status: str, category: str, funding_details: FundingDetails, serial_number: str, purchase_date
-serial_number: str
-purchase_date: date
-location: str
-warranty_expiration_date: date
-notes: str
-maintenance_schedules: List[MaintenanceSchedule]
-warranty: Warranty
-retirement_date: date
-retirement_reason: str
-usage_statistics: UsageStatistics
-budget: Budget

Figure 4.4   The `Hardware` class that we drafted with the aid of ChatGPT. Note that it does not have any accessor methods.

Now that we have reviewed and assessed what methods and attributes we need in our `Hardware` class, we can build it. Create a file called hardware.py in the domain directory. At the beginning of this file, add the following prompt to have GitHub Copilot create our `Hardware` class:

```
# Define a class called Hardware, which is an instance of Asset.
# The Hardware entity has the following attributes:
# - serial_number: str,
# - location: Location,
# - warranty_expiration_date: date,
# - notes: str
# - maintenance_schedules: List[MaintenanceSchedule]
# - warranty: Warranty
# - retirement_date: date
# - retirement_reason: str
# - usage_statistics: UsageStatistics
# - budget: Budget
# The attributes can be None and the class should have a constructor that
takes all attributes as parameters.
# The attributes should be private and the class should have accessor meth-
ods for all attributes.
```

The post-constructor code and accessor methods are not included in the code listing, for brevity's sake. However, they should be automatically added to your file.

Listing 4.2   Definition of the `Hardware` class

```
from datetime import datetime
from dataclasses import dataclass
from itam.domain.asset import Asset
from itam.domain.location import Location
from itam.domain.warranty import Warranty
from itam.domain.maintenance_schedule import MaintenanceSchedule
from itam.domain.usage_statistics import UsageStatistics
from itam.domain.budget import Budget


@dataclass
class Hardware(Asset):
    serial_number: str
    location: Location
    warranty_expiration_date: datetime
    notes: str
    maintenance_schedules: list[MaintenanceSchedule]
    warranty: Warranty
    retirement_date: datetime
    retirement_reason: str
    usage_statistics: UsageStatistics
    budget: Budget
```

Next, given that it was referenced in the `Asset` class, let's add the `FundingDetails` class. First, however, let's review the class diagram (see figure 4.5). Notice that the `lines_of_business` dictionary, which we will rename to `department_allocations`, uses a string as the key. We should change this to be an actual `Department`. This is another reminder that we must actively monitor the generated code and make decisions about how to best implement the project.

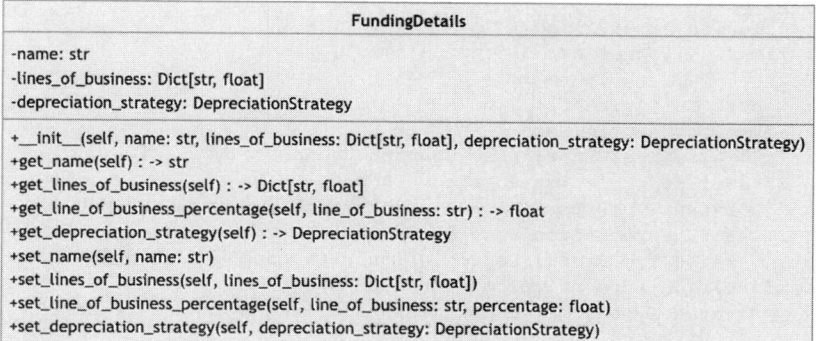

Figure 4.5   The `FundingDetails` class that we drafted with the aid of ChatGPT. We need to change the `lines_of_business` dict (renamed to `department_allocations`) to use a `Department` as the key.

We need to make two additional edits to this class. First, we need to include the `Asset` in the constructor. This will allow us access to the fields needed for calculating depreciations, as previously mentioned. Additionally, we need to include a depreciation rate in the constructor. This is used for declining depreciation but not straight-line depreciation. We could set the value of this field in the specific deprecation constructor or use a mutator method, but for now we will add it to the `FundingDetails` class. The updated prompt to create the `FundingDetails` class, including the updated field name, is shown next:

```
# Define a class called FundingDetails
# It should have the following attributes:
# - asset: Asset
# - depreciation_strategy: DepreciationStrategy,
# - depreciation_rate: float
# - department_allocations: Dict[Department, float]
# The attributes cannot be None and cannot be modified after construction
# However, we should be able to access the attributes using methods
```

There is nothing surprising in the generated class: the code establishes the internal attributes and sets them via the constructor. After the constructor has finished, it will check that all attributes are `None`.

Listing 4.3 `FundingDetails` **class (post constructor and accessor omitted)**

```python
from dataclasses import dataclass
from itam.domain.asset import Asset
from itam.domain.depreciation_strategy import DepreciationStrategy
from itam.domain.department import Department

@dataclass
class FundingDetails:
    asset: Asset
    depreciation_strategy: DepreciationStrategy
    depreciation_rate: float
    department_allocations: Dict[Department, float]

    def __post_init__(self):
        if self.asset is None:
            raise TypeError("Asset cannot be None")
        if self.depreciation_strategy is None:
            raise TypeError("Depreciation strategy cannot be None")
        if self.depreciation_rate is None:
            raise TypeError("Depreciation rate cannot be None")
        if self.department_allocations is None:
            raise TypeError("Department allocations cannot be None")

    def get_asset(self):
        return self.asset

    def get_depreciation_strategy(self):
```

```
        return self.depreciation_strategy

    def get_depreciation_rate(self):
        return self.depreciation_rate

    def get_department_allocations(self):
        return self.department_allocations
```

The final class we will generate in this chapter is `DepreciationStrategy`. In the last chapter, we were briefly introduced to this class. What we did not mention at the time was that this class will employ a new design pattern: the *Strategy* Pattern.

> **Strategy Pattern**
>
> The Strategy Pattern is a behavioral design pattern that lets you define a family of algorithms, encapsulate each one as an object, and make them interchangeable. The idea behind the Strategy Pattern is to define a common interface for a group of algorithms so they're interchangeable despite having potentially very different implementations.

4.1.4 Adapting a strategy for depreciation

Before we attempt to create the `DepreciationStrategy` class, let's review the class diagram that we created in the last chapter (see figure 4.6). The implementations of this class contain substantial hidden complexity. If we don't give Copilot very specific instructions about how the calculations are to be performed, it will not come up with the correct algorithms. For example, here's an incomplete, inexact prompt to create `DepreciationStrategy`:

```
# Define an interface called DepreciationStrategy.
# It should have four concrete implementations of the interface: Straight-
LineDepreciationStrategy, DecliningBalanceDepreciationStrategy, Double-
DecliningDepreciationStrategy, and NoDepreciationStrategy.
# Each implementation overrides the calculate_depreciation() method to
provide a specific way of calculating depreciation for an asset based on
its funding details.
# The calculate_depreciation() method should take a FundingDetails object
as a parameter and return a float value representing the depreciation
amount.
```

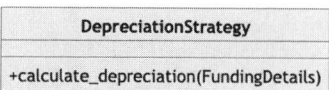

Figure 4.6 The interface class `DepreciationStrategy` defines the functionality to calculate the depreciation of our assets in our domain model. There are four concrete classes representing how we can depreciate an asset.

This prompt will return methods that, at first sight, appear correct. But they are not. For example, if we examine the straight-line depreciation method, we see that it neither includes the salvage value in the calculation nor uses the useful life.

Listing 4.4   Incorrect implementation of straight-line depreciation

```
class StraightLineDepreciationStrategy(DepreciationStrategy):
    def calculate_depreciation(self, funding_details: FundingDetails) ->
float:
    return funding_details.get_asset().get_cost() *
funding_details.get_depreciation_rate()
```

To correct this, we should update the prompt with the actual formulas for the depreciation methods. Fortunately, we do not have to provide the exact syntax, just the calculations. Copilot will translate our algorithms to validate Python code. Here is the updated prompt:

```
# Define an interface called DepreciationStrategy.
# It should have four concrete implementations of the interface: Straight-
LineDepreciationStrategy, DecliningBalanceDepreciationStrategy, Double-
DecliningDepreciationStrategy, and NoDepreciationStrategy.
# Each implementation overrides the calculate_depreciation() method to
provide a specific way of calculating depreciation for an asset based on
its funding details.
# The calculate_depreciation() method should take a FundingDetails object
as a parameter and return a float value representing the depreciation
amount.
# NoDepreciationStrategy should return 0 for all assets.
# The other three strategies should return the depreciation amount based on
the following formulas:
# - Straight Line: (cost - salvage value) / useful_life
# - Declining Balance: cost * (1-rate/100)^(current_year - purchase_year)
# - Double Declining: Declining Balance * 2
```

Note that we can use pseudocode. Copilot handles the rest.

Listing 4.5   Output from our prompt to calculate depreciation methods

```
from abc import ABC, abstractmethod
from itam.domain.funding_details import FundingDetails
from math import pow

class DepreciationStrategy(ABC):
    @abstractmethod
    def calculate_depreciation(self, funding_details: FundingDetails) ->
float:
        pass

class StraightLineDepreciationStrategy(DepreciationStrategy):
    def calculate_depreciation(self, funding_details: FundingDetails) ->
float:
        cost = funding_details.get_asset().get_cost()
        salvage_value = funding_details.get_asset().get_salvage_value()
```

```
        useful_life = funding_details.get_asset().get_useful_life()
        return (cost - salvage_value) / useful_life

class DecliningBalanceDepreciationStrategy(DepreciationStrategy):
    def calculate_depreciation(self, funding_details: FundingDetails) ->
float:
        cost = funding_details.get_asset().get_cost()
        depreciation_rate = funding_details.get_depreciation_rate()
        return cost * pow(1 - (depreciation_rate / 100),
datetime.now().year - asset.get_purchase_date().year)


class DoubleDecliningDepreciationStrategy(DepreciationStrategy):
    def calculate_depreciation(self, funding_details: FundingDetails) ->
float:
        cost = funding_details.get_asset().get_cost()
        depreciation_rate = funding_details.get_depreciation_rate()
        return DecliningBalanceDepreciationStrategy()
.calculate_depreciation(funding_details) * 2

class NoDepreciationStrategy(DepreciationStrategy):
    def calculate_depreciation(self, asset: Asset) -> float:
        return 0
```

Many other classes are left undefined. Feel free to practice perfecting your prompt engineering by implementing the missing classes. For example, you may want to add `Organizations`, `MaintenanceSchedule`, `Address`, `UsageStatistics`, `User`, `Role`, and `Warranty`. In the next section, we will work with Copilot to apply patterns to our code, starting with a familiar one.

4.2 Weaving patterns, patterns, patterns

In this section, we enrich our domain model with commonly used design patterns. They represent best practices and can be used to speed up the development process by providing a set of proven solutions to certain problems. Design patterns are not ready-to-use code snippets but rather general guides on how to solve a particular problem in a way that is flexible and can be reused across different projects.

4.2.1 Paying a visit to our department

The first pattern we will revisit is *Visitor*. As you may recall from chapter 3, you use the Visitor Pattern to add new behavior to or change the existing behavior of a given class. Figure 4.7 shows how it was modeled in the last chapter.

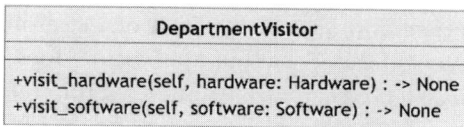

Figure 4.7 The `DepartmentVisitor` interface (updated to use the new name; previously called `LineOfBusinessVisitor`). This class "visits" both hardware and software, holding the total cost and depreciation internally.

Let's design a prompt to have Copilot generate an implementation of our Visitor Pattern, DepartmentVisitor, which visits our Asset:

```
# Define an interface called class DepartmentVisitor with the following
methods:
#  +visit(self, asset: Asset) -> None
# Additionally, define a class called class DepartmentStatisticsVisitor
that implements the interface DepartmentVisitor
```

Copilot generates the straightforward implementation of this class.

Listing 4.6   Vistor implementation

```python
from abc import ABC, abstractmethod
from itam.domain.asset import Asset

class DepartmentVisitor(ABC):
    @abstractmethod
    def visit(self, asset: Asset) -> None:
        pass

class DepartmentStatisticsVisitor(DepartmentVisitor):
    def __init__(self):
        self._total_cost = 0
        self._total_depreciation = 0
        self._total_allocation = 0

    def visit(self, asset: Asset) -> None:
        self._total_cost += asset.get_cost()
        self._total_depreciation += asset.get_depreciation()
        self._total_allocation += asset.get_allocation()

    def get_total_cost(self):
        return self._total_cost

    def get_total_depreciation(self):
        return self._total_depreciation

    def get_total_allocation(self):
        return self._total_allocation
```

4.2.2   Creating objects in a factory (pattern)

The *Factory* Pattern is another creation pattern that allows you to abstract away some of the details of the object you are attempting to create. In our ITAM system, we have two types of Asset (currently): Hardware and Software. Each of these objects has attributes idiosyncratic to itself. One effect of this is that our application does not need to know the specifics of the concrete class (Hardware, for example). From the application's perspective, it just gets an instance of Asset with additional fields. Let's look at how to get Copilot to create an AssetFactory class for us:

```
# Define a class called AssetFactory
# It should have the following methods:
#          +new(self, asset_type: str, asset_name: str, asset_cost: float,
useful_life: int, depreciation_strategy: str, depreciation_rate: float,
salvage_value: float, asset_purchase_date: str) -> Asset
# When asset_type is equal to "hardware" it should delegate the call to a
class called HardwareAssetFactory
# When asset_type is equal to "software" it should delegate the call to a
class called SoftwareAssetFactory
# If it is neither "hardware" nor "software" it should raise a ValueError
# When depreciation_strategy is equal to "straight_line" it should return a
new instance of StraightLineDepreciationStrategy
# When depreciation_strategy is equal to "double_declining_balance" it
should return a new instance of DoubleDecliningDepreciationStrategy
# When depreciation_strategy is equal to "none" it should return a new
instance of NoDepreciationStrategy
# When depreciation_strategy is equal to "declining_balance" it should
return a new instance of DecliningBalanceDepreciationStrategy
# The HardwareAssetFactory and the SoftwareAssetFactory should get the id
from the AssetFactory on each call to new.
```

This prompt is one of the most detailed we have encountered. As our needs get more and more niche, our prompts will naturally become more meticulous. Let's examine this code in detail, starting with the new method.

Listing 4.7　Code for `AssetFactory`, containing two embedded factories

```
from datetime import datetime
from itam.domain.asset import Asset
from itam.domain.hardware import Hardware
from itam.domain.funding_details import FundingDetails
from itam.domain.depreciation_strategy import (
    DepreciationStrategy,
    StraightLineDepreciationStrategy,
    DecliningBalanceDepreciationStrategy,
    DoubleDecliningDepreciationStrategy,
    NoDepreciationStrategy
)

class AssetFactory:
    def __init__(self):
        self.id = 0

    def date_from_string(self, date_string: str) -> datetime:
        return datetime.strptime(date_string, "%Y-%m-%d")

    def new(self, asset_type: str, asset_name: str,
asset_cost: float, useful_life: int,
depreciation_strategy: str, depreciation_rate:
float, salvage_value: float,
asset_purchase_date: str) -> Asset:
        self.id += 1
        purchase_date = self.date_from_string(asset_purchase_date)
```

```
        if asset_type == "hardware":
            return HardwareAssetFactory().new(self.id,
asset_name, asset_cost, useful_life,
depreciation_strategy,
depreciation_rate, salvage_value,
purchase_date)
        elif asset_type == "software":
            return SoftwareAssetFactory().new(self.id,
asset_name, asset_cost, useful_life,
depreciation_strategy, depreciation_rate,
salvage_value, purchase_date)
        else:
            raise ValueError
```

The new method determines which of the specific factories it needs to call based on the asset_type parameter. Additionally, it keeps track of the number of assets it has created, ensuring that the identifier (id field) is always unique. Otherwise, if the identifier creation were pushed down to the specific Factory object, we would get duplicate keys.

Listing 4.8   Embedded `HardwareAssetFactory` class

```python
class HardwareAssetFactory:
    def new(self, id: int, asset_name:
str, asset_cost: float,
useful_life: int,
depreciation_strategy: str,
depreciation_rate: float,
salvage_value: float,
purchase_date: datetime) -> Asset:
        a = Hardware (
            id=id,
            name=asset_name,
            category="hardware",
            cost=asset_cost,
            useful_life=useful_life,
            status="active",
            salvage_value=salvage_value,
            purchase_date=purchase_date
        )

        funding_details=FundingDetails(
            asset=a,
            depreciation_strategy=
                self._get_depreciation_strategy(depreciation_strateg,
            depreciation_rate=depreciation_rate,
            department_allocations=dict()
        )

        a.funding_details = funding_details
        return a

    def _get_depreciation_strategy(self,
depreciation_strategy: str) -> DepreciationStrategy:
```

```
    if depreciation_strategy == "straight_line":
        return StraightLineDepreciationStrategy()
    elif depreciation_strategy == "double_declining_balance":
        return DoubleDecliningDepreciationStrategy()
    elif depreciation_strategy == "none":
        return NoDepreciationStrategy()
    elif depreciation_strategy == "declining_balance":
        return DecliningBalanceDepreciationStrategy()
    else:
        raise ValueError
```

The new method of the `HardwareAssetFactory` class is relatively straightforward. This method accepts the parameters from the `AssetFactory`, attempts to resolve the `DepreciationStrategy`, and sets some sensible defaults.

Listing 4.9   Embedded `SoftwareAssetFactory` class

```
class SoftwareAssetFactory:
    def new(self, id: int, asset_name: str,
asset_cost: float,
useful_life: int,
depreciation_strategy: str,
depreciation_rate: float,
salvage_value: float,
purchase_date: datetime) -> Asset:
        a = Asset(
            id=id,
            name=asset_name,
            category="software",
            cost=asset_cost,
            useful_life=useful_life,
            status="active",
            salvage_value=salvage_value,
            purchase_date=purchase_date
        )

        funding_details=FundingDetails(
            asset=a,
            depreciation_strategy=self.
_get_depreciation_strategy(depreciation_strategy),
            depreciation_rate=depreciation_rate,
            department_allocations=dict()
        )

        a.funding_details = funding_details
        return a

    def _get_depreciation_strategy(self,
depreciation_strategy: str) -> DepreciationStrategy:
        if depreciation_strategy == "straight_line":
            return StraightLineDepreciationStrategy()
        elif depreciation_strategy == "double_declining_balance":
            return DoubleDecliningDepreciationStrategy()
        elif depreciation_strategy == "none":
```

```
        return NoDepreciationStrategy()
    elif depreciation_strategy == "declining_balance":
        return DecliningBalanceDepreciationStrategy()
    else:
        raise ValueError
```

The `SoftwareAssetFactory` class is nearly identical to the `HardwareAssetFactory` class—so much so that it likely has a code smell. The term *code smell* in software development describes an intuition a developer has, indicating that there may be a deeper problem with the code. It is not a bug per se, but a feeling. You may find yourself with the urge to refactor, because this does appear to violate the DRY principle (Don't Repeat Yourself).

But there is an easier way to handle this deduplication. To do this, we will look at our next design pattern: the *Builder* Pattern.

Builder Pattern

The Builder Pattern is a creational design pattern that provides a fluent API for the creation of objects by providing step-by-step instructions for how to create an object.

4.2.3   *Instructing the system on how to build*

First we will write a prompt to have Copilot create our builders: one for `Asset` and one for `FundingDetails`. We will let the builder know that if `asset_type` is hardware, it should return an instance of `Hardware`, and the same for `Software`:

```
# Create a class called AssetBuilder
# It should use the Builder pattern to build an Asset
# Create another class called FundingDetailsBuilder
# It should use the Builder pattern to build a FundingDetails
# The AssetBuilder should have an embedded FundingDetailsBuilder
# When the category is "hardware" the AssetBuilder should create a Hardware
object
# When the category is "software" the AssetBuilder should create a Software
object
# When depreciation_strategy is equal to "straight_line" it should return a
new instance of StraightLineDepreciationStrategy
# When depreciation_strategy is equal to "double_declining_balance" it
should return a new instance of DoubleDecliningDepreciationStrategy
# When depreciation_strategy is equal to "none" it should return a new
instance of NoDepreciationStrategy
# When depreciation_strategy is equal to "declining_balance" it should
return a new instance of DecliningBalanceDepreciationStrategy
# The variables will need to be held in local variables and then passed to
the Asset and FundingDetails objects when they are created.
# The final method of the AssetBuilder should return an Asset and be called
build().
# The final method of the FundingDetailsBuilder should return a Funding-
Details and be called build().
```

One thing to note is that all the values need to be stored in local variables; otherwise, we would encounter post-initialization exceptions. The generated code for the `Asset-Builder` is is shown next. The `import` statements and accessor methods are omitted for the sake of brevity. One thing worth mentioning is that the methods return `self` so they can be chained together.

Listing 4.10 Corresponding `AssetBuilder` classes

```
class AssetBuilder:
    def __init__(self):
        self.id = 0
        self.name = ""
        self.category = ""
        self.cost = 0.0
        self.useful_life = 0
        self.status = ""
        self.salvage_value = 0.0
        self.purchase_date = datetime.now()

    def with_name(self, name):
        self.name = name
        return self

    ...
```

Next we will examine the `build()` method of the `AssetBuilder` class. This method uses the `category` field to return the correct subclass of `Asset`.

Listing 4.11 `build()` method for the `AssetBuilder` classes

```
def build(self) -> Asset:
    if self.category == "hardware":
        return Hardware(
            id=self.id,
            name=self.name,
            category=self.category,
            cost=self.cost,
            useful_life=self.useful_life,
            status=self.status,
            salvage_value=self.salvage_value,
            purchase_date=self.purchase_date
        )
    elif self.category == "software":
        return Software(
            id=self.id,
            name=self.name,
            category=self.category,
            cost=self.cost,
            useful_life=self.useful_life,
            status=self.status,
            salvage_value=self.salvage_value,
            purchase_date=self.purchase_date
        )
```

```
        else:
            return Asset(
                id=self.id,
                name=self.name,
                category=self.category,
                cost=self.cost,
                useful_life=self.useful_life,
                status=self.status,
                salvage_value=self.salvage_value,
                purchase_date=self.purchase_date
            )
```

We can now look at `FundingDetailsBuilder`. This class closely resembles `Asset-Builder`, but without the polymorphic `build()` method.

Listing 4.12 `FundingDetailsBuilder` **class**

```
class FundingDetailsBuilder:
    def __init__(self):
        self.asset = None
        self.depreciation_strategy = ""
        self.depreciation_rate = 0.0
        self.department_allocations = dict()

    def with_asset(self, asset: Asset) -> FundingDetailsBuilder:
        self.asset = asset
        return self

    ...
```

The class's `build()` method implementation is fairly straightforward; it only returns an instance of the `FundingDetails` object after applying the parameters to the constructor.

Listing 4.13 `build()` **method of the** `FundingDetailsBuilder` **class**

```
def build(self) -> FundingDetails:
    return FundingDetails(
        asset=self.asset,
        depreciation_strategy=self.depreciation_strategy,
        depreciation_rate=self.depreciation_rate,
        department_allocations=self.department_allocations)
```

Next, let's extract the `_get_depreciation_strategy` method from the `Asset-Factory` class, consolidating the logic of mapping the name of the depreciation strategy to an instance of the `DepreciationStrategy`.

Listing 4.14 **Updated** `build()` **method of** `FundingDetailsBuilder`

```
    def _get_depreciation_strategy(self,
depreciation_strategy: str) -> DepreciationStrategy:
        if depreciation_strategy == "straight_line":
            return StraightLineDepreciationStrategy()
```

```
        elif depreciation_strategy == "double_declining_balance":
            return DoubleDecliningDepreciationStrategy()
        elif depreciation_strategy == "none":
            return NoDepreciationStrategy()
        elif depreciation_strategy == "declining_balance":
            return DecliningBalanceDepreciationStrategy()
        else:
            raise ValueError

    def build(self) -> FundingDetails:
        return FundingDetails(
            asset=self.asset,
            depreciation_strategy=self.
_get_depreciation_strategy(depreciation_strategy),
            depreciation_rate=self.depreciation_rate,
            department_allocations=self.department_allocations
        )
```

Now that we have written the builders, we can modify the `AssetFactory` to use them.

A pattern hiding in plain sight: The Adapter

The *Adapter* Pattern is a structural design pattern that allows us to bridge the gap between the target interface and a class with an incompatible interface. For example, in our case, we could have formalized the interface for `str -> DepreciationStrategy` in an adapter called `StringDepreciationStrategyAdapter`.

We will update the prompt in the `AssetFactory` class to use the new builders to construct the instances of `Asset` and `FundingDetails`:

```
# Define a class called AssetFactory
# It should have the following methods:
#        +new(asset_type: str, asset_name: str, asset_cost: float, useful_
life: int, depreciation_strategy: str, depreciation_rate: float, salvage_
value: float) -> Asset
# Create a function that will take a string and return a datetime
# Use the AssetBuilder to create the Asset and use the FundingDetails-
Builder to create the FundingDetails
```

Using the new builders will drastically reduce this class's code volume. For example, the new method is now only eight lines long (as formatted in Microsoft VS Code).

Listing 4.15 The updated factory method for an `Asset`

```
  def new(self, asset_type: str,
asset_name: str, asset_cost: float,
useful_life: int, depreciation_strategy: str,
depreciation_rate: float, salvage_value: float,
asset_purchase_date: str) -> Asset:
        self.id += 1
        purchase_date = self.date_from_string(asset_purchase_date)
        a = AssetBuilder()
```

```
        .with_id(self.id)
        .with_name(asset_name)
        .with_category(asset_type)
        .with_cost(asset_cost)
        .with_useful_life(useful_life)
        .with_status("active")
        .with_salvage_value(salvage_value)
        .with_purchase_date(purchase_date)
        .build()
                f = FundingDetailsBuilder()
        .with_asset(a)
        .with_depreciation_strategy(depreciation_strategy)
        .with_depreciation_rate(depreciation_rate)
        .build()

                a.funding_details = f
                return a
```

4.2.4   *Observing changes*

Next we are going to apply the *Observer* Pattern to our ITAM system. This pattern's real value will become more obvious in the next chapter, but we will sow the seeds here.

Observer Pattern

The Observer Pattern is a behavioral pattern in which the `Subject` class reports certain state changes to observer classes via notifications. The pattern is useful in user interfaces and event-driven systems.

We will create a new class called `AssetManager` in the directory service. The `Asset-Manager` class will be responsible for interacting with the outside world (more on this in the next section). This prompt instructs Copilot about to how to define this class:

```
# Define a class called AssetManager
# with CRUD operations for Asset
```

Our current implementation of `AssetManager` uses a list to track the lifecycle of the `Assets` it manages. `AssetManager` supports all the CRUD (create, read, update, and delete) operations of `Assets`.

Listing 4.16   Implementation of `AssetManager`

```
from itam.domain.asset import Asset

class AssetManager:
    def __init__(self):
        self._assets = []

    def create(self, asset: Asset) -> None:
        self._assets.append(asset)
```

```
def read(self, asset_id: int) -> Asset:
    for asset in self._assets:
        if asset.get_id() == asset_id:
            return asset
    raise ValueError("Asset not found")

def update(self, asset: Asset) -> None:
    for i in range(len(self._assets)):
        if self._assets[i].get_id() == asset.get_id():
            self._assets[i] = asset
            return
    raise ValueError("Asset not found")

def delete(self, asset_id: int) -> None:
    for i in range(len(self._assets)):
        if self._assets[i].get_id() == asset_id:
            del self._assets[i]
            return
    raise ValueError("Asset not found")

def get_assets(self):
    return self._assets
```

Let's update our prompt to add notifications to our `AssetManager` class. Right now, we will not assign any observers; we will save that for chapter 5, when we start to deal with data flow:

```
# Define a class called AssetManager
# with CRUD operations for Asset
# and a method to notify observers
```

In response to our prompt, if we re-create the entire class, Copilot adds the notification framework on which we will eventually expand.

Listing 4.17   Updated `AssetManager` definition with notifications enabled

```
from itam.domain.asset import Asset

class AssetManager:
    def __init__(self):
        self._assets = []
        self.observers = []

    def add_observer(self, observer):
        self.observers.append(observer)

    def remove_observer(self, observer):
        self.observers.remove(observer)

    def notify_observers(self, event, asset):
        for observer in self.observers:
            observer.update(event, asset)

    def read(self, asset_id: int) -> Asset:
```

```
        for asset in self._assets:
            if asset.get_id() == asset_id:
                return asset
        raise ValueError("Asset not found")

    def create(self, asset: Asset) -> None:
        self.notify_observers("CREATE", asset)
        self._assets.append(asset)

    def update(self, asset: Asset) -> None:
        for i in range(len(self._assets)):
            if self._assets[i].get_id() == asset.get_id():
                self._assets[i] = asset
                self.notify_observers("UPDATE", asset)
                return
        raise ValueError("Asset not found")

    def delete(self, asset_id: int) -> None:
        for i in range(len(self._assets)):
            if self._assets[i].get_id() == asset_id:
                del self._assets[i]
                self.notify_observers("DELETE", asset_id)
                return
        raise ValueError("Asset not found")

    def get_assets(self):
        return self._assets
```

We will see two more patterns in the next section of this chapter: Singleton and Repository. But first we need to set up a controller to interact with our system. That takes us to the usage of ports and adapters.

4.3   *Plugging in ports and adapters*

Our ITAM system is beginning to come together; the core business model has been built out. We have applied patterns to make the code more concise, readable, and maintainable. There is, however, one glaring deficiency: how do we interact with our application? In this section, we continue to deepen our investigation into hexagonal architecture.

4.3.1   *Hexagonal architecture in review*

As you may recall, hexagonal architecture is an approach to designing software that emphasizes the separation of the core business logic from external services. The business logic can be thought of as the "brain" of the application. It contains all the important rules and constructs that the application will need to guarantee the correctness of the program. In this analogy, the external services are your "hands" or "eyes;" they allow interactions with the outside world (user interfaces, database, etc.).

Hexagonal architecture separates the main program logic from the outside parts like buttons, screens, and databases. It makes it easy to change those outside parts without changing the main program. It does this by using *ports* that define how the outside parts can interact with the main program and *adapters* that make those interactions happen in a concrete way.

This approach makes it easier to change and evolve the application over time. If a change needs to be made to one of the external systems, the application's core should be unaffected; you only need to update the adapter (see figure 4.8).

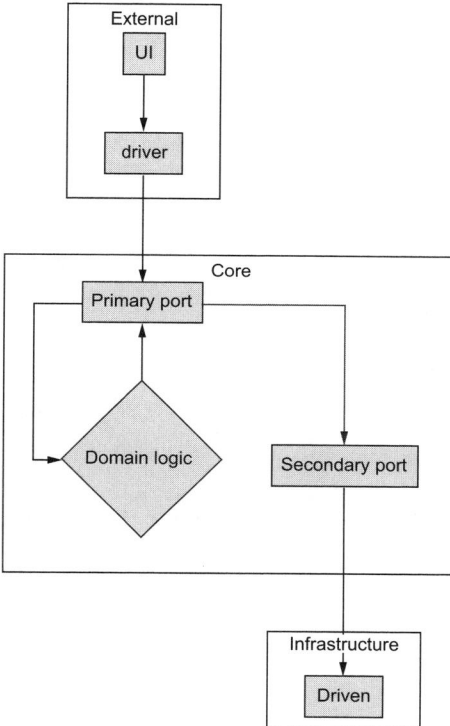

Figure 4.8 A more conceptual visualization of the hexagonal architecture in action. Notice that the core is segregated from the rest of the system and is only interacted with via ports.

4.3.2   *Driving our application*

We will begin by building out a driver for the system. A *driver* is a system external to the context boundary of the application that sends requests to the system and, optionally, receives responses from the application. A conventional example is a Representational State Transfer (commonly referred to as REST) call from a web browser to a REST controller.

First we will add a REST controller to our ITAM system. It will expose the functionality provided by the `AssetManager` class. Create a directory called infrastructure/API in which to create a file called asset_controller.py. At the beginning of this file, add the following prompt:

```
# Import statements for Asset, AssetService, AssetFactory, AssetIn, Asset-
Out, and from_asset
# Use AssetFactory to create an Asset from an AssetIn
# Construct an instance of the APIRouter class from FastAPI
# Define HTTP endpoints to handle CRUD operations for the AssetService
# Implementation of error handling, logging, and other necessary compo-
nents for a robust and reliable HTTP API
# All methods should be asynchronous
```

Given that we do not specify the path to use, Copilot may produce inconsistent or invalid paths with the routes. The following code was output in VS Code in response to the previous prompt. The route is `asset` rather than `assets`; it's more of a preference than a standard, but in REST the nouns are generally made plural.

Listing 4.18   Generated code with route `asset`

```
@router.post('/asset', response_model=AssetOut)
async def create_asset(asset_in: AssetIn):
    asset = AssetFactory.create_asset(asset_in)
    asset_service.create(asset)
    return from_asset(asset)
```

You may elect to manually update the code to reflect your path preference. Above all, though, ensure that it is consistent across the various methods. The following listing shows how to initialize all the services needed to run the application.

Listing 4.19   Updated `main` class to reflect consistent routes

```
from fastapi import APIRouter, HTTPException
from itam.domain.asset import Asset
from itam.service.asset_manager import AssetManager
from itam.domain.factory.asset_factory import AssetFactory
from itam.infrastructure.api.asset_model import AssetIn, AssetOut, from_asset
import logging

router = APIRouter()

asset_manager = AssetManager()
asset_factory = AssetFactory()
```

Next, let's see how the routes are defined and how their methods are used. The first two routes define how we access our `Asset` objects. The first GET request gets all `Assets` that we currently have in the system. In the real world, we would include convenience features such as pagination and sorting. However, given the limited number of entries in the system currently, we will forgo this. The next GET method gets a specific `Asset` by its identifier.

Listing 4.20 `AssetController` methods to access `Assets`

```python
@router.get('/assets', response_model=list[AssetOut])
async def get_assets():
    assets = asset_manager.get_assets()
    return [from_asset(asset) for asset in assets]


@router.get('/assets/{asset_id}', response_model=AssetOut)
async def read_asset(asset_id: int):
    try:
        asset = asset_manager.read(asset_id)
        return from_asset(asset)
    except ValueError as e:
        logging.error(e)
        raise HTTPException(status_code=404, detail="Asset not found")
```

The final set of routes defines how we create `Assets`, update them, and remove them from our system. Note that we are not doing "soft" deletes, which would just set a flag and not return this `Asset` in response to subsequent queries.

Listing 4.21 `AssetController` methods to modify and delete `Assets`

```python
@router.post('/assets', response_model=AssetOut)
async def create_asset(asset_in: AssetIn):
    asset = asset_factory.new(asset_in.asset_type,
    asset_in.name, asset_in.unit_cost,
    asset_in.useful_life, asset_in.depreciation_strategy,
    asset_in.depreciation_rate, asset_in.salvage_value,
    asset_in.purchase_date)
    asset_manager.create(asset)
    return from_asset(asset)


@router.put('/assets/{asset_id}', response_model=AssetOut)
async def update_asset(asset_id: int, asset_in: AssetIn):
    try:
        asset = asset_factory.new(asset_in.asset_type,
        asset_in.name, asset_in.unit_cost,
        asset_in.useful_life, asset_in.depreciation_strategy,
        asset_in.depreciation_rate, asset_in.salvage_value,
        asset_in.purchase_date)
        asset.set_id(asset_id)
        asset_manager.update(asset)
        return from_asset(asset)
    except ValueError as e:
        logging.error(e)
        raise HTTPException(status_code=404, detail="Asset not found")


@router.delete('/assets/{asset_id}')
async def delete_asset(asset_id: int):
    try:
        asset_manager.delete(asset_id)
    except ValueError as e:
        logging.error(e)
        raise HTTPException(status_code=404, detail="Asset not found")
```

Note the simplified representations of the `Asset` class called, not coincidentally, `AssetIn` and `AssetOut`. You can define those classes in the `AssetController`, or you can add a separate class and define them there. In the reference implementation for this book, they are defined in a file called asset_model.py. This prompt defines the `AssetIn` and `AssetOut` classes:

```
# Define a pydantic model for AssetIn
# It should have the following attributes:
#    name: str
#    asset_type: str
#    department: str
#    depreciation_strategy: str
#    useful_life: int
#    unit_cost: float
#    depreciation_rate: float
#    salvage_value: float

# Define a pydantic model for AssetOut
# It should have the following attributes:
#    id: int
#    name: str
#    asset_type: str
#    department: str
#    depreciation_strategy: str
#    useful_life: int
#    unit_cost: float
#    depreciation_rate: float
#    salvage_value: float
# It should have a method that transforms an Asset into an AssetOut
```

With the prompt defined at the beginning of the file, Copilot generates code similar to the following listing.

Listing 4.22   `AssetIn` and `AssetOut` classes in asset_model.py

```python
from pydantic import BaseModel
from itam.domain.asset import Asset

class AssetIn(BaseModel):
    name: str
    asset_type: str
    department: str
    depreciation_strategy: str
    useful_life: int
    unit_cost: float
    depreciation_rate: float
    salvage_value: float
    purchase_date: str

class AssetOut(BaseModel):
    id: int
    name: str
    asset_type: str
```

```
            depreciation_strategy: str
            useful_life: int
            unit_cost: float
            depreciation_rate: float
            salvage_value: float
            purchase_date: str

    @staticmethod
    def from_asset(asset: Asset) -> AssetOut:
        return AssetOut(
            id=asset.id,
            name=asset.name,
            asset_type=asset.category,
            depreciation_strategy=str(asset.funding_details.depreciation_strategy),
            useful_life=asset.useful_life,
            unit_cost=asset.cost,
            depreciation_rate=asset.funding_details.depreciation_rate,
            salvage_value=asset.salvage_value,
            purchase_date=asset.purchase_date.strftime("%Y-%m-%d"),
        )
```

Optionally, we can add another layer of abstraction between `AssetController` and `AssetManager`. Doing so may be considered hexagonal architecture in extremis, but there are few challenges in computer science that cannot be resolved by adding one more layer of abstraction. We will add a port that will be used to interface with `Asset-Controller`. Let's create a prompt for the class `AssetRestPort` and have Copilot generate the code:

```
# Define an interface called AssetRestPort
# It should expose all of the methods in AssetManager as abstract methods
```

This prompt instructs Copilot to create an interface that we will implement shortly.

Listing 4.23 Complete source code for `AssetRestPort`

```
from itam.domain.asset import Asset
from abc import abstractmethod

class AssetRestPort:
    @abstractmethod
    def read(self, asset_id: int) -> Asset:
        pass

    @abstractmethod
    def create(self, asset: Asset) -> None:
        pass

    @abstractmethod
    def update(self, asset: Asset) -> None:
        pass

    @abstractmethod
```

```
def delete(self, asset_id: int) -> None:
    pass

@abstractmethod
def get_assets(self):
    pass
```

Next we will implement this port with an adapter that will be used to interact with the controller to further abstract the components. We can swap out this adapter for another if we want to, for example, turn this into a command-line application. The prompt for `AssetRestAdapter` is as follows:

```
# Define an interface called AssetRestAdapter
# It should take an AssetManager as a parameter in its constructor
# It should expose all of the methods in AssetManager
# It should inherit from AssetRestPort
```

There are two important elements to this prompt. The first is that it implements the port interface that we defined previously. The second is that it wraps `AssetManager`'s functionality.

Listing 4.24 Source code for `AssetRestAdapter`

```
from itam.domain.asset import Asset
from itam.infrastructure.ports.asset_rest_port import AssetRestPort
from itam.service.asset_manager import AssetManager

class AssetRestAdapter(AssetRestPort):
    def __init__(self, asset_manager: AssetManager):
        self._asset_manager = asset_manager

    def read(self, asset_id: int) -> Asset:
        return self._asset_manager.read(asset_id)

    def create(self, asset: Asset) -> None:
        self._asset_manager.create(asset)

    def update(self, asset: Asset) -> None:
        self._asset_manager.update(asset)

    def delete(self, asset_id: int) -> None:
        self._asset_manager.delete(asset_id)

    def get_assets(self):
        return self._asset_manager.get_assets()
```

All that is left to do is to update `AssetController` to remove its direct invocation of the `AssetManager` methods and instead have `AssetController` invoke the methods of the adapter, which in turn invokes the methods of `AssetManager`. The key takeaway from the Ports and Adapters Pattern is that it abstracts the interaction between the driving parts of the system—in this case, the REST API—and the driven application: the business model and core of our system, `AssetManager`. To make this more explicit and as a preview, we will shortly modify this class again to add the port to the constructor.

Listing 4.25 Updated code for `AssetController` using `AssetRestAdapter`

```
router = APIRouter()

asset_rest_adapter = AssetRestAdapter(AssetManager())
asset_factory = AssetFactory()

@router.post('/assets', response_model=AssetOut)
async def create_asset(asset_in: AssetIn):
    asset = asset_factory.new(asset_in.asset_type,
        asset_in.name, asset_in.unit_cost,
        asset_in.useful_life, asset_in.depreciation_strategy,
        asset_in.depreciation_rate, asset_in.salvage_value,
        asset_in.purchase_date)
    asset_rest_adapter.create(asset)
    return from_asset(asset)
```

As previously mentioned, we will modify `AssetController` to remove all direct references to the `AssetManager`. Our current `AssetController`, although it does not directly invoke any `AssetManager` methods, does hold an indirect reference to `AssetManager`, because `AssetManager` is constructed in `AssetController`. Doing so further insulates `AssetManager` from changes in the drivers.

4.3.3 *Accessing our data and persisting our changes*

Abstractions in software are not merely an academic matter. These abstractions give us flexibility when it comes to satisfying requirements and making changes. They can hide complexity, encapsulating behavior behind seemingly simple interfaces. This brings us to our next pattern: the *Repository* Pattern.

Repository Pattern

The Repository Pattern is a design pattern that helps manage data by creating a separate place to handle tasks like getting, saving, updating, and deleting data. It connects the data source (such as a database or file) to the rest of the application, keeping data access code separate from other code.

In our ITAM project, the Repository Pattern will allow us to present a greatly simplified interface, masking the complexity of, in this case, our data access. From the perspective of the repository or `AssetManager`, our data access layer is just a series of methods. Behind the scenes, it may be a REST API, a Redis cache, MongoDB, a file, or a database of any flavor. Let's create a prompt that will set up our generic data access layer using the Repository Pattern:

```
# Create an abstract base class called BaseRepository that represents a
generic data access layer using the Repository pattern.
# The class should define common methods for CRUD operations such as cre-
ate, read, update, and delete.
# Make sure to use type hints for the input parameters and return values.
```

With this prompt, Copilot should have everything it needs to establish the contract that all implementations will honor. Let's examine the code.

Listing 4.26   Code for `BaseRepository`, our generic data access layer

```
from abc import ABC, abstractmethod
from typing import List, TypeVar, Generic

T = TypeVar('T')

class BaseRepository(ABC, Generic[T]):
    @abstractmethod
    def create(self, entity: T) -> None:
        pass

    @abstractmethod
    def read(self, entity_id: int) -> T:
        pass

    @abstractmethod
    def update(self, entity: T) -> None:
        pass

    @abstractmethod
    def delete(self, entity_id: int) -> None:
        pass

    @abstractmethod
    def get_entities(self) -> List[T]:
        pass
```

Copilot introduced a `Generic` type, allowing for some typing hints when it comes time to implement. If we express that the type should be an `Asset`, the method signature will demonstrate this. Our first attempt at an implementation will be an in-memory data store. This will allow us to perform an end-to-end test of our entire system. It also nicely demonstrates why abstractions are useful. Before long, we will add another implementation that uses Postgres. But first, the prompt:

```
# Define a class called InMemoryAssetRepository that inherits from the
BaseRepository abstract class.
# The InMemoryAssetRepository should be specific to managing Asset objects
using an in-memory list to store and update the assets.
# Implement the necessary methods for CRUD operations such as create, read,
update, and delete for Asset objects using the in-memory list.
# Make sure to use type hints for the input parameters and return values.
```

Our in-memory implementation will use a simple list to store `Assets`. We will be able to perform all CRUD operations. Additionally, Copilot will add typing hints for us, letting others know that it should accept and return `Assets`. That is what is meant by `Base-Repository[Asset]`: it's an implementation of a `BaseRepository` whose `Generic` type is `Asset`.

Listing 4.27   Code for `InMemoryAssetRepository`

```
from itam.infrastructure.repository.base_repository import BaseRepository
from itam.domain.asset import Asset

class InMemoryAssetRepository(BaseRepository[Asset]):
    def __init__(self):
        self._assets = []

    def create(self, asset: Asset) -> None:
        self._assets.append(asset)

    def read(self, asset_id: int) -> Asset:
        return next((asset for asset in self._assets
if asset.id == asset_id), None)

    def update(self, asset: Asset) -> None:
        for i in range(len(self._assets)):
            if self._assets[i].id == asset.id:
                self._assets[i] = asset
                break

    def delete(self, asset_id: int) -> None:
        self._assets = [asset for asset in self._assets
if asset.id != asset_id]

    def get_entities(self) -> list[Asset]:
        return self._assets
```

Finally, we will update `AssetManager` to delegate the CRUD operations of the `Assets` to a `BaseRepository` instance (`_repository`). The full source code follows, including the prompt at the beginning of the file.

Listing 4.28   `AssetManager` using `InMemoryAssetRepository`

```
# Define a class called AssetManager
# with CRUD operations for Asset
# and a method to notify observers whenever an asset is created, updated or
deleted
# The AssetManager should use an instance of the InMemoryAssetRepository
class for data access and CRUD operations on Asset objects.
# Implement methods for creating, reading, updating, and deleting assets
using the AssetRepository instance.
# Please include type hints for the input parameters and return values.
# The methods should be named create, read, update, get_assets, and delete.

from itam.domain.asset import Asset
```

```
from itam.infrastructure.repository.in_memory_asset_repository import
InMemoryAssetRepository

class AssetManager:
    def __init__(self):
        self._repository = InMemoryAssetRepository()

    def create(self, asset: Asset) -> Asset:
        self._repository.create(asset)
        return asset

    def read(self, asset_id: int) -> Asset:
        return self._repository.read(asset_id)

    def update(self, asset: Asset) -> Asset:
        self._repository.update(asset)
        return asset

    def get_assets(self) -> list[Asset]:
        return self._repository.get_entities()

    def delete(self, asset_id: int) -> None:
        self._repository.delete(asset_id)
```

At this point, we have a core business domain that is untouched directly by our system. We have ports by which requests can come in. We also have ports by which we can store the data (at least while the system is running). We should be able to test the system end to end by running it, POSTing requests to the creation end point, and reading from the GET end points. Once we have confirmed that the system works end to end, we can tackle the problem that our data is only persisted in memory; we can now hook up an actual database. To do this, we introduce the final pattern of this chapter: the *Singleton* Pattern. A singleton, conceptually, is very simple to grok; there should only ever be one instance of it running. It is good for many use cases: logging, caching, configuration settings, or a database connection manager.

> **Singleton Pattern**
>
> The Singleton Pattern is a design pattern that ensures a class has only one instance and provides a global access point to that instance. It is used when you want to have a single object shared across different parts of your program instead of creating multiple instances of the same class.

4.3.4 *Centralizing (and externalizing) our data access*

We will ask Copilot to create a singleton class for us to manage our database's connections. We should never hardcode usernames or passwords (or any connection details, for that matter) in our source code, not only because it is inherently less secure but also because the details will likely differ depending on the environment (DEV versus

QA versus PROD). We will therefore ask Copilot to accept these values as environmental variables and configure the connections using them:

```
# Create a Python class called DatabaseConnection using the Singleton
pattern to manage a single connection to a PostgreSQL database using
SQLAlchemy.
# The class should read the database username, password, and connection
string from environment variables
# The environment variables should be named: DB_USERNAME, DB_PASSWORD,
DB_HOST, DB_PORT, and DB_NAME
```

We are asking Copilot to employ SQLAlchemy, an object-relational mapping (ORM) tool, to perform the actions against the database. Copilot will adroitly assemble our source code. The `@staticmethod` keyword creates a method that belongs to a class rather than the instance of the class. This keyword is used to get the instance of the `DatabaseConnection` class. Because a static method cannot modify the instance data, it can be used to ensure that only one instance of this class is ever running and is thus a singleton. The constructor initializes the connection to the database using string interpolation with environment variables.

Listing 4.29 Implementation of a `DatabaseConnection`

```
from sqlalchemy import create_engine
from sqlalchemy.orm import sessionmaker
import os

class DatabaseConnection:
    __instance = None
    @staticmethod
    def get_instance():
        if DatabaseConnection.__instance == None:
            DatabaseConnection()
        return DatabaseConnection.__instance

    def __init__(self):
        if DatabaseConnection.__instance != None:
            raise Exception("This class is a singleton!")
        else:
            DatabaseConnection.__instance = self
            self.engine =
create_engine(f"postgresql://
{os.environ['DB_USERNAME']}:
{os.environ['DB_PASSWORD']}@
{os.environ['DB_HOST']}:
{os.environ['DB_PORT']}/
{os.environ['DB_NAME']}")
            self.Session = sessionmaker(bind=self.engine)

    def get_session(self):
        return self.Session()
```

Now that we can get a connection to our database, we need to create a repository that will use this connection to store and retrieve our `Asset` objects. We will create a class that does just that called `SQLAlchemyAssetRepository`.

Listing 4.30   Prompt and code for the `SQLAlchemyAssetRepository` class

```
# Define a class called SQLAlchemyAssetRepository that implements the
AssetRepository interface for data access using SQLAlchemy.
# The class should handle the CRUD operations (create, read, update, and
delete) for assets, storing and retrieving them in a PostgreSQL database
using SQLAlchemy.

from itam.domain.asset import Asset
from itam.infrastructure.repository.base_repository import BaseRepository
from sqlalchemy.orm import Session

class SQLAlchemyAssetRepository(BaseRepository[Asset]):
    def __init__(self, session: Session):
        self._session = session

    def create(self, asset: Asset) -> Asset:
        self._session.add(asset)
        self._session.commit()
        return asset

    def read(self, asset_id: int) -> Asset:
        return self._session.query(Asset)
.filter(Asset.id == asset_id).first()

    def update(self, asset: Asset) -> Asset:
        self._session.query(Asset)
.filter(Asset.id == asset.id).update(asset)
        self._session.commit()
        return asset

    def get_assets(self) -> list[Asset]:
        return self._session.query(Asset).all()

    def delete(self, asset_id: int) -> None:
        self._session.query(Asset).filter(Asset.id == asset_id).delete()
        self._session.commit()
```

Next we will refactor `AssetController` to allow us to pass in `AssetRestPort`. By doing this, we can swap out the driven aspect of our application. This refactor further abstracts the driver from the business core.

Listing 4.31   Updated `AssetController` that exposes routes

```
from itam.infrastructure.ports.asset_rest_port import AssetRestPort
import logging

class AssetController:
    def __init__(self, asset_rest_port:  AssetRestPort):
```

```
            self._asset_factory = AssetFactory()
            self._asset_rest_port = asset_rest_port
            ...

        def get_router(self):
            return self._router

        async def get_assets(self):
            return  [ from_asset(a) for a in self._asset_rest_port.get_assets()]

        async def get_asset(self, asset_id: int):
            asset = self._asset_rest_port.read(asset_id)
            if asset is None:
                raise HTTPException(status_code=404, detail="Asset not found")
            return from_asset(asset)

        async def create_asset(self, asset_in: AssetIn):
            asset = self._asset_factory.new(
asset_in.asset_type,
asset_in.name,
asset_in.unit_cost,
asset_in.useful_life,
asset_in.depreciation_strategy,
asset_in.depreciation_rate,
asset_in.salvage_value,
asset_in.purchase_date)
            self._asset_rest_port.create(asset)
            return from_asset(asset)

        async def update_asset(self, asset_id: int, asset_in: AssetIn):
            asset = self._asset_factory.new(
asset_in.asset_type,
asset_in.name,
asset_in.unit_cost,
asset_in.useful_life,
asset_in.depreciation_strategy,
asset_in.depreciation_rate,
asset_in.salvage_value,
asset_in.purchase_date)

            asset.id = asset_id
            asset = self._asset_rest_port.update(asset)
            if asset is None:
                raise HTTPException(status_code=404, detail="Asset not found")
            return from_asset(asset)

        async def delete_asset(self, asset_id: int):
            asset = self._asset_rest_port.read(asset_id)
            if asset is None:
                raise HTTPException(status_code=404, detail="Asset not found")
            self._asset_rest_port.delete(asset_id)
            return from_asset(asset)
```

We can now consolidate the initialization logic of our application into the main.py file. This is the big payoff. Our system will have layering, facilitating the swapping out of components as needed or when requirements change.

Listing 4.32   Final version of main.py, wiring our application together

```
from fastapi import FastAPI
from itam.infrastructure.api.asset_controller import AssetController
#from itam.infrastructure.repository.in_memory_asset_repository
    import InMemoryAssetRepository
from itam.infrastructure.repository.sqlalchemy_asset_repository
    import SQLAlchemyAssetRepository
from itam.infrastructure.database.database_connection
    import DatabaseConnection
from itam.service.asset_manager import AssetManager
from itam.infrastructure.adapters.asset_rest_adapter import AssetRestAdapter
import uvicorn

app = FastAPI()
session = DatabaseConnection().get_session()
#repository = InMemoryAssetRepository()
repository = SQLAlchemyAssetRepository(session)
asset_manager = AssetManager(repository)
asset_rest_adapter = AssetRestAdapter(asset_manager)
asset_controller = AssetController(asset_rest_adapter)
app.include_router(asset_controller.get_router())

if __name__ == '__main__':
    uvicorn.run(app, host='0.0.0.0', port=8000)
```

Congratulations! We now have a running system that persists data to our database.

Summary

- The Decorator Pattern is a structural design pattern that allows you to add new object behavior or modify existing behavior dynamically without changing the existing class. This is done by wrapping the current object in the decorating object.
- The Visitor Pattern adds new behavior to changes the existing behavior of a given class.
- The Factory Pattern is another creation pattern that allows you to abstract away some of the details of the object you are attempting to create.
- The Builder Pattern is a creational design pattern that provides a fluent API for the creation of objects by providing step-by-step instructions for creating those objects.
- The Adapter Pattern is a structural design pattern that allows you to bridge the gap between the target interface and a class with an incompatible interface.
- The Observer Pattern is a behavioral pattern in which the subject class reports certain state changes to observer classes via notifications.

- Hexagonal architecture separates the main program logic from outer parts like buttons, screens, and databases. It makes changing outer parts easy without changing the main program.

- The Repository Pattern is a design pattern that helps manage data by creating a separate place to handle tasks like getting, saving, updating, and deleting data. It connects the data source (such as a database or file) to the rest of the application, keeping data access code separate from other code.

- The Singleton Pattern is a design pattern that ensures a class has only one instance and provides a global access point to that instance. It is used when you want a single object to be shared across different parts of your program instead of creating multiple instances of the same class.

Managing data with GitHub Copilot and Copilot Chat

5

This chapter covers

- Persisting data into a relational database
- Streaming data using Apache Kafka
- Incorporating event-driven principles
- Analyzing data to monitor the location using Spark

The last chapter laid the foundation for our information technology asset management (ITAM) system. However, this application will not fulfill our requirements without data. Data is the lifeblood of every application. That is what this chapter is all about: the various ways we can use generative AI to create data, stream data, transform data, react to data, and learn from data.

Perceptive individuals may have noticed in the last chapter that our data access pattern would not have worked as it was incomplete. The opening section of this chapter will address this. After that, we will set up our database, fix the classes that access this data, and load some sample data to use in the rest of the chapter.

5.1   *Amassing our dataset*

Our first task will be to construct a substantial corpus of data to assist our experimentation in the remainder of the chapter. First we will use GitHub Copilot to generate 1,000 rows of asset information. We will soon find, however, that this may not be the tool best suited to this task. A key driver behind using these tools is the idea of discovery: testing their boundaries, pushing against them, and occasionally pushing back. But the journey is often where the joy is found. Once we have found this edge, we will be introduced to a new, previously unseen tool: GitHub Copilot Chat. Finally, when we have created our list of assets, we will add location information for those assets, again using GitHub Copilot Chat.

We need to get our database running before building our initial dataset. Docker makes this task trivial, allowing us to quickly spin up an empty PostgreSQL (or other RDBMS/NoSQL server) with minimal effort. Have you forgotten the command to do this? No worries—we can ask Copilot. Open a new file called data/initial_data_load.sql and enter the following prompt at the top of your newly minted SQL file:

```
-- Question: What is the command to run a docker container, running Postgre-
SQL for a database called itam_db. I would like to specify the password for
this database.
```

Copilot will slowly reveal the Docker command:

```
--Answer: docker run --name itam_db
   -e POSTGRES_PASSWORD=postgres -d
   -p 5432:5432 postgres
```

Once you run this command at your terminal or command line, we can build out our dataset. You should be able to connect to the locally running database. Notice that a database called `itam_db` is running in it. However, this database has no schema, tables, or data. Let's first set up a new schema.

In our initial_data_load.sql, we will add a prompt to have Copilot draft the schema creation command. The following prompt (and response from Copilot) will allow you to create a new schema called `itam` if executed from within your database client application (e.g., DataGrip, SQuirreL, pdAdmin, or even using the Docker `exec` command `docker exec -i itam_db psql -U postgres -c "create schema itam"`):

```
-- create a schema called itam
create schema itam;
```

Next, we should add a user for use in our application. This user will be able to perform CRUD (create, read, update, delete) operations on our data but will not be able to affect the structure of the database tables or procedures.

NOTE   The lines that start with double dashes (--) are comments in SQL. Commenting out these lines is optional from Copilot's perspective, as it will generate solutions without the comments; it makes it easier to copy and paste the code directly into our database tool of choice.

While we are at it, we will also add an administrative account to perform the operations that our read-write users cannot, such as creating or dropping tables.

Listing 5.1   Prompt to create new users

```
-- create two users called itam_user and itam_admin. itam_user should be able
to read from and write to the tables in the itam schema. itam_admin should be
able to read from and write to the tables in the itam schema and create and
drop tables in the itam schema.
create user itam_user with password 'itam_user';
create user itam_admin with password 'itam_admin';
grant usage on schema itam to itam_user;
grant usage on schema itam to itam_admin;
grant select, insert, update, delete on all tables in schema itam to itam_user;
grant select, insert, update, delete on all tables in schema itam to itam_admin;
grant usage, drop on schema itam to itam_admin;
```

Next we will grant ownership of this schema to the itam_admin account. Transferring this ownership will ensure that only this account can change the table structure (the data definition):

```
-- grant ownership of the itam schema to itam_admin
alter schema itam owner to itam_admin;
```

With the setup, account creation, and ownership of the system out of the way, we can start to focus on the data. We will begin by adding the reference data, which supports the assets: the depreciation strategies. This data is more static in nature; it changes less frequently, if at all. Let's define and store these strategies.

Listing 5.2   Prompt to create the `depreciation_strategy` table

```
-- create a table called depreciation_strategy in the itam schema. the table
should have the following columns: id (int), name (varchar), and description
(varchar). the table should have a primary key on id.
-- id needs to be in quotes because it is a reserved word in postgresql
-- there are two values for depreciation_strategy: straight line and double
declining balance
create table itam.depreciation_strategy (
    "id" int primary key,
    "name" varchar,
    "description" varchar
);
```

We will use a sequence as this table's primary key. Although this is not strictly necessary for a table that will not be very large and that has known values we can and will enter manually, adding this sequence will allow us to work with Copilot more and have it make some suggestions. Moreover, it is amusing to ask Copilot questions and have Copilot answer in a text file.

Listing 5.3 Prompt to create a sequence to use as primary key

```
-- create a sequence called depreciation_strategy_seq, which should start
at 1 and increment by 1 and should be used as the primary key for the
depreciation_strategy table.
create sequence itam.depreciation_strategy_seq start 1 increment 1;
```

Naturally, with the sequence in our proverbial hand, we need to know how to associate the sequence with the primary key column of the `depreciation_strategy` table. Luckily, Copilot has the answer.

Listing 5.4 Asking Copilot how to associate the sequence with the primary key

```
-- question: how do I make the sequence the primary key for the depreciation_
strategy table?

-- answer: use the following command
alter table itam.depreciation_strategy
    alter column "id"
    set default
    nextval('itam.depreciation_strategy_seq'
        ::regclass);
```

Finally, we complete this table by inserting the following static entries into it. We will only use two depreciation strategies for now: straight-line and double declining balance.

Listing 5.5 Adding the static entries to the `depreciation_strategy` table

```
insert into depreciation_strategy (id, name, description)
    values (1, 'straight line',
    'straight line');

insert into depreciation_strategy (id, name, description)
    values (2, 'double declining balance',
    'double declining balance');
```

Next we will move on to the `funding_details` table. This information tells us how we financed our equipment, the resale value, and instructions for what should be done with an asset once its useful life is over. The sequence of steps will be identical to what we did for the depreciation strategies, with the exception that we will not add static entries, as this data is directly related to an individual asset. We will define the table, create the sequence, and apply that sequence to the table, for which it functions as the primary key.

Listing 5.6   Complete code listing for the `funding_details` **table**

```
-- create a table called funding_details in the itam schema. the table should
have the following columns: id (int), name (varchar),depreciation_strategy_id
(int) and depreciation_rate (float). the table should have a primary key on
id.
-- depreciation_strategy_id is a foreign key to the depreciation_strategy
table.
-- id needs to be in quotes because it is a reserved word in postgresql
create table itam.funding_details (
    "id" int primary key,
    "name" varchar,
    "depreciation_strategy_id" int,
    "depreciation_rate" float
);


-- create a sequence called funding_details_seq, which should start at 1 and
increment by 1 and should be used as the primary key for the funding_details
table.
create sequence itam.funding_details_seq start 1 increment 1;

alter table itam.funding_details
alter column "id"
set default
nextval('itam.funding_details_seq'
    ::regclass);
```

The final information that we will define and generate is the assets themselves. This listing, too, is redundant but included for completeness. Finally, we create the table, make the sequence, and use it as the primary key.

Listing 5.7   Complete code listing for the `assets` **table**

```
-- create a table called assets in the itam schema. the table should have the
following columns:
-- id (int), name (varchar), status (varchar), category (varchar), cost
(float), useful_life (int), salvage_value (float), purchase_date (date),
funding_details_id (int). The table should have a primary key on id and a
foreign key on funding_details_id.
-- id needs to be in quotes because it is a reserved word in postgresql
-- the table should have a sequence called assets_id_seq, which should start
at 1 and increment by 1 and should be used as the primary key for the assets
table.
create table itam.assets (
    "id" int primary key,
    "name" varchar,
    "status" varchar,
    "category" varchar,
    "cost" float,
    "useful_life" int,
    "salvage_value" float,
    "purchase_date" date,
    "funding_details_id" int
);
```

```
-- create a sequence called assets_seq, which should start at 1 and increment
by 1 and should be used as the primary key for the assets table.
create sequence itam.assets_seq start 1 increment 1;

alter table itam.assets alter column "id"
set default
nextval('itam.assets_seq'::
    regclass);
```

With the tables defined and created, we will now focus on creating the data. In our text file, we instruct Copilot with parameters for the dataset we are looking for. Copilot will likely attempt to assist you in outlining the attributes surrounding your new dataset.

Listing 5.8 Creating a dataset for the assets table

```
-- Generate a dataset of assets for an ITAM system. The dataset should
include the following columns: id (int), name (varchar), status (varchar),
category (varchar), cost (float), useful_life (int), salvage_value (float),
purchase_date (date), funding_details_id (int). The dataset should have 1000
rows, sorted by id. Each row should have the following characteristics:
-- - id should be a unique integer and sequential starting at 1.
-- - name should be a random string of characters between 1 and 50 characters
long.
-- - status should be a random selection from the following valid asset
statuses: in use, in storage, disposed of, in repair, in transit, other.
-- - category should be a random selection from the following valid
categories: hardware, software, other.
-- - cost should be a random float between 0 and 100000.
-- - useful_life should be a random int between 1 and 10.
-- - salvage_value should be a random float greater than 0 but less than the
cost of the asset.
-- - purchase_date should be a random date between 1/1/2019 and 12/31/2022.
-- - funding_details_id should be a random integer either 1 or 2.
-- The dataset should be saved as a CSV file named assets.csv in the data
directory. The file should have a header row and the columns should have the
following data types: id (int), name (varchar), status (varchar), category
(varchar), cost (float), useful_life (float), salvage_value (float), funding_
details_id (int)
```

The solution that Copilot provides is novel. It builds a large series using a Postgres built-in function, meaning this solution would not be portable. However, given that this is the database we will use, it is an appropriate enough solution. The resulting dataset is refined. We would have gotten better results if we had used Python and asked for Copilot's assistance in coding a script to generate a file to load into Postgres. However, given that this dataset is only for playing with the application, we do not need to be overly concerned with the data quality for now—although in the real world, data quality is everything.

Listing 5.9   Copilot's response: an `insert` statement built off of a series

```
insert into itam.assets (id, name, status,
    category, cost, useful_life, salvage_value,
    purchase_date, funding_details_id)
select
    id,
    name,
    status,
    category,
    cost,
    useful_life,
    salvage_value,
    purchase_date,
    funding_details_id
from (
    select
        row_number() over (order by random()) as id,
        md5(random()::text) as name,
        case
            when random() < 0.2 then 'in use'
            when random() < 0.4 then 'in storage'
            when random() < 0.6 then 'disposed of'
            when random() < 0.8 then 'in repair'
            when random() < 0.9 then 'in transit'
            else 'other'
        end as status,
        case
            when random() < 0.5 then 'hardware'
            when random() < 0.9 then 'software'
            else 'other'
        end as category,
        random() * 100000 as cost,
        (random() * 100)::int as useful_life,
        random() * (random() * 100000) as salvage_value,
        -- generate a random date between 1/1/2019 and 12/31/2022
        -- this does not work please fix
        -- '2019-01-01'::date + random() *
            ('2022-12-31'::date - '2019-01-01'::date)
            as purchase_date,
        '2019-01-01'::date + (random() *
          (DATE '2022-12-31' - DATE '2019-01-01')
          ::integer)::integer as purchase_date
        case
            when random() < 0.5 then 1
            else 2
        end as funding_details_id
    from generate_series(1, 1000)
) as assets;
```

If we switch back to ChatGPT for a minute, we can get a second opinion about how to create such a dataset. ChatGPT suggests the Python library `faker`. The `faker` package is used to generate fake data, such as common English first names. `numpy` is used to generate the random float values for cost, useful life, and salvage value. `pandas` is used to manage the data in a DataFrame (the table). Additionally, we can save the Data-Frame to a CSV file using the method df.to_csv('assets.csv', index=False).

Listing 5.10 **ChatGPT suggests** `Faker` **to generate the fake dataset**

```python
import pandas as pd
import numpy as np
import random
from faker import Faker

# Create Faker object
fake = Faker()

# Define our valid statuses, categories, funding_details and depreciation_
strategies
valid_statuses = ['in use', 'in storage',
'disposed', 'in repair', 'in transit', 'other']
valid_categories = ['hardware']
valid_funding_details = ['purchased']
valid_depreciation_strategies = ['straight line']

# Generate the data
data = {
    'id': list(range(1, 1001)),
    'name': [fake.first_name() for _ in range(1000)],
    'status': [random.choice(valid_statuses) for _ in range(1000)],
    'category': [random.choice(valid_categories) for _ in range(1000)],
    'cost': np.random.uniform(0, 100000, 1000),
    'useful_life': np.random.uniform(1, 10, 1000),
    'salvage_value': np.random.uniform(0, 10000, 1000),
    'funding_details': [random.choice(valid_funding_details)
 for _ in range(1000)],
    'depreciation_strategy': [random.choice(
    valid_depreciation_strategies)
    for _ in range(1000)],
}

# Create DataFrame
df = pd.DataFrame(data)

# Ensure the DataFrame is sorted by id
df = df.sort_values('id')

# Show the DataFrame
print(df)
```

For each of these assets, we will need funding details as well: how they were financed (purchased, in this case) and the depreciation details. Unsurprisingly, we get a similar solution from Copilot: generate a series of entries using a prompt similar to the one we used for the assets. We will need to ensure that for each of the asset identifiers (1–1000), we have a corresponding funding details entry. Otherwise we risk getting null pointers when running this code.

Listing 5.11   Creating a dataset for the `funding_details` table

```
-- Generate a dataset of funding details for an ITAM system. The dataset
should include the following columns: id (int), name (varchar), depreciation_
strategy_id (int), depreciation_rate (float). The dataset should have 1000
rows, sorted by id.
-- Each row should have the following characteristics:
-- - id should be a unique integer and sequential starting at 1.
-- - name should be a random string of characters between 1 and 10 characters
long.
-- - depreciation_strategy_id should be a random integer either 1 or 2.
-- - depreciation_rate should be a random float between 0 and .4.

insert into itam.funding_details (id, name,
    depreciation_strategy_id, depreciation_rate)
select
    id,
    name,
    depreciation_strategy_id,
    depreciation_rate
from (
    select
        row_number() over (order by random()) as id,
        md5(random()::text) as name,
        case
            when random() < 0.5 then 1
            else 2
        end as depreciation_strategy_id,
        random() * 0.4 as depreciation_rate
    from generate_series(1, 1000)
) as funding_details;
```

With the dataset generated and stored in the database, we should be able to wire up the remainder of our application to store and display assets using the REST APIs. However, because we previously stripped out all the metadata for SQLAlchemy during our build phase (see chapter 4), we need a way to wire this metadata with our adapters differently.

At this point we have reached the edge of Copilot's capabilities. We are perplexed by what comes next and how we can solve our most recent dilemma. Tempting as it is, we cannot give up and go home. Therefore, it is time to introduce the most recent addition to the Copilot product suite: Copilot Chat. Copilot Chat is a GPT-4 model embedded in an IDE (currently supported only by Visual Studio Code). We will open the chat dialog and ask how to keep our business model clean while still using SQLAlchemy's object-relational model (ORM) features. Figure 5.1 shows the response from ChatGPT.

Copilot Chat suggests that we create a separate data access layer. This approach maps nicely onto the ports and adapters approach we have used thus far. In addition, Copilot Chat recommends modeling these classes similarly to the domain classes but including the metadata required for ORM functionality to work correctly. The resulting code is shown in listing 5.12.

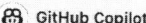 **GitHub Copilot**

If you don't want to include any SQLAlchemy properties in your domain model, you can create a separate data access layer (DAL) that handles all interactions with the database. This way, your domain model can remain independent of any specific database implementation.

Here's an example of how you can create a DAL using SQLAlchemy:

Figure 5.1 GitHub Copilot Chat's solution for how to solve our most recent quandary

Listing 5.12   ORM support outside of the domain classes

```python
Base  = declarative_base()

class FundingDetailsModel(Base):
    __tablename__ = 'funding_details'
    id = Column(Integer, primary_key=True)
    depreciation_rate = Column(Float)
    depreciation_strategy_id = Column(Integer)

    def get_depreciation_strategy(self) -> DepreciationStrategy:
        if self.depreciation_strategy_id is 1:
            return StraightLineDepreciationStrategy()
        else:
            return DoubleDecliningDepreciationStrategy()

class AssetModel(Base):
    __tablename__ = 'assets'
    id = Column(Integer, primary_key=True)
    name = Column(String)
    status = Column(String)
    category = Column(String)
    cost = Column(Float)
    useful_life = Column(Float)
    salvage_value = Column(Float)
    purchase_date = Column(Date)
    funding_details_id = Column(Integer, ForeignKey('funding_details.id'))
    funding_details = relationship('FundingDetailsModel')
```

Now that the external model classes have been created, we must map these ORM instances to our domain model before returning them to the system's core. This may seem like over-engineered code for such a simple application, but it gives us great flexibility in how our domain model can operate. For example, our model can perform complex operations beyond just CRUD. We would be limited to these operations if we kept our domain model identity to the model used in the data access layer.

Next we will use Copilot and Copilot Chat to explore incorporating event-driven ideas into our application. Event-driven concepts will allow us to track our IT assets in real time: their location, status, and market value, for example.

5.2   *Monitoring our assets in real time with Kafka*

We will monitor our assets in real time to motivate our exploration of using generative AI in conjunction with event-driven architecture. We will take it as a given that some system external to the ISAM system fires events as our assets move from one location to another.

To delve into ITAM events, we will need to configure a few additional services. In this case, we will use Apache Kafka. Apache Kafka is a distributed streaming platform that is used to build real-time data pipelines and streaming apps. It's designed to handle data streams from multiple sources and deliver them to multiple consumers, effectively acting as a middleman for our real-time data.

To start, we will ask Copilot Chat how to run Kafka locally using Docker. Apache Kafka has an undeserved reputation for being difficult to install and configure, and running in Docker will allow us to side-step this controversy. Using Copilot Chat, we can produce a Docker Compose file. However, as is often the case, the versions are very old, to the point of not supporting some hardware. Listing 5.13 is an updated listing from Confluent's (the company that offers commercial support for Kafka) official GitHub repository. Notice that the Docker Compose file's contents include both Kafka and Zookeeper. Zookeeper is a distributed coordination service that Kafka uses to manage and coordinate the brokers in the cluster, at least for now. Future versions aim to remove dependency on Zookeeper.

Listing 5.13   Docker Compose file to launch Kafka with Zookeeper

```
version: '2.1'

services:
  zookeeper:
    image: confluentinc/cp-zookeeper:7.3.2
    container_name: zookeeper
    ports:
      - "2181:2181"
    environment:
      ZOOKEEPER_CLIENT_PORT: 2181
      ZOOKEEPER_SERVER_ID: 1
      ZOOKEEPER_SERVERS: zoo1:2888:3888

  kafka:
    image: confluentinc/cp-kafka:7.3.2
    hostname: kafka
    container_name: kafka
    ports:
      - "9092:9092"
      - "29092:29092"
      - "9999:9999"
    environment:
      KAFKA_ADVERTISED_LISTENERS:
            INTERNAL://kafka:19092,EXTERNAL://
            ${DOCKER_HOST_IP:127.0.0.1}:9092,
            DOCKER://host.docker.internal:29092
```

```
        KAFKA_LISTENER_SECURITY_PROTOCOL_MAP:
INTERNAL:PLAINTEXT,EXTERNAL:PLAINTEXT,
DOCKER:PLAINTEXT
        KAFKA_INTER_BROKER_LISTENER_NAME: INTERNAL
        KAFKA_ZOOKEEPER_CONNECT: "zookeeper:2181"
        KAFKA_BROKER_ID: 1
        KAFKA_LOG4J_LOGGERS: "kafka.controller=
            INFO,kafka.producer.async
            .DefaultEventHandler=INFO,
            state.change.logger=INFO"
        KAFKA_OFFSETS_TOPIC_REPLICATION_FACTOR: 1
        KAFKA_TRANSACTION_STATE_LOG_REPLICATION_FACTOR: 1
        KAFKA_TRANSACTION_STATE_LOG_MIN_ISR: 1
        KAFKA_JMX_PORT: 9999
        KAFKA_JMX_HOSTNAME: ${DOCKER_HOST_IP:-127.0.0.1}
        KAFKA_AUTHORIZER_CLASS_NAME: kafka.security.authorizer.AclAuthorizer
        KAFKA_ALLOW_EVERYONE_IF_NO_ACL_FOUND: "true"
    depends_on:
    - zookeeper
```

With our new Kafka instance running, we now need a consumer that will pull the updated locations off the topic `asset_location` (which we will create shortly) and update the inventory in the database. Again, we can ask Copilot Chat to provide us with a suggestion for how to use Python to subscribe to the topic:

 In our ITAM project, we would like a Python consumer for the asset_location Kafka topic. Once it receives a new updated location, it should update the domain model to reflect the new location. How should we do this?

The code that Copilot Chat generates creates a consumer, listens to the topic, and uses a reference to the `AssetManager` class to update the location of the affected asset.

Listing 5.14 Copilot Chat code to monitor assets' locations

```python
from kafka import KafkaConsumer
from asset_manager import AssetManager

consumer = KafkaConsumer(
    'asset_location',
    bootstrap_servers=['localhost:9092'],
    auto_offset_reset='earliest',
    enable_auto_commit=True,
    group_id='my-group',
    value_deserializer=lambda x:
            tuple(map(float, x.decode('utf-8')
            .split(','))))
)

asset_manager = AssetManager()

for message in consumer:
    asset_id, latitude, longitude = message.value
    asset_manager.update_asset_location(asset_id, (latitude, longitude))
```

However, should the adapter be aware of `AssetManager`? The `AssetManager` does not directly sit inside the domain model; it is a critical intermediary. This coupling level between `AssetManager` and the adapter could arguably violate the hexagon in the hexagonal architecture model. Let's have Copilot Chat weigh in. We can ask it this:

 Given that this project uses hexagonal architecture, is it a good idea to have an adapter aware of the AssetManager?

Looking at figure 5.2, it appears that Copilot Chat agrees that this would indeed be considered a breach of the contractual responsibility of an adapter. We could add a new port to our `AssetManager` class that would use the Kafka port. However, let's see if Copilot Chat has any other suggestions:

 We do not want the Kafka consumer to interact directly with the AssetManager. Are there any ways to accomplish this?

GitHub Copilot

In a hexagonal architecture, the adapters are responsible for translating external input and output to and from the domain model. The domain model should not depend on the adapters, but the adapters may depend on the domain model.

In the case of a Kafka adapter that listens for messages on the `asset_location` topic and updates the domain model with the new location, it is reasonable for the adapter to depend on the `AssetManager` class. The adapter would translate the Kafka message into a domain event that the `AssetManager` can handle, and then call the appropriate method on the `AssetManager` to update the domain model.

However, it is important to ensure that the adapter does not tightly couple with the `AssetManager` class. One way to achieve this is to define an interface or protocol in the domain layer that the adapter can depend on, rather than depending directly on the `AssetManager` class. The interface or protocol would define the methods that the adapter can call to update the domain model, and the `AssetManager` class would implement this interface or protocol.

This approach allows the domain model to remain decoupled from the adapters, while still allowing the adapters to interact with the domain model in a controlled and well-defined way.

Figure 5.2   GitHub Copilot Chat's acceptance that it is, in fact, imperfect

Copilot Chat suggests that we apply the `Mediator` pattern, which resembles a port and adapter combination.

Mediator Pattern

The Mediator design pattern is a behavioral pattern that promotes loose coupling between objects by encapsulating their interactions in a mediator object. The mediator object acts as a central hub that facilitates communication between objects without the objects having to know about each other.

Let's first take a look at the `Mediator` class that Copilot Chat generates. The class sits between `AssetManager` and the Kafka consumer.

Listing 5.15 `Mediator` **class between** `AssetManager` **and Kafka consumer**

```
class AssetLocationMediator:
    def __init__(self):
        self.handlers = {}

    def register_handler(self, event_type, handler):
        if event_type not in self.handlers:
            self.handlers[event_type] = []
        self.handlers[event_type].append(handler)

    def publish(self, event):
        event_type = type(event)
        if event_type in self.handlers:
            for handler in self.handlers[event_type]:
                handler(event)
```

This implementation closely resembles a message queue or message publisher, which is precisely the point: decoupling.

> **NOTE** Eagle-eyed readers will likely notice that we are playing a little fast and loose with the distinction between an `Asset` and an asset of type `Hardware`. In the original domain model, only `Hardware` had a location. Generally, we do not think of software as having a location. Of course, you could say that software is installed in its location, but it is arguable how convincing this argument is. As this project continues, we flatten the domain model for simplicity's sake, as polymorphic structures in a persistence layer are a distractingly complex topic.

Now that we have a strategy to decouple the Kafka consumer from `AssetManager`, we should update the Kafka consumer to take advantage of it. We need to pass the mediator into the class in its constructor. This way, `AssetManager` and the consumer will have access to the same instance, and messages can freely flow back and forth— or rather, in this case, the flow will be unidirectional. You should note that we intend to read and write JSON on this topic, so our value deserializer needs to understand this.

Listing 5.16 **Incorporating the mediator into the Kafka consumer class**

```
from kafka import KafkaConsumer
from itam.domain.events.asset_location_updated import AssetLocationUpdated
import json

class AssetLocationKafkaConsumer:
    def __init__(self, mediator):
        self.mediator = mediator

        self.consumer = KafkaConsumer(
            'asset_location',
            bootstrap_servers=['localhost:9092'],
```

```
                enable_auto_commit=True,
                group_id='itam-group',
                value_deserializer=lambda m: json.loads(m.decode('utf-8'))
        )

    def poll(self):
        print("Polling for asset location updates")
        for message in self.consumer:
            asset_id = message.value['asset_id']
            latitude = message.value['latitude']
            longitude = message.value['longitude']
            timestamp = message.value['timestamp']
            event = AssetLocationUpdated(asset_id, latitude, longitude,
timestamp)
            self.mediator.publish(event)
```

Next we will examine the changes that the `AssetManager` class requires to incorporate the ability to track these locations.

> **NOTE**   To run this project in its entirety, you would need to modify the `Asset-Manager`, `SQLAlchemyAssetRepository`, and `Asset` classes and also create a new table in your database called `itam.asset_locations`. The complete and updated source code is available on the book's website (www.manning.com/ books/ai-powered-developer) and in the book's GitHub repository (https:// github.com/nathanbcrocker/ai_assisted_dev_public). For now, we will focus on the changes needed to get the events flowing through our system and use the repository for reference if the reader so chooses.

Figure 5.3 shows the changes required to the `AssetManager` class to begin to track the location of our assets in real time.

AssetManager
-BaseRepository[Asset] _repository
-AssetLocationMediator mediator
+__init__(base_repository: BaseRepository[Asset], mediator: AssetlocationMediator): None
+update_asset_location(event: AssetlocationUpdated): None

Figure 5.3   `AssetManager` **requires the addition of another constructor parameter and a method to handle the updates to its location objects.**

There are two required changes for the `AssetManager` class. First, we need to add the `AssetLocationMediator` to the constructor, registering it to handle the `Asset-LocationUpdated` event. And second, we need to add a method that will handle this event. In this case, we call the method `update_asset_location`. The abridged code is shown next.

> **Listing 5.17   Updated constructor and an event handler for `AssetManager`**

```
from itam.infrastructure.mediators.asset_location_mediator import

class AssetManager:
    def __init__(self, base_repository:
            BaseRepository[Asset],
            mediator: AssetLocationMediator):
        self._repository = base_repository
        self.mediator = mediator
        self.mediator.register_handler(
            AssetLocationUpdated,
            self.update_asset_location)

    def update_asset_location(self, event: AssetLocationUpdated) -> None:
        asset = self.read(event.asset_id)
        asset.add_location(event.latitude,
            event.longitude, event.timestamp)
        #self.update(asset)
        print(f"Asset {asset.id} location updated
            to {event.latitude}, {event.longitude}
            at {event.timestamp}")
```

The `add_location` method of the `Asset` class merely appends the new `Location` to the end of a list of `Locations`. More sophisticated domain models may include a `current_location` attribute, relegating the rest to a list of historical locations; however, given that we are trying to get our events flowing through the system, it behooves us to keep things simple.

There is only one final item on our to-do list: create the topic. How do we do this? That is a good question. Fortunately, all the tools we need are available in our running Docker container. So, let's log in to our Kafka Docker instance. We use the following command (assuming that your Docker instance is named `kafka`):

```
docker exec -it kafka /bin/bash
```

The first thing to check is whether any topics are already created. We can do that with the following command:

```
kafka-topics --list --bootstrap-server localhost:9092
```

This command lists all the existing topics running on this Kafka cluster. As you can see, there aren't any.

Given the need for a topic, let's create it. Use the following command:

```
kafka-topics --create --bootstrap-server localhost:9092
    --replication-factor 1
    --partitions 1
    --topic asset_location
```

If you run the `kafka-topics --list` command again, you will see the new topic. The partitions and replication-factor instructions we included in the create-topic command inform Kafka that we want one partition and a replication factor of 1. If we were setting this up for production or any purpose other than testing, we would likely want them to be greater than that to ensure the availability of data. Table 5.1 provides you with some of the commonly used Kafka commands that you will need for this and other projects.

Table 5.1   Summary of Kafka console commands

Action	Command
Create	`kafka-topics --create --bootstrap-server localhost:9092 --replication-factor 1 --partitions 1 --topic asset_location`
Read	`kafka-console-consumer --broker-list localhost:9092 --topic asset_location -from-beginning`
Write	`kafka-console-producer --broker-list localhost:9092 --topic asset_location`
Delete	`kafka-topics --delete --topic asset_location --bootstrap-server localhost:9092`
List	`kafka-topics --list --bootstrap-server localhost:9092`

Now comes the fun part: observing the application in action. Kafka comes with a console producer that will allow us to publish messages to Kafka from standard input. To do this, launch the console producer with the following command:

```
kafka-console-producer --broker-list localhost:9092 --topic asset_location
```

You will enter an interactive session allowing you to publish a message with every line. Let's publish a few messages simulating our asset moving around or near Chicago.

Listing 5.18   Entries for the Kafka console producer

```
{"asset_id": 1, "latitude": 41.8781, "longitude": -87.6298,
    "timestamp": "2022-01-01T00:00:00Z"}
{"asset_id": 1, "latitude": 41.9000, "longitude": -87.6244,
    "timestamp": "2022-01-01T00:10:00Z"}
{"asset_id": 1, "latitude": 41.8676, "longitude": -87.6270,
    "timestamp": "2022-01-01T00:20:00Z"}
{"asset_id": 1, "latitude": 41.8788, "longitude": -87.6359,
    "timestamp": "2022-01-01T00:30:00Z"}
{"asset_id": 1, "latitude": 41.8740, "longitude": -87.6298, "timestamp":
"2022-01-01T00:40:00Z"}
```

As you enter these messages, you should see the output from your application indicating that the location has been updated.

Deleting a topic

For the sake of completeness, there is one more command you should be aware of. You might make a mistake when entering these messages, and an invalid message could potentially break your consumer. One possible solution is to delete the topic. Deleting a topic may sound dramatic, but it will solve the problem. So here is that command:

```
kafka-topics --delete --topic asset_location --bootstrap-server
localhost:9092
```

In this section, we have added the ability to see changes in the location of our `Assets` in real-time tracking using Apache Kafka. In the final section of this chapter, we will work with Copilot Chat to extend the capacity by monitoring our assets in real time and attempting to determine if they are where they should be. We will explore using Spark and Kafka together to accomplish this analysis. Once completed, we will win the thanks of our Information Security team, who fear that too much of our core business and intellectual property exists on and in these `Assets`.

5.3 *Analyzing, learning, and tracking with Apache Spark*

Real-time tracking of assets is a business-critical function. Your IT assets contain sensitive business data, client lists, sales figures, profit-and-loss (PnL) projections, and sales strategies, among many other items. A lost asset can be an existential event for a company. Therefore, careful management and monitoring are priority one for many InfoSec professionals. In this section, we aim to make their jobs substantially easier. Modern data platforms make it trivial to track your assets in real time and send notifications if questionable conditions arise. Let's get into it.

Apache Spark is a powerful open source data-processing engine built around speed, ease of use, and sophisticated analytics. It was developed to provide an improved alternative to MapReduce for processing big datasets and can handle batch and real-time analytics. Spark provides APIs for Scala, Java, Python, and R and a built-in module for SQL queries. Its core data structure, the resilient distributed dataset (RDD), enables fault-tolerant operation and allows data to be processed in parallel across a cluster of computers.

Spark also includes several libraries to broaden its capabilities, including MLlib for machine learning, Spark Streaming for processing live data streams, and Spark SQL and DataFrames for processing structured data. These tools make it well-suited for tasks ranging from machine learning to real-time data streaming and batch processing. Its in-memory processing capabilities make Spark significantly faster than its predecessor, so it is a popular choice for big data processing.

First we will ask Copilot Chat to recommend a strategy for using Apache Spark to track our assets:

 Let's imagine that our company is in Chicago. We want to create a class called AssetLocationSparkAdapter that will continuously stream AssetLocation json messages from a Kafka topic called asset_location. An AssetLocation has the following attributes asset_id: int, latitude: float, longitude: float, and timestamp: datetime. The AssetLocations are stored in a Postgres database in a table called itam.asset_locations. AssetLocationSparkAdapter should calculate if the new AssetLocation is more than 25 miles from Chicago. If it is, then it should write a message to the console. This should be using the latest version of Spark. How would we do this?

Copilot Chat generates a class that you should be able to put into a file called asset_location_spark_adapter.py in the infrastructure package. Helpfully, it also includes comments for each line, so you should find the generated code easy to follow. The import statements include the Spark libraries as well as geopy.

```
from pyspark.sql import SparkSession
from pyspark.sql.functions import from_json, col, expr
from pyspark.sql.types import StructType,
    StructField, IntegerType, DoubleType,
    TimestampType
from geopy.distance import distance
```

The class begins with an overstuffed constructor that defines the schema Spark will use when it translates the JSON to a DataFrame.

> **NOTE**   The `AssetLocationSparkAdapter`, as defined, is a blocking process. Therefore, your FastAPI application will not "fully" boot until the Spark process has been killed. You want this to be a standalone process, or you need to introduce an asynchronous framework to have these two processes run concomitantly.

Next it starts up a local Spark instance/session that will allow Spark to connect to the Kafka topic and continuously stream in the records.

Listing 5.20   `AssessLocationSparkAdapter`, which processes the Kafka topic

```
class AssetLocationSparkAdapter:
    def __init__(self):
        # Define the schema for the incoming JSON data
        self.schema = StructType([
            StructField("asset_id", IntegerType()),
            StructField("latitude", DoubleType()),
            StructField("longitude", DoubleType()),
            StructField("timestamp", TimestampType())
        ])

        # Create a SparkSession
        self.spark = SparkSession.builder \
            .appName("AssetLocationSparkAdapter") \
            .getOrCreate()

        # Create a streaming DataFrame from the asset_location topic
        self.df = self.spark \
            .readStream \
            .format("kafka") \
            .option("kafka.bootstrap.servers", "localhost:9092") \
            .option("subscribe", "asset_location") \
            .option("startingOffsets", "earliest") \
            .load() \
            .selectExpr("CAST(value AS STRING)")

        # Parse the incoming JSON data
```

```
        self.parsed_stream = self.df \
            .select(from_json(col("value"), self.schema).alias("data")) \
            .select("data.*")
```

The final section of the `AssetLocationSparkAdapter` class calculates the distance from the asset's current location to Chicago. If the difference is greater than 25 miles, it sends the result set to the console. Additionally, it provides a method to start and stop the adapter.

Listing 5.21 Calculating the distance from the `Asset` location to Chicago

```
        # Calculate the distance between the current location and Chicago for
each asset
        self.distance = self.parsed_stream \
            .withColumn("distance",
            expr("calculate_distance(latitude,
            longitude, 41.8781, -87.6298)")) \
            .select(col("asset_id"), col("timestamp"), col("distance")) \
            .filter(col("distance") > 25)

        # Write the results to the console
        self.query = self.distance \
            .writeStream \
            .outputMode("append") \
            .format("console") \
            .start()

    def run(self):
        # Start the streaming query
        self.query.awaitTermination()

    def stop(self):
        # Stop the streaming query and SparkSession
        self.query.stop()
        self.spark.stop()
```

The `calculate_distance` method takes the longitude and latitude of the asset's location and determines the distance from Chicago using the `geopy.distance` function.

Listing 5.22 Function to calculate the distance between Chi-town and `Asset`

```
def calculate_distance(lat1, lon1, lat2, lon2):
    return distance((lat1, lon1), (lat2, lon2)).miles
```

In this instance, the code that Copilot Chat produced had some problems preventing it from running locally. After running it locally, encountering these problems, and trolling Stack Overflow, you would find a solution to the two main problems with the code: a missing environmental variable for running locally and failing to register your UDF (User Defined Function). Fortunately, you do not need to do the testing and research—a solution is provided in the following listing.

Listing 5.23   Edits required to run the application locally

```
os.environ['PYSPARK_SUBMIT_ARGS'] =
    '--packages org.apache.spark:
        spark-streaming-kafka-0-10_2.12:3.2.0,
        org.apache.spark:
        spark-sql-kafka-0-10_2.12:3.2.0
        pyspark-shell'

class AssetLocationSparkAdapter:
    def __init__(self):
        # Create a SparkSession
        self.spark = SparkSession.builder \
            .appName("AssetLocationSparkAdapter") \
            .getOrCreate()
        self.spark.udf.register("calculate_distance", calculate_distance)
```

Finally, to run your Spark application, update main.py with the following code in the main function.

Listing 5.24   Updates to the `main` function

```
if __name__ == "__main__":
    adapter = AssetLocationSparkAdapter()
    adapter.run()
```

As you enter locations for your asset into the Kafka console producer that are further than 25 miles from downtown Chicago, you will notice that entries are written to the console. It would be trivial to update the class to output these results to Twilio's SMS API or an email service such as SendGrid.

Listing 5.25   The streaming output from your asset location

```
+--------+-------------------+------------------+
|asset_id|          timestamp|          distance|
+--------+-------------------+------------------+
|       1|2021-12-31 20:30:00| 712.8314662207446|
+--------+-------------------+------------------+
```

Congratulations! You are tracking your assets in real time and sending real-time alerts in case your corporate resources grow legs and walk away.

Summary

- GitHub Copilot Chat is an innovative tool that brings together the comprehensive language understanding of ChatGPT and the handy features of Copilot. It's a noteworthy development in the realm of programming assistance, particularly for providing detailed and contextually relevant suggestions in real time, fostering a more efficient coding experience.
- The Mediator design pattern is a distinct behavioral pattern that facilitates a high level of decoupling between objects, thus enhancing the modularity of your

code. By encompassing the interactions between objects in a mediator object, objects can communicate indirectly, which reduces dependencies and promotes code reusability and ease of modification.

- Apache Kafka is a robust, distributed streaming platform engineered for creating real-time data pipelines and streaming applications. It can effectively handle data streams from a multitude of sources and transmit them to various consumers, making it an ideal solution for use cases that require handling substantial volumes of real-time or near-real-time data. It's important to remember that Kafka is optimized for append-only, immutable data and not for use cases that need record updates or deletions, or complex querying.

- Apache Spark is a high-performance, distributed data processing engine renowned for its speed, user-friendliness, and advanced analytics capabilities. It's highly suitable for scenarios necessitating real-time data processing or for operations on enormous datasets. However, for simpler tasks such as basic analytics and straightforward aggregations, a traditional relational database may be a more appropriate choice.

- Generative AI, despite its rapid evolution, is not infallible. It's crucial to meticulously review all generated output to ensure that it aligns with your specific requirements and quality standards. Generative AI is not a substitute for deep domain knowledge or coding expertise, but it significantly enhances productivity by providing valuable insights and reducing the time spent on routine tasks.

Part 3

The feedback

In part 3, we highlight the critical role of testing, quality assessment, and explanation in AI-augmented software development. This section focuses on ensuring the reliability and robustness of software built with LLMs. It covers the processes involved in bug hunting and code translation, emphasizing the importance of thorough testing and quality control. Using AI, developers can generate clear explanations of AI-generated code, facilitating better understanding and collaboration within development teams. This part underscores the necessity of maintaining high standards in software quality and provides strategies for achieving this in an AI-driven environment.

Testing, assessing, and explaining with large language models

This chapter will explore a critical aspect of software engineering: testing. The act of testing software serves multiple essential purposes. First and foremost, it aids in the identification of bugs, errors, and problems that can potentially affect the software's functionality, usability, or performance. Furthermore, it ensures that the software adheres to the required quality standards. By conducting thorough tests, we can verify whether the software meets the specified requirements, functions as intended, and produces the expected outcomes. Through comprehensive testing, developers can evaluate software's reliability, accuracy, efficiency, security, and compatibility across various platforms and environments. Detecting and resolving software defects early in the development process can result in significant time and cost savings.

Once we have finished formulating our tests, we will evaluate the quality of our code. You will be introduced to several metrics that are helpful in assessing software quality and complexity. Additionally, if we need clarification on the purpose of our code or are reviewing it for the first time, we will seek an explanation to ensure thorough understanding.

6.1 Testing, testing ... one, two, three types

Testing plays a vital role in software engineering; therefore, we will explore various types of testing in detail. These include unit tests, integration tests, and behavior tests. To start, we will use Copilot Chat to help us create a *unit test*.

> **DEFINITION**   A *unit test* focuses on testing individual components or units of code to ensure that they function correctly in isolation. Developers usually run unit tests to help identify bugs and problems in specific software units.

6.1.1 Unit testing

In this section, we will create unit tests to test our software components. Several unit-testing frameworks are available for Python. Each has unique features and is suitable for different scenarios. We will examine each of them briefly before settling on a specific framework based on the recommendation provided by our AI tool.

The first framework is `unittest`. This is Python's standard library for creating unit tests. It comes bundled with Python and doesn't need to be installed separately. `unittest` provides a rich set of assertions and is great for writing simple to complex test cases, but it can be verbose. It is a good choice for writing basic unit tests, especially if you don't want to introduce additional dependencies in your project. It's useful in any scenario where you need to confirm the functionality of individual units of code in isolation from the rest of the system.

Next, let's examine `pytest`. It is a popular third-party library that can be used for unit testing, although it's versatile enough to handle more than just unit tests. It requires less boilerplate code than `unittest` and has powerful features like fixtures for setup and teardown, parameterized testing, and the ability to run `unittest` and `nose` test suites. `pytest` is great for both simple and complex unit test cases. It's also useful for functional and integration tests. If you value simplicity and ease of use, and your project is not restricted to using only the Python standard library, `pytest` is an excellent choice.

`nose2` is the successor to the deprecated `nose` testing framework. It extends `unittest` and makes testing easier. It's known for its test discovery feature, which automatically finds your project's tests so you don't have to manually list them. `nose2` is good for larger projects where test discovery can save time. Like `pytest`, it can run `unittest` test suites, so it's also a good choice if you're migrating from `unittest` but want to keep your existing tests.

Finally, there is doctest. This is another module that's part of the Python standard library. It's not a full-featured testing framework like the others, but it allows you to write tests directly in your docstrings. doctest is best suited for simple cases where you want to demonstrate how to use a function or module and confirm that the example code works as expected. It's a great way to ensure that your documentation stays up to date with your code.

Copilot Chat recommended that we use unittest, so we will. You might try to ask it yourself and see if it reaches a different conclusion, which it may, depending on how you frame the question.

First we will define test cases by creating classes that inherit from the unittest .TestCase class. In writing our first unit test, we will uncover a rather pernicious bug that has thus far eluded us; we will get to that shortly. Finally, we are going to test the correctness of the DepartmentStatisticsVisitor class.

We start with a prompt asking Copilot Chat to create a unit test for Department-StatisticsVisitor. The response will be a reminder of the importance of context. Copilot Chat, given that we began a new chat session, will attempt to create this unit test, but it lacks the definition of any of our classes.

Listing 6.1 First attempt to define a unit test

```python
import unittest
from department_visitor import DepartmentStatisticsVisitor

class TestDepartmentStatisticsVisitor(unittest.TestCase):
    def test_visit_department(self):
        visitor = DepartmentStatisticsVisitor()
        department = {'name': 'Sales', 'employees':
            [{'name': 'John', 'salary': 50000},
             {'name': 'Jane', 'salary': 60000}]}
        visitor.visit_department(department)
        self.assertEqual(visitor.total_salaries, 110000)
        self.assertEqual(visitor.num_employees, 2)
        self.assertEqual(visitor.avg_salary, 55000)
```

We proceed by inputting definitions into Copilot Chat so that it can refine the test case. We can tell it more about the visitor class:

```
The DepartmentStatisticsVisitor class visits to determine the total asset
depreciation based off of the asset allocation for each department
```

With this updated information, Copilot Chat can better estimate how our unit test should function.

Listing 6.2 The result of a unit test prompt

```python
import unittest
from department_visitor import DepartmentStatisticsVisitor, Asset

class TestDepartmentStatisticsVisitor(unittest.TestCase):
    def test_visit(self):
```

```
visitor = DepartmentStatisticsVisitor()
asset1 = Asset(1000, 500, 0.5)
asset2 = Asset(2000, 1000, 0.3)
visitor.visit(asset1)
visitor.visit(asset2)
self.assertEqual(visitor.get_total_cost(), 3000)
self.assertEqual(visitor.get_total_depreciation(), 1500)
self.assertEqual(visitor.get_total_allocation(), 0.8)
```

The unit test is close to what we need; however, the definition of `Asset` is incorrect. We can enter the proper definition from our asset.py class, and Copilot Chat will continue to refine the unit test.

Listing 6.3   Next attempt to define a unit test, with `Asset` definition

```
import unittest
from datetime import date
from typing import List
from dataclasses import dataclass

@dataclass
class Location:
    name: str
    address: str

@dataclass
class Asset:
    id: int
    name: str
    status: str
    category: str
    cost: float
    useful_life: int
    salvage_value: float
    purchase_date: date
    locations: List[Location]

class TestAsset(unittest.TestCase):
    def test_asset(self):
        location1 = Location('Office', '123 Main St')
        location2 = Location('Warehouse', '456 Elm St')
        asset = Asset(1, 'Computer',
            'In use', 'Hardware',
            1000.0, 3, 100.0, date.today(),
            [location1, location2])
        self.assertEqual(asset.id, 1)
        self.assertEqual(asset.name, 'Computer')
        self.assertEqual(asset.status, 'In use')
        self.assertEqual(asset.category, 'Hardware')
        self.assertEqual(asset.cost, 1000.0)
        self.assertEqual(asset.useful_life, 3)
        self.assertEqual(asset.salvage_value, 100.0)
        self.assertEqual(asset.purchase_date, date.today())
        self.assertEqual(asset.locations, [location1, location2])
```

This is closer. We also need to remind Copilot Chat that the `Asset` class has a class called `FundingDetails`. Let's provide the definition of `FundingDetails` and inform Copilot Chat that it should be part of `Asset`.

Listing 6.4 Third attempt at a unit test, which comes reasonably close

```python
import unittest
from department_visitor import
    DepartmentStatisticsVisitor, Asset,
    FundingDetails
from datetime import date
from typing import List, Dict
from dataclasses import dataclass

@dataclass
class Location:
    name: str
    address: str

class TestDepartmentStatisticsVisitor(unittest.TestCase):
    def test_visit(self):
        visitor = DepartmentStatisticsVisitor()
        location1 = Location('Office', '123 Main St')
        location2 = Location('Warehouse', '456 Elm St')
        asset1 = Asset(1, 'Computer', 'In use',
            'Hardware', 1000.0, 3,
            100.0, date.today(),
            [location1, location2])
        asset2 = Asset(2, 'Printer', 'In use',
            'Hardware', 500.0, 2, 50.0,
            date.today(), [location1])
        funding_details1 = FundingDetails(
            asset1, 'Straight Line',
            0.33, { 'IT': 0.5, 'HR': 0.5 })
        funding_details2 = FundingDetails(
            asset2, 'Double Declining Balance',
            0.25, { 'IT': 0.3, 'HR': 0.7 })
        visitor.visit(asset1, funding_details1)
        visitor.visit(asset2, funding_details2)
        self.assertEqual(visitor.get_total_cost(), 1500.0)
        self.assertEqual(visitor.get_total_depreciation(), 550.0)
        self.assertEqual(visitor.get_total_allocation(), 0.8)
```

All that remains is to manually update the `import` statements.

> **NOTE** Let this exercise be a cautionary tale in the usage of large language models: coercing them to behave with respect to highly focused tasks can be very challenging, to the point of not being worth the effort. In the real world, no one will blame you for abandoning the prompt engineering and going back to just coding out this test. However, with some persistence, you can build a template library that you can use to build a suite of unit tests for similarly shaped classes. Also note that Copilot Chat can and will generate a test for the file in the editor

window if you instruct it to `Generate (a) unit test for my code`, but it will mock all objects/properties that are not directly part of the class under test. Depending on what you are attempting to test, the utility of this feature may be questionable. Another common problem specific to Python is that the indentation is frequently incorrect with code copied from Copilot Chat.

When we attempt to run this test, we discover that there is a *circular dependency* between the visitor, asset, funding details, and depreciation strategy. A circular dependency is a situation in which two or more modules or components depend on each other directly or indirectly. In our case, when Python tries to instantiate `Asset`, it loads the definition of `FundingDetails`. We can fix this by moving away from a direct instantiation or reference to the `FundingDetails` class.

Listing 6.5   Updated `Asset`, no direct reference to `FundingDetails`

```
@dataclass
class Asset():
    id: int
    name: str
    status: str
    category: str
    cost: float
    useful_life: int
    salvage_value: float
    purchase_date: date
    locations: List[Location]
    funding_details: None or 'itam.domain.funding_details.FundingDetails'
```

We need to do the same for the `FundingDetails` class. It should not directly reference the `DepreciationStrategy` class.

Listing 6.6   `FundingDetails`, no direct ref to `DepreciationStrategy`

```
@dataclass
class FundingDetails:
    depreciation_rate: float
    department_allocations: Dict[Department, float]
    depreciation_strategy: DepreciationStrategy or 'itam.domain.depreciation_
strategy.DepreciationStrategy'
    asset: None or 'itam.domain.asset.Asset'
```

As we've seen, we were able to create a unit test using Copilot Chat. However, we would likely have been able to create it more easily if we had written it without Copilot. The tool is surprisingly good at providing guidance as to when and how to test your code, but the implementation (at least currently) leaves something to be desired.

In the real world, we would continue to add unit tests to build up a substantial body of tests. How many tests is *substantial*, you ask? We will explore this shortly. However, we first turn our attention to the next type of test: the *integration test*.

DEFINITION *Integration testing* involves testing the interaction between different components or modules of the software to ensure that they work together seamlessly. It verifies that the integrated system functions as expected and detects any inconsistencies or communication problems between modules.

6.1.2 Integration testing

In this section, we will develop an integration test that will allow us to test the end-to-end system. Fortunately, `fastapi` comes with its own test client, which will aid us in creating this test.

We begin by copying in the definition of `AssetController` into the Copilot Chat window. We can then ask Copilot Chat how to create an integration test for this controller. Given that we included the routes in the definition, Copilot Chat should be able to provide us with accurate integration tests. We need to specify that we will use the `InMemoryAssetRepository` class or fix this after the test has been generated.

Listing 6.7 Copilot Chat-generated integration test of `AssetController`

```python
from fastapi.testclient import TestClient
from itam.infrastructure.adapters.memory_asset_repository import
MemoryAssetRepository
from itam.infrastructure.ports.asset_rest_port import AssetRestPort
from itam.interfaces.asset_controller import AssetController

def test_get_assets():
    # Create an instance of the InMemoryAssetRepository
    asset_repository = InMemoryAssetRepository()

    # Add some assets to the repository
    asset_repository.create(Asset(name="Asset 1", unit_cost=1000))
    asset_repository.create(Asset(name="Asset 2", unit_cost=2000))

    # Create an instance of the AssetRestPort using the MemoryAssetRepository
    asset_rest_port = AssetRestPort(asset_repository)

    # Create an instance of the AssetController using the AssetRestPort
    asset_controller = AssetController(asset_rest_port)

    # Create a TestClient instance using the AssetController's router
    client = TestClient(asset_controller.get_router())

    # Send a GET request to the /assets endpoint
    response = client.get("/assets")

    # Check that the response status code is 200 OK
    assert response.status_code == 200

    # Check that the response body contains the expected assets
    assert response.json() == [
        {"id": 1, "name": "Asset 1", "unit_cost": 1000},
        {"id": 2, "name": "Asset 2", "unit_cost": 2000},
```

We will now turn our attention to the final type of testing that we'll examine: *behavior testing*.

> **DEFINITION**   *Behavior testing* focuses on the behavior of a system as a whole from the perspective of an end user. It is typically used to test the functionality of a system and to ensure that the system meets the requirements and specifications defined for it.

6.1.3   *Behavior testing*

In a sense, all testing is behavior testing, as tests verify the behavior of the system. However, behavior testing is unique in some respects. Let's summarize the different types of testing that we have encountered thus far and contrast them against behavior tests.

Unit testing focuses on testing individual units or components of a system in isolation, typically using automated tests. Unit tests are designed to test the functionality of individual functions or methods and to ensure that they behave correctly under a variety of conditions.

Integration testing, on the other hand, focuses on testing the interactions between different components or units of a system. Integration testing is typically used to test the interfaces between different components or units and to ensure that they work together correctly. Integration testing can be performed manually or using automated tests, and it typically involves testing the interactions between different components or units of a system rather than the system as a whole.

Behavioral testing focuses on defining the behavior of the software in terms of user stories or scenarios. These scenarios are written in a specific format called *given-when-then* (GWT) and are used to drive the development process. The GWT format describes the preconditions (given), the actions (when), and the expected outcomes (then) of a particular scenario.

As we progress with our testing, we may find that some behaviors or components are difficult to set up in our test. Additionally, it may be tricky to isolate the behavior of a particular object or module and test the interactions between different objects. To address this limitation, we can use a *mock object*.

> **DEFINITION**   A *mock object* is a test double that simulates the behavior of a real object in a controlled way. Mock objects can also be used to simulate error conditions or edge cases that are difficult to reproduce with real objects. They can be created manually using a mocking library such as `unittest.mock` or `pytest-mock`. These libraries provide functions and classes for creating and configuring mock objects. Mock objects can be configured to return specific values or raise specific exceptions when their methods are called. They can also be used to record the calls made to their methods so that you can verify that the correct methods were called with the correct parameters.

We will incorporate mock objects into the prompt to create a behavior test for `AssetManager`:

 We have a class called AssetManager. AssetManager's constructor takes two classes BaseRepository and AssetLocationMediator. The BaseRepository is a repository in which Assets are stored. We want to use InMemoryAssetRepository, which is a subclass of BaseRepository that stores the Assets in memory. Use a mock object for AssetLocationMediator. The AssetManager stores Assets using the method create and gets all of the Assets using the method get_assets. An asset has 10 required positional arguments: 'id', 'name', 'status', 'category', 'cost', 'useful_life', 'salvage_value', 'purchase_date', 'locations', and 'funding_details'. Use named parameters to make it clear which param is going where. Create a BDD script that will add two Assets to the AssetManager, confirming that all Assets cost $4000.00. This should be implemented in Python. Take it step by step, telling us the tools and libraries you will use.

Copilot Chat tells us that we need to create a new file (a *feature file*) called `asset_manager.feature`. In this file, we will define `AssetManager`'s attributes (and any supporting classes). For example, the feature file defines a scenario that adds two assets to `AssetManager`, confirms that the total cost of all assets is $4,000.00, and mocks the `AssetLocationMediator` class.

Listing 6.8 `asset_manager.feature` file according to Copilot Chat

```
Feature: Asset Manager
  As an IT Asset Manager
  I want to be able to manage assets
  So that I can keep track of all IT assets in my organization

  Scenario: Add two assets to the Asset Manager
    Given the Asset Manager is running
    And the InMemoryAssetRepository is initialized
    And the AssetLocationMediator is mocked
    When I create an asset with a cost of $2000.00
    And I create another asset with a cost of $2000.00
    Then the total cost of all assets should be $4000.00
```

We need to create a directory called features at the root of our project and place this file in that directory. Additionally, we need to add a subdirectory called steps. Next we create a new Python file called steps.py and place it in the steps directory. This Python file defines the step implementations for the scenario in the feature file. The `Asset-Manager`, `InMemoryAssetRepository`, `AssetLocationMediator`, and `Asset` classes are imported, and six functions are defined to correspond to the steps in the scenario. These functions use the context object to store and retrieve data between steps. The `Mock` class from the `unittest.mock` library is used to create a mock object for the `AssetLocationMediator` class. The `Asset` class is instantiated using named parameters to clarify which parameter belongs to which attribute. If we ask Copilot Chat for the contents of the steps.py file, we will see output similar to the following listing.

```python
from behave import given, when, then
from itam.service.asset_manager import AssetManager
from itam.infrastructure.repository.in_memory_asset_repository
    import InMemoryAssetRepository
from itam.domain.asset import Asset
from itam.infrastructure.mediators.asset_location_mediator
    import AssetLocationMediator
from unittest.mock import Mock

@given('the Asset Manager is running')
def step_impl(context):
    context.asset_repository = InMemoryAssetRepository()
    context.asset_location_mediator = Mock(spec=AssetLocationMediator)
    context.asset_manager = AssetManager(
            context.asset_repository,
            context.asset_location_mediator)

@given('the InMemoryAssetRepository is initialized')
def step_impl(context):
    pass

@given('the AssetLocationMediator is mocked')
def step_impl(context):
    pass

@when('I create an asset with a cost of ${cost}')
def step_impl(context, cost):
    asset = Asset(id=1, name='Test Asset 1', status='Available',
        category='Test Category', cost=float(cost), useful_life=5,
        salvage_value=0, purchase_date='2022-01-01',
        locations=['Test Location'],
        funding_details={'Test Funding': 1000})
    context.asset_manager.create(asset)

@when('I create another asset with a cost of ${cost}')
def step_impl(context, cost):
    asset = Asset(id=2, name='Test Asset 2', status='Available',
        category='Test Category', cost=float(cost), useful_life=5,
        salvage_value=0, purchase_date='2022-01-01',
        locations=['Test Location'],
        funding_details={'Test Funding': 1000})
    context.asset_manager.create(asset)

@then('the total cost of all assets need to be ${total_cost}')
def step_impl(context, total_cost):
    assets = context.asset_manager.get_assets()
    assert sum(asset.cost for asset in assets) == float(total_cost)
```

If you do not have it installed already, you need to install the behave library using pip: pip install behave. Additionally, add it to the requirements.txt file to ensure that it will be pulled in when we later build a deployable version of this application. We run the behavior test by issuing the following command from the root directory of our project.

Listing 6.10 Running the behavior test, and the resulting output

```
% behave features
Feature: Asset Manager # features/asset_manager.feature:1
  As an IT Asset Manager
  I want to be able to manage assets
  So that I can keep track of all IT assets in my organization
  Scenario: Add two assets to the Asset Manager
    # features/asset_manager.feature:6
    Given the Asset Manager is running
# features/steps/steps.py:8 0.000s
    And the InMemoryAssetRepository is initialized
# features/steps/steps.py:14 0.000s
    And the AssetLocationMediator is mocked
# features/steps/steps.py:18 0.000s
    When I create an asset with a cost of $2000.00
# features/steps/steps.py:22 0.000s
    And I create another asset with a cost of $2000.00
# features/steps/steps.py:27 0.000s
    Then the total cost of all assets should be $4000.00
# features/steps/steps.py:32 0.000s

1 feature passed, 0 failed, 0 skipped
1 scenario passed, 0 failed, 0 skipped
6 steps passed, 0 failed, 0 skipped, 0 undefined
Took 0m0.001s
```

In this section, we have laid a foundation for good software development by using three types of tests: unit, integration, and behavior. Some may quibble that it came very late in the development lifecycle of this project, and they would not be wrong. In the real world, we develop our tests as we develop our code. Some may argue that we need to build our tests *before* our code. You may or may not hold this belief, but either way, you need to test early and test often.

In the next section, we dive into some metrics that can be used to determine the overall quality of our software, and we will ask Copilot to help us assess the quality of our code thus far.

6.2 *Assessing quality*

Understanding the performance, reliability, maintainability, and overall quality of software applications is a crucial aspect of software engineering. This section delves into the fascinating and intricate domain of software quality metrics—the quantitative standards and benchmarks that guide our understanding of the quality of a software system.

Software quality metrics are essential tools that allow stakeholders—developers, testers, managers, and users—to assess a software product's state, identifying its strengths and areas for improvement. They provide an empirical foundation for various processes such as product development, testing, debugging, maintenance, and improvement initiatives. By quantifying specific characteristics of the software, these metrics provide a tangible means to understand the otherwise abstract concept of software quality.

In this section, we explore several important categories of software quality metrics, including product metrics, process metrics, and project metrics. We'll analyze their significance, methodologies for their calculation, and how they can be effectively utilized to evaluate and enhance software quality. This exploration will include both static metrics, which are applied to the static software system, and dynamic metrics, which assess the system's behavior during execution.

Software quality metrics not only contribute to the technical soundness of a software system but also help ensure customer satisfaction, profitability, and long-term business success. Therefore, developing an understanding of these metrics is invaluable to anyone involved in the field of software development, from engineers and project managers to executives and software users.

We will examine a few common measures of complexity and maintainability of the class or code. Complex software can be difficult to comprehend, which makes it challenging for developers, particularly new ones, to grasp how different parts of the software interact with each other. This can slow down the onboarding process and development time.

Complex code often leads to more maintenance: modifications or bug fixes can take longer because it's harder to predict the effects of changing a single piece of the system. This can result in higher costs over the software's lifecycle.

Complex software also tends to be more error-prone. Because it's harder to understand, developers are more likely to introduce bugs when making changes. Also, complex code can have many interdependencies, and a change in one area may have unexpected effects elsewhere.

The more complex the software, the more test cases are required to achieve thorough testing. It may also be harder to write these test cases due to the complexity of the logic involved.

Writing simple and maintainable code should be one of our highest priorities. Observing the change in the metric that accompanies our code should aid us in this endeavor. Toward this objective, the first metric that we can (and should) use is *cyclomatic complexity*.

> **DEFINITION** *Cyclomatic complexity* is a metric that quantifies the number of independent paths through a software module. It measures the complexity of decision-making in the code, including loops, conditionals, and branches. A higher cyclomatic complexity value indicates increased complexity and suggests the potential for more bugs and challenges in understanding and maintaining the code.

Enter the following prompt anywhere in the file department_visitor.py. Copilot will immediately output the answer:

```
# Question: What is the cyclomatic complexity of the class Department-
StatisticsVisitor?
# Answer: 1
```

Copilot tells us that the complexity of this class is 1. You may or may not be aware of the meaning of this value. If the latter, you can ask Copilot to elaborate:

```
# Question: Is 1 an excellent cyclomatic complexity?
# Answer: Yes
```

```
# Question: Why is 1 a good value for cyclomatic complexity?
# Answer: Because it is low
```

Copilot informs us that cyclomatic complexity is good if it is low. Intuitively, this makes sense. Code with low complexity means it is simpler to understand and therefore reason about. It is likely easier to maintain as well. Next we will explore the *Halstead complexity measures*.

DEFINITION   *Halstead complexity measures* assess the complexity of a software program based on the number of unique operators and operands used in the code. These measures include metrics such as program length (N1), program vocabulary (n1), volume (V), difficulty (D), effort (E), and others. These metrics provide insights into the size and cognitive complexity of the code.

Similar to last time, we will start with a prompt asking Copilot to determine the Halstead complexity measure for our visitor class:

```
# Question: What is the Halstead Complexity Measure of the class Department-
StatisticsVisitor?
# Answer: 2
```

```
# Question: What is the Halstead Difficulty Measure of the class Department-
StatisticsVisitor?
# Answer: 1
```

```
# Question: Is 2 a good Halstead Complexity Measure?
# Answer: Yes
```

```
# Question: Is 1 a good Halstead Difficulty Measure?
# Answer: Yes
```

```
# Question: What is a bad Halstead Difficulty Measure?
# Answer: 10
```

```
# Question: What is a bad Halstead Complexity Measure?
# Answer: 10


# Question: What does a high Halstead Difficulty Measure mean?
# Answer: It means the code is hard to understand
```

You may want to continue this Q&A session for a while to see what information can be gleaned from Copilot. Once you are ready to continue, there is one more metric to explore: the *maintainability index*.

> **DEFINITION**   The *maintainability index* is a composite metric that combines several factors, including cyclomatic complexity, lines of code, and Halstead complexity measures, to provide an overall measure of software maintainability. A higher maintainability index suggests easier maintenance and potentially lower complexity.

Start a similar discussion for the maintainability index in the visitor file:

```
# Question: What is the maintainability index of the class Department-
StatisticsVisitor?
# Answer: 100


# Question: Do we want a high Maintainability Index or low Maintainability
Index?
# Answer: high


# Question: Why do we want a high Maintainability Index?
# Answer: Because it is easier to maintain
```

If we get a low maintainability index, we can refactor to reduce this number.

A metric is useful in that it gives us a nail to hang our hat on; that is, we can take that measure and perform some action to improve it. Metrics move us beyond pure aesthetics or the subjectivity of an individual. A metric is real, actionable data. But Copilot has (at least) one more trick up its proverbial sleeve. Copilot is capable of doing more than just writing and assessing our code: it can also address the code's flaws. Let's bug hunt.

6.3   *Hunting for bugs*

In this section, we will use an elementary (albeit contrived) example to demonstrate how we can use Copilot to find and fix problems in our code. This code is supposed to loop a the list of integers and calculate the sum. However, there is a "blink and you'll miss it" bug: the sum is assigned the value of i rather than adding the value of i to the running total.

Listing 6.11 Looping over a list of integers and calculating the sum

```
l = [1, 2, 3, 4, 5]

if __name__ == '__main__':
    sum = 0
    for i in l:
        sum = i

    print("sum is", sum)
```

To debug this problem, we will introduce a new tool: Copilot Labs. Prior to Copilot Chat, Copilot Labs was the only means by which certain features were available in an IDE (specifically, Visual Studio Code). For example, we need to use Copilot Labs to find and fix bugs. The main advantage that Copilot Labs still offers today is that it can access the highlighted contents of your editor pane. This feature allows Copilot Labs to operate directly on the editable code in your IDE.

Once you install the extension into your IDE, you should see a Copilot Labs toolkit on the left side of the IDE, as shown in figure 6.1. If you need a reminder about how to install an extension into your IDE, see appendices A–C for instructions.

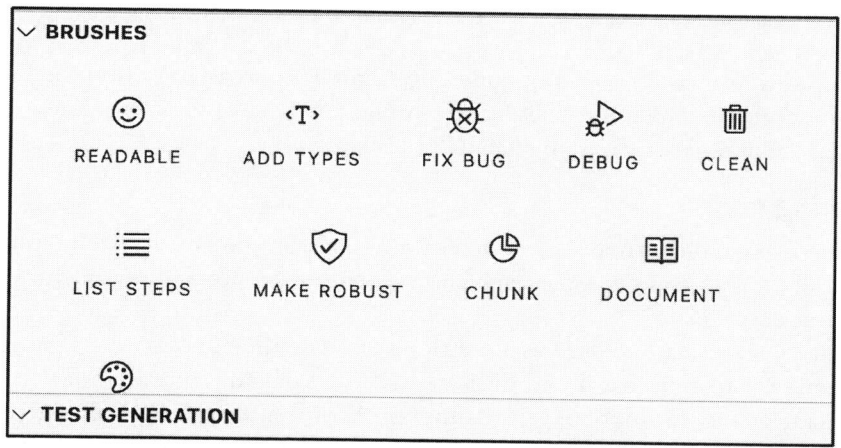

Figure 6.1   The Copilot Labs toolkit menu, which includes options for finding and fixing bugs. The toolkit also provides facilities to enhance your code as well as document it.

We will temporarily change the contents of the main.py file to the code listed in listing 6.11. Once you have made this change, highlight the code and click the Fix Bug button in the Copilot Labs toolkit. You should see output like that in figure 6.2. Copilot Labs was able to determine the problem in this code and provides a suggestion as to how to fix it.

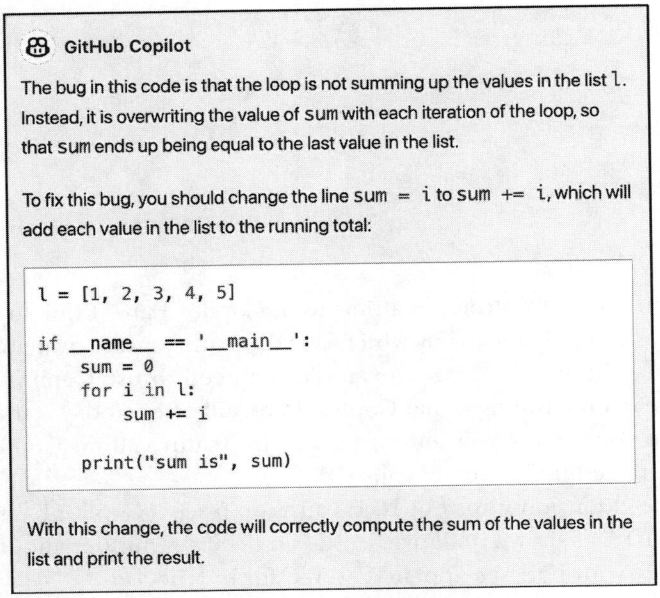

> **GitHub Copilot**
>
> The bug in this code is that the loop is not summing up the values in the list l. Instead, it is overwriting the value of sum with each iteration of the loop, so that sum ends up being equal to the last value in the list.
>
> To fix this bug, you should change the line sum = i to sum += i, which will add each value in the list to the running total:
>
> ```
> l = [1, 2, 3, 4, 5]
>
> if __name__ == '__main__':
>     sum = 0
>     for i in l:
>         sum += i
>
>     print("sum is", sum)
> ```
>
> With this change, the code will correctly compute the sum of the values in the list and print the result.

Figure 6.2   Copilot Labs, using the GPT model, has identified the bug and how to address it.

Alternatively, you could copy this code into ChatGPT and ask it to find the bug. However, it is arguable that doing so is less convenient as you would have to know there was a bug in your code before asking ChatGPT to fix it.

6.4   *Covering code*

Code coverage is a measure of how much of your code is being exercised by your tests. It is typically expressed as a percentage and represents the proportion of your code that your tests execute.

Code coverage can be used as a metric to evaluate the effectiveness of your tests. If your code coverage is low, it may indicate that parts of your code are not being tested, which can lead to uncaught bugs and other problems. Alternatively, with high code coverage, you can rest assured that your code is well-tested. This does not guarantee that your code is bug-free, but it should give you a high degree of confidence that if there are bugs, they will be caught in a test.

To determine the code coverage in our Python project, we will use the code coverage tool provided in the coverage library. The coverage library works by instrumenting our code to collect coverage data as it runs. It can collect coverage data for any Python code, including tests, scripts, and modules. By using a code coverage tool like coverage, we can better understand how much of our code is being exercised by our tests and identify areas of our code that may need more testing.

First, let's install `coverage` using pip: `pip install coverage`. Next, let's run our tests with coverage: `coverage run -m pytest`. This runs your tests and collects coverage data.

Now we will generate a coverage report (see figure 6.3). The coverage report shows the code coverage for each file in our project. We can create a text-based coverage report using the `coverage report` command or generate an HTML version of the report using the `coverage html` command. The HTML version of the report is in the htmlcov directory.

Coverage report: 70%

coverage.py v7.2.7, created at 2023-06-07 21:02 -0400

Module	statements	missing	excluded	coverage
itam/__init__.py	4	0	0	100%
itam/domain/__init__.py	12	0	0	100%
itam/domain/address.py	16	8	0	50%
itam/domain/asset.py	54	14	0	74%
itam/domain/budget.py	17	6	0	65%
itam/domain/department.py	7	0	0	100%
itam/domain/depreciation_strategy.py	25	2	0	92%
itam/domain/events/asset_location_updated.py	7	4	0	43%
itam/domain/funding_details.py	18	2	0	89%
itam/domain/hardware.py	34	9	0	74%
itam/domain/location.py	11	0	0	100%
itam/domain/maintenance_schedule.py	20	10	0	50%
itam/domain/organization.py	8	2	0	75%
itam/domain/role.py	10	4	0	60%
itam/domain/software.py	30	14	0	53%
itam/domain/usage_statistics.py	52	27	0	48%
itam/domain/user.py	22	11	0	50%
itam/domain/warranty.py	20	10	0	50%
itam/infrastructure/__init__.py	7	0	0	100%

Figure 6.3 The code coverage report showing the coverage for each file in our ITAM system project

Code coverage of 70% is a good start. In the real world, we would continue working with our team and generative AI pals to bring this measure up into the high 90s. Now we will transition to a new topic: using generative AI to describe a code listing to us.

6.5   *Transliterating code—from code to descriptions*

Often, we are handed existing source code. Determining the exact entry point of this code, the purpose of the code, and the overall structure of a brownfield project can be challenging. Fortunately, this is one of the areas in which generative AIs truly excel: translating code into textual descriptions.

To begin, we will copy the (buggy) code from the previous section into the Copilot Chat dialog box, prefixed with the following prompt (see figure 6.4):

 What does this code do?

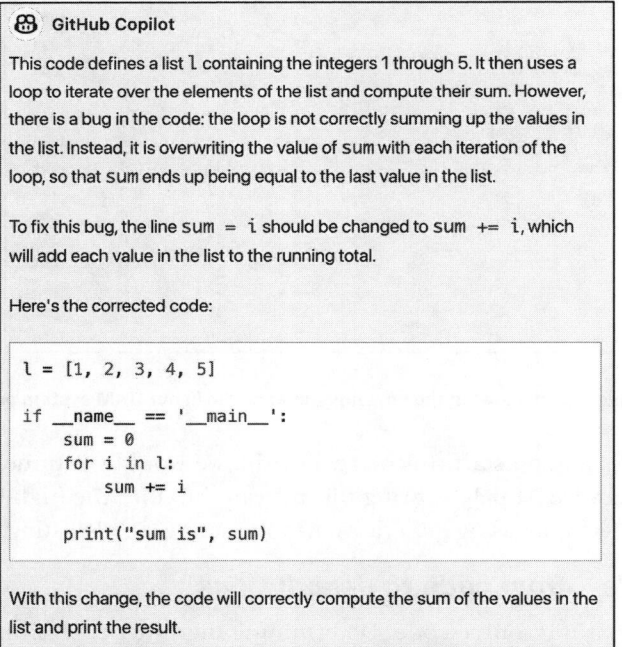

```
What does this code do?

l = [1, 2, 3, 4, 5]

if __name__ == '__main__':
   sum = 0
   for i in l:
     sum = i

   print("sum is", sum)
```

Figure 6.4   The buggy code from the last section with a prompt asking Copilot Chat to explain this code to us

What is striking about the explanation in figure 6.5 is that Copilot Chat detects a bug in the code and offers suggestions for how to fix it.

GitHub Copilot

This code defines a list `l` containing the integers 1 through 5. It then uses a loop to iterate over the elements of the list and compute their sum. However, there is a bug in the code: the loop is not correctly summing up the values in the list. Instead, it is overwriting the value of `sum` with each iteration of the loop, so that `sum` ends up being equal to the last value in the list.

To fix this bug, the line `sum = i` should be changed to `sum += i`, which will add each value in the list to the running total.

Here's the corrected code:

```
l = [1, 2, 3, 4, 5]

if __name__ == '__main__':
    sum = 0
    for i in l:
        sum += i

    print("sum is", sum)
```

With this change, the code will correctly compute the sum of the values in the list and print the result.

Figure 6.5   Copilot Chat explains the code's purpose, identifies the bug, and suggests a fix.

Next we will ask it something more challenging: to explain the behavior test from listing 6.9 into the Copilot Chat window, and ask it what this class does. You will likely receive a response similar to the following.

Listing 6.12 Copilot Chat explaining the behavior test we wrote earlier

The code you provided is not a class but a series of step definitions for a Behavior-Driven Development (BDD) test using the Behave framework in Python. These steps correspond to a specific scenario written in Gherkin language (Given, When, Then format).

These step definitions describe how to interact with an AssetManager class and an InMemoryAssetRepository class. They're meant to test the creation of assets and the calculation of the total cost of all assets.

Let's go through each step:

@given('the Asset Manager is running'): This sets up the initial state for the test. It initializes the AssetManager with an InMemoryAssetRepository (which presumably stores assets in memory during the execution of the test) and a mocked AssetLocationMediator.

@given('the InMemoryAssetRepository is initialized') and @given('the AssetLocationMediator is mocked'): These steps appear to be placeholders, as they don't execute any actions.

@when('I create an asset with a cost of ${cost}') and @when('I create another asset with a cost of ${cost}'): These steps create Asset instances with the given cost and add them to the AssetManager.

@then('the total cost of all assets should be ${total_cost}'): This step retrieves all the assets from the AssetManager, calculates the total cost, and checks that it matches the expected total cost.

This sequence of steps allows the user to test the process of creating assets and validating the total cost of all assets in the AssetManager.

```
# Question: What does this method do?
# Answer: This code defines an asynchronous method get_asset that
  takes an integer asset_id as input. The method first calls the
  _asset_rest_port.read method with the asset_id to retrieve an
  asset from a REST API. If the asset is not found (i.e., the
  REST API returns None), the method raises an
  HTTPException with a 404 status code and a "Asset not
  found" detail message. Otherwise, the method returns the
  asset converted to a domain object using the from_asset
  function. The implementation of the from_asset function is
  not shown in the code snippet.
```

```
async def get_asset(self, asset_id: int):
    asset = self._asset_rest_port.read(asset_id)
    if asset is None:
        raise HTTPException(status_code=404, detail="Asset not found")
    return from_asset(asset)
```

6.6   *Translating from one language to another*

As remote as this may seem, you may find yourself looking through a code base written in a programming language with which you have only a passing familiarity. Alternatively, you may pine for a specific function from another language to be available in your current language. For example, what would the `Asset` and `FundingDetails` classes look like if they were rewritten in JavaScript? Well, let's ask Copilot Chat.

Listing 6.13   `Asset` and `FundingDetails` translated to JavaScript.

```javascript
class Asset {
  constructor(id, name, status, category, cost,
        useful_life, salvage_value,
        purchase_date, locations,
        funding_details) {
    this.id = id;
    this.name = name;
    this.status = status;
    this.category = category;
    this.cost = cost;
    this.useful_life = useful_life;
    this.salvage_value = salvage_value;
    this.purchase_date = purchase_date;
    this.locations = locations;
    this.funding_details = funding_details;
  }
}

class FundingDetails {
  constructor(asset, funding_source, funding_amount) {
    this.asset = asset;
    this.funding_source = funding_source;
    this.funding_amount = funding_amount;
  }
}
```

You may think that translating a class or two is too easy. Well, we will attempt something more complex:

 What would the AssetManager behavior test look like if written in JavaScript?

Listing 6.14   `AssetManager` behavior test translated into JavaScript

```javascript
const AssetManager = require('./asset_manager');
const Asset = require('./asset');

describe('AssetManager', () => {
  let assetManager;

  beforeEach(() => {
    assetManager = new AssetManager();
  });
```

```javascript
describe('addAsset', () => {
  it('should add an asset to the asset list', () => {
    const asset = new Asset(1, 'Computer', 'Active',
        'Hardware', 1000.0, 5, 100.0,
        new Date(), [], null);
    assetManager.addAsset(asset);
    expect(assetManager.assets.length).toBe(1);
    expect(assetManager.assets[0]).toBe(asset);
  });
});

describe('removeAsset', () => {
  it('should remove an asset from the asset list', () => {
    const asset = new Asset(1, 'Computer', 'Active',
        'Hardware', 1000.0, 5, 100.0,
        new Date(), [], null);
    assetManager.addAsset(asset);
    assetManager.removeAsset(asset);
    expect(assetManager.assets.length).toBe(0);
  });
});

describe('getAssetById', () => {
  it('should return the asset with the given ID', () => {
    const asset1 = new Asset(1, 'Computer', 'Active',
        'Hardware', 1000.0, 5, 100.0,
        new Date(), [], null);
    const asset2 = new Asset(2, 'Printer', 'Active',
        'Hardware', 500.0, 3, 50.0,
        new Date(), [], null);
    assetManager.addAsset(asset1);
    assetManager.addAsset(asset2);
    const result = assetManager.getAssetById(2);
    expect(result).toBe(asset2);
  });

  it('should return null if no asset with the given ID is found', () => {
    const result = assetManager.getAssetById(1);
    expect(result).toBeNull();
  });
});
});
```

Additionally, you may wish to have GPT rewrite the code in idiomatic JavaScript. You need only say

 Write AssetManager in idiomatic JavaScript

Copilot Chat will inform you that it will define the `AssetManager` class using the class syntax introduced in ES6.

Listing 6.15   `AssetManager` class rewritten in idiomatic JavaScript

```javascript
class AssetManager {
  constructor() {
    this.assets = [];
  }

  addAsset(asset) {
    this.assets.push(asset);
  }

  removeAsset(asset) {
    const index = this.assets.indexOf(asset);
    if (index !== -1) {
      this.assets.splice(index, 1);
    }
  }

  getAssetById(id) {
    return this.assets.find(asset => asset.id === id) || null;
  }
}
```

Here's an example of what the `AssetManager` behavior test might look like in Java-Script using the Jest testing framework (which Copilot Chat included without our suggestion).

Listing 6.16   `AssetManager` behavior test in idiomatic JavaScript

```javascript
const AssetManager = require('./asset_manager');
const Asset = require('./asset');
describe('AssetManager', () => {
  let assetManager;
  beforeEach(() => {
    assetManager = new AssetManager();
  });
  describe('addAsset', () => {
    it('should add an asset to the asset list', () => {
      const asset = new Asset(1, 'Computer', 'Active',
            'Hardware', 1000.0, 5, 100.0,
            new Date(), [], null);
      assetManager.addAsset(asset);
      expect(assetManager.assets.length).toBe(1);
      expect(assetManager.assets[0]).toBe(asset);
    });
  });
  describe('removeAsset', () => {
    it('should remove an asset from the asset list', () => {
      const asset = new Asset(1, 'Computer', 'Active',
            'Hardware', 1000.0, 5, 100.0,
            new Date(), [], null);
      assetManager.addAsset(asset);
      assetManager.removeAsset(asset);
      expect(assetManager.assets.length).toBe(0);
```

```
        });
    });
    describe('getAssetById', () => {
        it('should return the asset with the given ID', () => {
            const asset1 = new Asset(1, 'Computer', 'Active',
                'Hardware', 1000.0, 5, 100.0,
                new Date(), [], null);
            const asset2 = new Asset(2, 'Printer', 'Active',
                'Hardware', 500.0, 3, 50.0,
                new Date(), [], null);
            assetManager.addAsset(asset1);
            assetManager.addAsset(asset2);
            const result = assetManager.getAssetById(2);
            expect(result).toBe(asset2);
        });
        it('should return null if no asset with the given ID is found', () => {
            const result = assetManager.getAssetById(1);
            expect(result).toBeNull();
        });
    });
});
```

In this example, we use the Jest testing framework to define a set of behavior tests for the `AssetManager` class. We are using the `describe` library to determine test suites and individual tests.

In each test, we create an instance of the `AssetManager` class and perform some operation on it, such as adding or removing an asset. We then use the `expect` function to make assertions about the behavior of the `AssetManager` class, such as checking that an asset was added to the asset list or that an asset was removed from the asset list. Note that the syntax for defining classes and constructors is slightly different in JavaScript than in Python, and we are using the required function to import the `AssetManager` and `Asset` classes from their respective modules.

Finally, time for the big finale: we will start a new ChatGPT 4.0 session and paste in our Mermaid diagram from chapter 3. Lead with this prompt:

 Here is a mermaid diagram of my application. Please implement in Golang.

Marvel as it returns the code, rendered in Golang.

Listing 6.17 Asset class rewritten in idiomatic Golang

```
type Asset struct {
    id             int
    name           string
    status         string
    category       string
    fundingDetails *FundingDetails
}

func NewAsset(name, status, category string,
    fundingDetails *FundingDetails) *Asset {
```

```
    return &Asset{
        name:          name,
        status:        status,
        category:      category,
        fundingDetails: fundingDetails,
    }
}
```

Next, tell it to switch to Java.

Listing 6.18 **Asset** class rewritten in idiomatic Java

```
class Asset {
    private int id;
    private String name;
    private String status;
    private String category;
    private FundingDetails fundingDetails;

    public Asset(String name, String status, String category, FundingDetails
fundingDetails) {
        this.name = name;
        this.status = status;
        this.category = category;
        this.fundingDetails = fundingDetails;
    }
}
```

Summary

- Unit testing focuses on testing individual components or units of code to identify bugs and problems in specific units. Unit tests will be the most numerous in your codebase.
- Integration testing tests the interaction between different components or modules of the software to ensure seamless integration and detect communication problems.
- Behavior testing tests a system's functionality from an end user's perspective, ensuring that it meets requirements and specifications.
- Mock objects simulate the behavior of natural objects in a controlled way and are useful for testing and simulating error conditions. Mock objects are especially good at mimicking parts of the system that are needed for the test to run but are outside the scope of the test: for example, if your class has a constructor argument for a database, but you do not want to test the database directly because the data may change, causing your test to be inconclusive, nonrepeatable, or nondeterministic.
- Cyclomatic complexity measures the number of independent paths through a software module, indicating complexity and potential for bugs.
- Halstead complexity measures assess software complexity based on unique operators and operands, providing insights into code size and cognitive complexity.

- The maintainability index combines factors like cyclomatic complexity, lines of code, and Halstead measures to evaluate software maintainability.

- Code coverage is a metric for evaluating test effectiveness, indicating the extent to which code is tested and the potential for uncaught bugs. Generally, higher is better.

- Large language models allow you to navigate code in an unfamiliar programming language or translate features from another language in the current or preferred one.

Part 4

Into the world

In part 4, we address the practical aspects of deploying and managing AI-integrated software in real-world environments. This section covers coding infrastructure and deployment strategies, from building Docker images to setting up continuous integration and continuous deployment (CI/CD) pipelines with tools like GitHub Actions. It also emphasizes secure application development, discussing threat modeling and the implementation of security best practices. Additionally, this part of the book explores the concept of democratizing access to AI by hosting your own LLM and utilizing platforms like GPT-4All. By providing practical guidance on deployment and security, this part prepares developers to successfully bring their AI-powered applications to market.

Coding infrastructure and managing deployments

7

This chapter covers

- Creating a Dockerfile with the assistance of Copilot
- Drafting your infrastructure as code using large language models
- Managing Docker images with a container registry
- Harnessing the power of Kubernetes
- Releasing your code effortlessly using GitHub Actions

There is nothing more demoralizing than having an application sit unused. For this reason, fast-tracking a well-tested application to production is the stated goal of every competent developer. Because we spent the last chapter testing our product, it is now ready for launch.

This chapter will focus on that pivotal moment of transitioning from development to product launch. During this critical phase, understanding deployment strategies and best practices becomes essential to ensure a successful product launch.

With our application successfully secured and tested, it's time to shift our attention toward launching the product. To this end, we will use the powerful capabilities of large language models (LLMs) to explore various deployment options tailored to cloud infrastructure.

By harnessing the power of LLMs and embracing their deployment options and methodologies, we can confidently navigate the complex landscape of launching our product, delivering a robust and scalable solution to our customers while using the benefits of cloud computing.

First, we will develop deployment files for Docker. We will explore how to create Docker images and define deployment files. Additionally, we will discuss best practices for containerizing our application and achieving seamless deployment.

Next, we will use Terraform to define our infrastructure as code and automate the deployment of Elastic Compute Cloud (EC2) instances on Amazon Web Services (AWS). We will demonstrate how to write Terraform scripts to provision and deploy our application on EC2 instances, ensuring consistent and reproducible infrastructure setups.

Then we will utilize LLMs to deploy our application onto Kubernetes (AWS Elastic Kubernetes Service [EKS]/Elastic Container Service [ECS]). We will have GitHub Copilot create the appropriate Kubernetes deployment files to streamline our deployment process and efficiently manage our application's lifecycle. Given the relative simplicity of our application, we will not need a Kubernetes package manager like Helm. However, as the complexities and dependencies of services grow, you may want to explore it as one option. Fortunately, Copilot can write Helm charts for you as well!

Finally, we will briefly showcase migrating from local to automated deployments using GitHub actions. We can automate our build and deployment processes by integrating LLMs with this widespread continuous integration and deployment (CI/CD) tool, ensuring faster and more efficient deployments.

> **NOTE** This chapter uses AWS as our cloud provider, but the principles and practices covered in the chapter can be adapted and applied to other cloud platforms and even on-premises infrastructure without virtualization (bare metal), allowing us to adapt and scale your product deployment strategy as your business needs evolve. You will find that by employing LLMs and using infrastructure as code, you can (partially) mitigate the vendor lock-in that is very common to cloud platforms.

Note that if you choose to deploy this (or any application) to AWS, there will be a cost associated with your activity. AWS and most cloud providers give you free trials to learn their platforms (Google Cloud Platform and Azure, for example), but once those credits have expired, you may get hit with a rather unexpectedly large bill. If you decide to follow along in this chapter, you need to set threshold alerts for an amount you can comfortably afford. Section 1.9 of Andreas Wittig and Michael Wittig's *Amazon Web Services in Action, Third Edition* (Manning, 2023; www.manning.com/books/amazon-web-services-in-action-third-edition) is an excellent resource for setting up such a billing notification alert.

7.1 *Building a Docker image and "deploying" it locally*

As you may remember from chapter 6, Docker is a containerization platform that allows you to run applications with little or no installation of an application (outside of Docker) in the traditional sense. Unlike a virtual machine, which simulates an entire operating system, a container shares the host system's kernel (the core part of the operating system) and uses the host system's operating system's capabilities while isolating the application processes and file systems from the host. This lets you run multiple isolated applications on a single host system, each with its own environment and resource limits. Figure 7.1 gives you a sense of the relationship between the Docker runtime and the host.

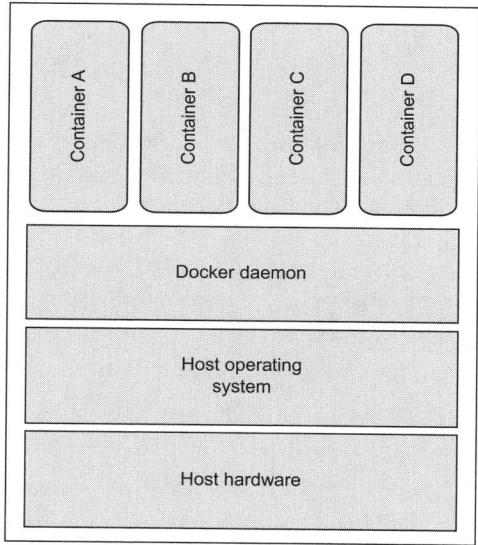

Figure 7.1 Docker makes use of the host's operating system while isolating each of the containers. This makes Docker containers lightweight compared to virtual machines, as they do not require a full OS to run.

One of the more exciting features, from a production readiness perspective, is that Docker makes it easier to run applications that can self-heal in some sense. If they fail or fall over at runtime, you can configure them to restart without intervention. In this section, we will use Copilot to create the file (called a *Dockerfile*) from which we will build our *Docker image*.

DEFINITION *Docker images* are like blueprints for Docker containers. They are portable, including all the dependencies (libraries, environment variables, code, etc.) required for the application to run.

Running Docker instances are called Docker *containers*. Given their lightweight nature, we can run multiple containers on a single host without a problem. We can do this because the containerization technology shares the OS kernel, operating in an isolated user space.

> **NOTE**   Originally, I wanted to use AWS CodeWhisperer as the LLM for this chapter. It seemed logical, given the intended cloud platform. However, at the time of this writing, AWS CodeWhisperer only supports programming in a programming language. It does not have facilities for infrastructure as code.

We will begin with the following prompt to have Copilot draft the Dockerfile for us:

```
# Create a Dockerfile for this Python app. The main class is main.py. Use
Python 3.10 and install
# the dependencies using the requirements.txt file in this directory. The
app should run on port 8080.
```

You may be left with an empty file (other than this comment). Support for infrastructure as code is ever-evolving (not unlike the LLM ecosystem in general). According to Copilot Chat, GitHub Copilot is capable of creating a Dockerfile for you—but you have to goad it with the following steps:

1 In the Dockerfile, type `FROM python:` and wait for Copilot to suggest a version of Python to use. Select the version you want to use.
2 Type `WORKDIR /app` to set the working directory for the container.
3 Type `COPY . /app` to copy the contents of your project into the container.
4 Type `RUN pip install --trusted-host pypi.python.org -r requirements .txt` to install the dependencies for your project.
5 Type `EXPOSE 8080` to expose port 8080 for the container.
6 Type `CMD ["python", "main.py"]` to specify the command to run when the container starts.

Alternatively, you may want to copy and paste the same prompt that you previously wrote into the Dockerfile into the Copilot Chat prompt window. Copilot Chat will give you the desired content for the Dockerfile.

Listing 7.1   Dockerfile to build a Docker image

```
FROM python:3.10-slim-buster
WORKDIR /app
COPY . /app
RUN pip install --trusted-host pypi.python.org -r requirements.txt
EXPOSE 8080
CMD ["python", "main.py"]
```

With a Dockerfile, we will build an image for deploying and running our application. We can enter the following command to build our application (run from the directory where the Dockerfile lives, and do not forget the trailing dot). You will need internet access to download the dependencies and create the image:

```
docker build -t itam:latest .
```

Building a Docker image can run for a few seconds to a few minutes, depending on which images and packages are installed on your system and your internet connection speed. Your patience will be rewarded, as you will shortly have an application you can install nearly anywhere from the lowliest commodity hardware to the most oversized hardware offered by your favorite cloud provider. Before running it anywhere, however, you need to try to get it running locally. If you've forgotten the command, Copilot Chat will happily and helpfully assist:

```
docker run -p 8000:8000 -d --name itam itam:latest
```

You can confirm that your Docker container is running by issuing this command at the command line: `docker ps | grep itam`. You should see the running instance.

7.2 Standing up infrastructure by copiloting Terraform

Using a Docker image on your computer is useful when creating and testing an app. But when it comes time to launch your application, you need a machine with a little more heft than local computers. In this section, we'll use GitHub Copilot to help us set up and control our AWS infrastructure by having Copilot write the requisite deployment descriptors for an infrastructure-as-code tool called Terraform. Terraform is made by HashiCorp and lets us write what we want our infrastructure to look like using a domain-specific language (DSL). This DSL saves us from having to understand all the complexities and intricacies that each cloud service provider uses to provision hardware. Additionally, it allows us to store and version our infrastructure using infrastructure as code.

To start, we want to create a file called ec2.tf and add the prompt to inform Copilot that we intend this to be a Terraform file and how we want our infrastructure stood up. Notice that Copilot needs us to enter the first word of a given line before it can be cajoled to continue.

> **Listing 7.2   Example Terraform file, including instance size**

```
# Create a Terraform file that provisions an AWS EC2 instance of type
t2.micro, installs the Docker daemon, and returns the instance's hostname.
provider "aws" {
  region = "us-west-2"
}

resource "aws_instance" "example" {
  ami           = "ami-0c55b159cbfafe1f0"
  instance_type = "t2.micro"
}
```

You may find that Copilot skips over one small but crucial detail: it does not provide code for installing and provisioning Docker. Given that Docker is required for running our application, we need to correct this oversight. In fact, you may need to update the file manually to include the command to install Docker, like this:

```
resource "aws_instance" "example" {
  ami           = "ami-0c55b159cbfafe1f0"
  instance_type = "t2.micro"

  user_data = <<-EOF
              #!/bin/bash
              sudo yum update -y
              sudo yum install -y docker
              sudo service docker start
              sudo usermod -a -G docker ec2-user
              sudo docker run -d -p 80:80 nginx
              EOF
}
```

Copilot should produce a complete Terraform file that resembles the following listing. Your code probably does not exactly match the listing, but that's fine as long as it contains the key features: the provider, the instance, the script to add the Docker daemon, the key pair, and the security group.

Listing 7.3   Terraform file to create the smallest EC2 instance available

```
# Create a Terraform file that provisions an AWS EC2 instance of type
t2.micro, installs the Docker daemon, and returns the hostname of the
instance.
provider "aws" {
  region = "us-west-2"
}

resource "aws_instance" "example" {
  ami           = "ami-0c55b159cbfafe1f0"
  instance_type = "t2.micro"

  user_data = <<-EOF
              #!/bin/bash
              sudo yum update -y
              sudo yum install -y docker
              sudo service docker start
              sudo usermod -a -G docker ec2-user
              sudo docker run -d -p 80:80 nginx
              EOF
  connection {
      type        = "ssh"
      user        = "ec2-user"
      private_key = file("~/.ssh/id_rsa")
      host        = self.public_ip
  }

  lifecycle {
      create_before_destroy = true
  }
```

```
    depends_on = [aws_security_group.allow_http]
}

resource "aws_security_group" "allow_http" {
  name        = "allow_http"
  description = "Allow HTTP inbound traffic"
  vpc_id      = "vpc-12345678"

  ingress {
    description = "HTTP from VPC"
    from_port   = 80
    to_port     = 80
    protocol    = "tcp"
    cidr_blocks = ["0.0.0.0/0"]
    }
}

output "public_dns" {
  value = aws_instance.example.public_dns
    }
```

If you are using the default Virtual Private Cloud (VPC), the vpc_id entry is not strictly necessary. You will find that many of the default configurations and conventions chosen by the AWS team make sense; if you have stricter security requirements, or if you know everything about your infrastructure and assume nothing, you might consider setting up a new VPC from scratch using Terraform. You need to change the key pair entry on line 21 to be a key pair to which you have access.

Once you have completed this file satisfactorily, run the terraform init command. This command initializes a new or existing Terraform working directory. It downloads and installs the required provider plugins and modules specified in your configuration files and gets everything ready to go.

Next you will have Terraform explain the changes that it intends to make. You do this with the terraform plan command. This command creates an execution plan for your infrastructure changes: it shows you what changes Terraform will make to your infrastructure when you apply your configuration files. The plan will show you which resources will be created, modified, or destroyed and any other changes that will be made to your infrastructure.

> **NOTE** You may get an error when running terraform plan for the first time: "Error: configuring Terraform AWS Provider: no valid credential sources for Terraform AWS Provider found." You get this error when Terraform attempts to connect to AWS but cannot supply AWS with proper credentials. To address this problem, you will need to create (or edit) the file called ~/.aws/credentials and add your ITAM AWS Access Key ID and AWS Secret Access Key credentials. You can find more details on how to accomplish this correctly in section 4.2.2, "Configuring the CLI," of *Amazon Web Services in Action, Third Edition*.

Finally, to apply the Terraform changes, you use the terraform apply command. Terraform will then read the configuration files in the current directory and apply any changes to your infrastructure. If you have made any changes to your configuration files since the last time you ran `terraform apply`—for example, if you need to start up a new database instance or change the size of your EC2—Terraform will show you a preview of the changes that will be made and prompt you to confirm before applying the changes.

If you apply these changes, in a manner of minutes you will have a brand-new EC2 instance running in your VPC. However, this is only half of the equation. Having computing power at your fingertips is fantastic, but you need something to apply this power. In this case, we can use this EC2 instance to run our ISAM system. The following section briefly demonstrates transferring a locally built image to another machine.

7.3   *Moving a Docker image around (the hard way)*

First we will export a Docker image from our local machines and load it onto a remote machine. We will use the commands `docker save` and `load` to accomplish this. You can use the `docker save` command on your local machine to save the image to a tar archive. The following command will save the image to a tar archive named <image -name>.tar:

```
docker save -o <image-name>.tar <image-name>:<tag>
```

Next, transfer the tar archive to the remote machine using a file transfer protocol such as Secure Copy Protocol (SCP) or Secure File Transfer Protocol (SFTP). You can use the `docker load` command on the remote machine to load the image from the tar archive: `docker load -i <image-name>.tar`. This will load the image into the local Docker image cache on the remote machine. Once the image has been loaded, use the `docker run` command to start the image and run the Docker container, as you did after you built it. Then add this image to your Docker compose file, in which you have the Postgres database and Kafka instances.

> **NOTE**   This discussion of Terraform is heavily abridged. When you are ready to get serious with Terraform, your go-to resource should be Scott Winkler's *Terraform in Action* (Manning, 2021; www.manning.com/books/terraform-in-action).

This section examined how to package up images and load them on remote hosts. This process is scriptable, but with the advent of container registries, it is now easier than ever to manage deployments without slinging them all around the internet. In the next section, we will explore one such tool: Amazon's Elastic Container Registry (ECR).

7.4   *Moving a Docker image around (the easy way)*

Docker images, the blueprints for our containers, are a fundamental building block of containerized applications. Managing them correctly ensures that we maintain clean, efficient, and organized development and deployment workflows. Amazon ECR serves as a fully managed Docker container registry that makes it easy for developers to store, manage, and deploy Docker container images.

First, let's dive into pushing Docker images to ECR. This process is vital to making your images accessible for use and deployment. We'll walk through setting up your local environment, authenticating with ECR, and pushing your image. Before we can move an image to ECR, we must create a repository to house that image. This can be done from the AWS Management Console or, as we will do shortly, using the AWS command line interface (CLI). The command to create a new repository for an image is

```
aws ecr create-repository --repository-name itam
```

Next you need to tag your Docker image with the ECR repository URL and the image name. You may want to call it `latest` or use semantic versioning. Tagging will allow you to easily roll back or forward versions of your system. Tag your application image `latest` using the following command:

```
docker tag itam:latest
123456789012.dkr.ecr.us-west-2.amazonaws.com/itam:latest
```

Now, authenticate Docker to the ECR registry using the `aws ecr get-login -password` command. This will generate a Docker `login` command that you can use to authenticate Docker to the registry. The command to log in is

```
aws ecr get-login-password --region us-west-2 |
docker login --username AWS --password-stdin
123456789012.dkr.ecr.us-west-2.amazonaws.com
```

Finally, push the Docker image to the ECR registry using the `docker push` command:

```
docker push 123456789012.dkr.ecr.us-west-2.amazonaws.com/itam:latest
```

Once the image is in your registry, your deployment options have greatly increased. You could, for example, write a bash script that will log on to the EC2 instance and perform a `docker pull` to download and run the image on that EC2. Alternatively, you may want to adopt a more bulletproof deployment pattern. In the next section, we're going to walk through the process of setting up and launching our application on a powerful cloud service called Elastic Kubernetes Service (EKS). EKS is a managed Kubernetes service provided by AWS. Let's dive in!

7.5 *Deploying our application onto AWS Elastic Kubernetes Service*

Kubernetes confers many benefits over simply running Docker images on EC2 instances. For one, managing and scaling our application becomes considerably more straightforward with Kubernetes. Also, with Kubernetes, we do not have to spend a lot of additional time thinking about what our infrastructure should look like. Plus, thanks to its automatic management of the lifecycles of its images, known as *pods*, our application will essentially be self-healing. This means if something goes wrong, Kubernetes can automatically fix it, keeping our application running smoothly at all times.

First we need a deployment descriptor written in YAML (Yet Another Markup Language or YAML Ain't Markup Language, depending on who you ask), which will describe the state we want our ITAM system to be in at all times. This file (typically called deployment.yaml) will provide the template against which Kubernetes will compare the current running system, making corrections as needed.

Listing 7.4   Kubernetes deployment file for the ITAM system

```
# Create a Kubernetes deployment file for the itam application. The image
name is itam:latest
# The deployment will run on port 8000

apiVersion: apps/v1
kind: Deployment
metadata:
  name: itam-deployment
  labels:
    app: itam
spec:
  replicas: 1
  selector:
    matchLabels:
      app: itam
  template:
    metadata:
      labels:
        app: itam
    spec:
      containers:
      - name: itam
        image: itam:latest
        imagePullPolicy: Always
        ports:
        - containerPort: 8000
```

This will not work, however. Kubernetes will not be able to find the image that we reference in the deployment descriptor file. To correct this, we need to tell Kubernetes to use our newly minted ECR. Fortunately, this is not as challenging as it may sound. We just have to update the image entry in our file to point to the ECR image, as well as grant EKS permissions to access ECR (okay, maybe it is a little trickier, but it is manageable).

First, update the deployment YAML to use the ECR image:

`image: 123456789012.dkr.ecr.us-west-2.amazonaws.com/itam:latest.`

Then you would need to define a policy for EKS to use and apply the policy using either the AWS CLI or the Identity and Access Management (IAM) Management Console. Although applying the policy is (slightly) outside of the scope of this book, you can use Copilot to define it. The resulting policy will resemble the following listing.

Listing 7.5   IAM policy to allow EKS to pull images from ECR

```
{
  "Version": "2012-10-17",
  "Statement": [
    {
      "Sid": "AllowPull",
      "Effect": "Allow",
      "Principal": {
        "AWS": "arn:aws:iam::<aws_account_id>:role/<role>"
      },
      "Action": [
        "ecr:GetDownloadUrlForLayer",
        "ecr:BatchGetImage",
        "ecr:BatchCheckLayerAvailability"
      ],
      "Resource": "arn:aws:ecr:<region>:<aws_account_id>:
repository/<repository_name>"
    }
  ]
}
```

Once the EKS can pull down the image from ECR, you will see a pod start to run. However, you have no way to access this pod externally. You need to create a service. In Kubernetes, a *service* is an abstraction that defines a logical set of pods (the smallest and simplest unit in the Kubernetes object model that you create or deploy) and a policy to access them.

Services enable communication between different parts of an application and between different applications. They help distribute network traffic and load balance by exposing the pods to the network and other pods in Kubernetes.

Listing 7.6   Kubernetes services file to enable external access for our application

```
# Please create a service for the application that uses a load balancer type
egress
apiVersion: v1
kind: Service
metadata:
  name: itam-service
spec:
  type: LoadBalancer
  selector:
    app: itam
  ports:
  - name: http
    port: 80
    targetPort: 8000
```

Kubernetes is responsible for routing all requests from this ingress through the service to the running pods, regardless of what host they are running on. This allows for seamless failover. Kubernetes expects things to fail. It banks on it. As a result, many of the best practices in distributed systems are baked into Kubernetes. Getting to Kube is a significant first step to having a reliable, highly available system. In the next section, we will examine how to ease the burden of getting our application onto Kubernetes repeatably and continuously. We will look at building out a small deployment pipeline using GitHub actions.

7.6   Setting up a continuous integration/continuous deployment pipeline in GitHub Actions

If releasing is hard, it will not be done often. This limits our ability to add value to the application and thus to our stakeholders. However, automating the deployment process significantly reduces the time to release. This allows for more frequent releases, accelerating the pace of development and enabling faster delivery of features to users. Continuous integration/continuous deployment (CI/CD) pipelines limit the risk associated with deployment. By making smaller, more frequent updates, any problems that arise can be isolated and fixed quickly, minimizing the potential effect on the end users. These pipelines facilitate seamless integration of code changes and expedite deployment, simplifying the software release process.

GitHub Actions allows us to construct customized CI/CD pipelines directly in our GitHub repositories. This makes the development workflow more efficient and enables the automation of various steps, freeing us to focus on coding rather than the logistics of integration and deployment.

This section provides a concise introduction to setting up a CI/CD pipeline using GitHub Actions and GitHub Copilot. Note that this will not be a comprehensive guide but rather a survey that introduces the potential benefits and general workflow. This should serve as a primer, giving you an insight into how these tools can be used to optimize your software development process.

First, create a file in your project in the path .github/workflows. Note the leading dot. You can call this file itam.yaml or whatever you desire. On the first line of this file, add the following prompt:

```
# Create a GitHub Actions workflow that builds the ITAM application on
every merge to the main branch and deploys it to EKS.
```

NOTE   Like many of the infrastructure-related tasks that we have put to Copilot in this chapter, Copilot needs a lot of assistance in creating this file for us. We need to be aware of the structure of this file and how to begin every line. It makes sense in cases such as this one to ask ChatGPT or Copilot Chat to build the file for us.

The first part of this file outlines when this action should take place. The on:push instruction denotes that when a git push occurs to the main branch, this action should be executed. There is a single job in this file, one with several steps. This job "build" uses an embedded function `login-ecr` to log into our ECR.

Listing 7.7 Beginning of GitHub Actions file to build our application

```
# Create a GitHub Actions workflow that builds the ITAM application on every
merge to the main branch and deploys it to EKS.
name: Build and Deploy to EKS

on:
  push:
    branches:
      - main
jobs:
```

The build job will first check out the code from our GitHub repository. It uses the code written in the module `actions/checkout` version 2. Similarly, it will next grab the EKS CLI and configure the credentials to connect to EKS. Note that the AWS access key and secret are values that are automatically passed into the application. GitHub Actions uses a built-in secret management system to store sensitive data such as API keys, passwords, and certificates. This system is integrated into the GitHub platform and allows you to add, remove, or update secrets (and other sensitive data) at both the repository and organization levels. Secrets are encrypted before they're stored and are not shown in logs or available for download. They're only exposed as environment variables to the GitHub Actions runner, making it a secure way to handle sensitive data.

Likewise, you can create environmental parameters and use them in your actions. For example, look at the variable `ECR_REGISTRY`. This variable is created using the output from the `login-ecr` function. In this case, you still need to hardcode the ECR in your Actions file. However, you should do this because of consistency and the need to manage it in only one place in the file. Most of these steps should seem familiar, as we have used them throughout the chapter. That is the magic of automation: it does it for you.

Listing 7.8 Build and deploy steps of our GitHub Actions file

```
build:
  runs-on: ubuntu-latest

  steps:
  - name: Checkout code
    uses: actions/checkout@v2

  - name: Set up EKS CLI
    uses: aws-actions/amazon-eks-cli@v0.1.0

  - name: Configure AWS credentials
    uses: aws-actions/configure-aws-credentials@v1
    with:
      aws-access-key-id: ${{ secrets.AWS_ACCESS_KEY_ID }}
      aws-secret-access-key: ${{ secrets.AWS_SECRET_ACCESS_KEY }}
      aws-region: us-west-2

  - name: Build and push Docker image
```

```
  env:
    ECR_REGISTRY: ${{ steps.login-ecr.outputs.registry }}
    ECR_REPOSITORY: itam
    IMAGE_TAG: ${{ github.sha }}
  run: |
    docker build -t $ECR_REGISTRY/$ECR_REPOSITORY:$IMAGE_TAG .
    docker push $ECR_REGISTRY/$ECR_REPOSITORY:$IMAGE_TAG

- name: Deploy to EKS
  env:
    ECR_REGISTRY: ${{ steps.login-ecr.outputs.registry }}
    ECR_REPOSITORY: itam
    IMAGE_TAG: ${{ github.sha }}
  run: |
    envsubst < k8s/deployment.yaml | kubectl apply -f -
    envsubst < k8s/service.yaml | kubectl apply -f -
```

The final part of the file logs in to AWS ECR. The steps in the Actions file invoke this action. On completion, it returns the output to the calling function.

```
login-ecr:
  runs-on: ubuntu-latest
  steps:
  - name: Login to Amazon ECR
    id: login-ecr
    uses: aws-actions/amazon-ecr-login@v1
    with:
      registry: <your-ecr-registry>
      aws-access-key-id: ${{ secrets.AWS_ACCESS_KEY_ID }}
      aws-secret-access-key: ${{ secrets.AWS_SECRET_ACCESS_KEY }}
```

Exploring code-as-infrastructure has enabled us to understand its vital role in any project and how it can be better managed through code. Tools like Terraform provide streamlined solutions for managing infrastructure, and GitHub's code-centric features aid in maintaining the overall workflow.

Introducing CI/CD pipelines, primarily through platforms like GitHub Actions, highlights the importance of automating the software delivery process. Automating such processes increases the speed and reliability of the software development life cycle and minimizes the chances of human errors.

The journey of managing infrastructure as code is ever-evolving, with new tools and practices emerging. It requires a constant learning and adaptation mindset. This chapter has given you a glimpse of the benefits and possibilities.

Summary

- You learned about the transition from application development to product launch, covering deployment strategies, best practices for cloud infrastructure, and the use of Docker and Terraform for managing and containerizing applications efficiently.

- The chapter explained how to manage application deployment via Kubernetes, including creating YAML deployment descriptors, forming services for network traffic distribution, and deploying on AWS's Elastic Kubernetes Service (EKS).

- You discovered how to adapt deployment methods to different environments, whether on various cloud platforms or on premises, and how GitHub Copilot can assist in creating Dockerfiles and Terraform files accurately.

- Finally, we explored the process of exporting Docker images to remote machines, pushing them to Amazon's Elastic Container Registry (ECR), and migrating to automated deployments using GitHub Actions.

Secure application development with ChatGPT

In the evolving software development landscape, security concerns have escalated from an afterthought to being integral to a project's design and implementation phases. Despite this elevated attention, developers often find it challenging to keep pace with the rapidly changing sphere of application security. This chapter offers a comprehensive understanding of how AI, specifically ChatGPT, can be embedded into various stages of the application development process to strengthen application security, providing a novel set of tools for building more secure software applications.

As we delve into this subject, we'll explore how ChatGPT can be incorporated into various stages of the application development process for the ISAM application, written in Python using FastAPI. We'll discuss how this AI model can help identify vulnerabilities, contribute to threat modeling, assess application design for potential insecurities, understand and apply security best practices.

The objective of this chapter is not to position ChatGPT as a silver bullet for all security concerns but rather to showcase its potential as a powerful tool in the developer's security toolkit. We will learn how to proactively identify and manage threats, keeping in mind the holistic goal of creating not just functional software but secure software. In this journey, we will navigate topics such as modeling threats, incorporating security in the development lifecycle, the role of AI in security, and much more. Let's get started!

Security is not a feature

Secure applications start with the design. It is not a feature, although it is often treated as such. Generative AIs are tools that can be used to assess and improve the security of your application, but they will not replace input from a security expert, nor will they make you one. For more information on designing secure applications, refer to *Secure by Design* by Dan Bergh Johnsson, Daniel Deogun, and Daniel Sawano (Manning, 2019; www.manning.com/books/secure-by-design).

The (fallacious) mental model of the software life cycle, in which security is treated as a feature to be prioritized and deprioritized as needed in the project or as an add-in to be performed at some point in the lifecycle. Security, however, is a mindset that needs to be front and center during all phases.

8.1 Modeling threats with ChatGPT

Threat modeling is a structured approach that helps teams understand, prioritize, and manage potential threats in a system. By simulating the mindset of an attacker, threat modeling systematically identifies vulnerabilities, evaluates the potential effect, and determines mitigation strategies. Rooted in the design phase but relevant throughout the entire software development lifecycle, threat modeling acts as a crucial bridge between high-level security policies and on-the-ground practices.

Threat modeling is not a one-time process. As new vulnerabilities are discovered, your system and the external environment change, so you must revisit and update your threat model.

8.1.1   *Why it matters in today's development landscape*

Before we delve into threat modeling using ChatGPT, we need to take a step back to understand why we would want to do this in the first place. With a greater emphasis on security in today's development landscape, we must be mindful of factors that have significantly reshaped how software is developed, deployed, and accessed. As more services go digital, there's a broader attack surface. Everything from online banking to health records, e-commerce, and even government services is now available online, making them potential targets.

Additionally, cyber threats are not static. New vulnerabilities emerge daily, and attackers are continually devising new methods. The danger has never been more significant, with the rise of state-sponsored attacks, ransomware, and cyber espionage.

Modern architecture is significantly more complex than before, as applications commonly utilize microservices, third-party APIs, and cloud infrastructures. This complexity can introduce multiple potential points of vulnerability. Systems are not standalone but interconnected with other systems, creating a domino effect. A breach in one can provide a stepping-stone to compromise others.

Security breaches

Beyond immediate financial implications, a security breach can erode trust, harm a company's reputation, lead to legal consequences, and result in a loss of customers or business opportunities. Further, with regulations like the General Data Protection Regulation (GDPR) in Europe and the California Consumer Privacy Act (CCPA) in the United States, organizations have an increased responsibility to protect user data. Noncompliance can result in substantial penalties.

In an interconnected, digital-first world, security is not just an IT concern but a fundamental business imperative. Ensuring that applications are developed with security in mind from the ground up reduces risk and costs, builds trust, and provides systems continuity.

8.1.2   *How ChatGPT can aid in threat modeling*

Now that we can appreciate the why, let us turn to how we can utilize ChatGPT to understand the cybersecurity threats that surround us, their effects, and potential mitigation techniques. ChatGPT has an extensive knowledge base of basic cybersecurity concepts; it can define standard terms and explain complex attack vectors to you in whatever level of detail is appropriate to your cybersecurity journey. You can begin by asking it to explain cybersecurity principles, what a SQL injection attack is (but not how to perform one!), or what clickjacking is.

As an informal approach to modeling threats, you can pose detailed hypothetical scenarios to ChatGPT and ask for potential threats or vulnerabilities that may arise in those situations. Start very general and refine as the process continues. For example, you might enter the following prompt:

If I'm developing a cloud-based web application for e-commerce, what threats should I be aware of?

Then drill in, triangulating around specific threats:

 How might an attacker session hijack a user's cart in my e-commerce application?

Next, you can engage with ChatGPT to understand how to assess the risks associated with various threats. This can help you prioritize which threats to address first. With an understanding of some of the threats potentially directed at your system, you can engage ChatGPT about potential countermeasures, best practices, and mitigation strategies:

 How do I assess the risk of a DDoS attack for my online service?

And then,

 What are the best practices to prevent cross-site scripting attacks?

You need to periodically engage with ChatGPT to refresh your knowledge or ask about any new concepts or strategies you've come across.

One quick warning, however: as always, you must be aware of ChatGPT's limitations. It doesn't have real-time threat intelligence or knowledge beyond its last update. For the latest threats, always consult up-to-date resources. Although ChatGPT is a valuable tool, always cross-reference its insights with other authoritative sources. Cybersecurity rapidly evolves, and staying updated with multiple trusted sources is crucial. After discussing a specific threat with ChatGPT, you may want to consult the latest documentation from organizations like the Open Worldwide Application Security Project (OWASP), the National Institute of Standards and Technology (NIST), and other recognized cybersecurity entities.

Finally, interactive brainstorming sessions with ChatGPT can help you effectively generate ideas, understand complex concepts, or refine strategies, especially in areas like cybersecurity. Here's how you can structure and execute such sessions:

1 Clearly state the goal of the brainstorming session. For instance, it could be identifying potential vulnerabilities in a system, generating security measures for a new application, or discussing strategies to improve user data protection.
2 Begin the session by providing ChatGPT with a detailed context. If it's about a specific system or application, describe its architecture, components, functionalities, and any known problems or concerns. You may, for example, say

 I'm working on a web-based e-commerce platform using a microservices architecture with Docker containers. We're looking to identify potential security threats.

Based on ChatGPT's responses, delve deeper into specific areas of interest or concern. For example, you may say

> NC   Tell me more about container security best practices.

or ask

> NC   How can I secure communication between microservices?

3   Present hypothetical scenarios to ChatGPT, and ask for feedback or solutions. This can help anticipate potential challenges or threats:

> NC   Imagine an attacker gains access to one of the containers; what steps should be taken?"

4   Engage with ChatGPT by playing the devil's advocate. Question or counter the ideas or suggestions it provides, to stimulate further thought and explore different angles:

> NC   What if I were to use a third-party authentication service? How would that change the security landscape?

5   Ask ChatGPT for concrete steps or action items to implement the suggested solutions. You might, for example, inquire,

> NC   Given the security concerns you mentioned, what are the specific steps I should take to mitigate them?

NOTE   As the brainstorming progresses, document the ideas, suggestions, and strategies provided by ChatGPT. They will be invaluable for reviewing and implementing after the session. Brainstorming is most effective when iterative. Based on what you learn in one session, you may refine your questions, adjust your approach, or explore new areas in subsequent sessions.

Figure 8.1 shows the security feedback loop performed during a brainstorming session.

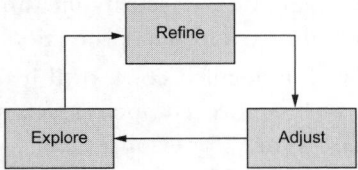

Figure 8.1   The workflow of a brainstorming session with ChatGPT

As your project or scenario progresses, revisit the discussion with ChatGPT to account for any changes, updates, or new challenges. Recent updates allow you to upload your system design documentation and have ChatGPT scrutinize this design for potential threats and common vulnerabilities in the same way that it can assess code.

By using ChatGPT in this semistructured manner, you can benefit from its expansive knowledge base and receive valuable feedback and insights for your scenarios. Always remember to cross-reference suggestions with up-to-date resources and experts in the relevant field.

8.1.3   *Case study: Simulating threat modeling with ChatGPT*

In addition to scenario analysis and interactive brainstorming sessions with ChatGPT, you may decide to apply a formal methodology, one that is commonly used by cyber security professionals: STRIDE. STRIDE is a threat modeling methodology introduced by Microsoft to help identify potential security threats in systems or applications. You can use ChatGPT and STRIDE to simulate threats and triage accordingly.

STRIDE

The acronym STRIDE stands for spoofing, tampering, repudiation, information disclosure, and denial of service:

- *Spoofing*—Impersonating something or someone else. This can mean taking on the identity of a user, a device, or even a system to gain unauthorized access. For example, an attacker may spoof a media access control (MAC) address to impersonate a device on a network.
- *Tampering*—Unauthorized modification of data or code. For example, an attacker may modify a transmitted data packet in a man-in-the-middle attack.
- *Repudiation*—The ability of malicious (or careless) users to deny that they performed specific actions, even if they did, due to lack of evidence of those actions. For example, a user may deny placing an order or changing some data.
- *Information disclosure*—The exposure of information to individuals who aren't supposed to have access to it. For example, a database misconfiguration may expose sensitive user data to the public.
- *Denial of service (DoS)*—Making a resource unavailable or unresponsive to its intended users. This can be achieved by overwhelming a system's resources or exploiting specific vulnerabilities. For example, during a DDoS attack, an attacker may flood a website with traffic, causing it to become slow or entirely unresponsive.
- *Elevation of Privilege*—An unprivileged user gains elevated rights, often allowing them to control the entire system or perform tasks they are not authorized to do.

Throughout this book, we have been developing part of a ITAM system. As a reminder, this system is used to manage and optimize an organization's IT assets. In this section, we will apply STRIDE to our application, using ChatGPT to assist in modeling the threats against this system.

Let us start with spoofing:

 Within the context of our ITAM system, how might our system be spoofed?

ChatGPT may respond with something similar to the following listing.

> **Listing 8.1   ChatGPT explanation of how spoofing may affect our application**

MAC Address Spoofing: Most ITAM systems rely on MAC addresses to identify and manage devices on a network. An attacker might spoof the MAC address of an authorized device to gain unauthorized access or to mask a rogue device's presence.
IP Address Spoofing: An attacker could bypass network security measures or divert traffic by masquerading as a trusted IP address. This could lead to unauthorized access to the ITAM system or even denial-of-service attacks.
DNS Spoofing (Cache Poisoning): If the ITAM system relies on domain names for accessing updates or related resources, DNS spoofing can redirect the ITAM server to malicious sites, potentially compromising the system.
Device Identifier Spoofing: Beyond MAC addresses, devices may have other unique identifiers. Spoofing these can allow unauthorized devices to appear as legitimate assets in the ITAM inventory.
User Agent Spoofing: If the ITAM system is accessed via web browsers, attackers can spoof user agent strings to mimic authorized devices or browsers, potentially bypassing certain security checks.
Fake Asset Registration: A malicious actor might introduce fake assets into the system, leading to inaccurate asset tracking, skewed analytics, and potential security loopholes.
Spoofed Update Servers: If your ITAM solution fetches updates from remote servers, attackers could spoof these servers, delivering malicious updates or software.
Phishing & Social Engineering: While not a technical spoofing method per se, attackers can still spoof emails or other communications, pretending to be ITAM administrators or vendors. Unsuspecting employees might then provide sensitive ITAM data.

Additionally, it may respond with common prevention or mitigation steps.

> **Listing 8.2   ChatGPT outlining mechanisms to prevent such exploits**

Network Security: Implement network segmentation, strong firewalls, and Intrusion Detection Systems (IDS) to monitor and block suspicious activities.
Encryption: Encrypt data in transit to protect against man-in-the-middle attacks that could lead to spoofing.
Dynamic Identification: Rotate device identifiers periodically or use dynamic identifiers.
DNS Security: Implement DNS Security Extensions (DNSSEC) to ensure the authenticity of DNS responses.
Authentication and Authorization: Require multi-factor authentication (MFA) for ITAM system access and ensure strict role-based access control.
Regular Audits: Audit the ITAM database frequently to identify discrepancies or rogue assets.
User Education: Regularly train IT personnel and employees about the risks of spoofing and the importance of verifying communications.

Rather than enumerate the entirety of STRIDE, let's next move to repudiation. This is the least intuitive of all attacks and the most misunderstood:

 Within the context of our ITAM system, how might our system be affected by repudiation?

ChatGPT may respond with a definition of this risk in the context of our system.

Listing 8.3   ChatGPT defining repudiation through the lens of cybersecurity
---

```
Repudiation, in a cybersecurity context, refers to the ability of a user
(or system) to deny having performed a specific action, even if they did
perform it. Regarding ITAM (Information Technology Asset Management) systems,
repudiation can pose challenges regarding accountability, traceability, and
compliance. Let's explore how repudiation might affect an ITAM system:
```

It then catalogs these various repudiation risks that may affect our ITAM system.

Listing 8.4   Possible repudiation risks as outlined by ChatGPT

```
Denial of Asset Changes: A user might make unauthorized changes to an asset's
status or details in the ITAM system and later deny having made such changes.
This can lead to inaccuracies in asset tracking, causing potential compliance
issues and operational inefficiencies.
Lack of Accountability: If actions within the ITAM system are not
appropriately logged or if logs can be altered without a trace, it becomes
challenging to hold individuals accountable for their actions. This can
result in unauthorized software installations, hardware misallocations, or
asset misuse without any accountability.
Financial Discrepancies: Repudiation can lead to financial implications. For
instance, if an employee claims they never received a particular hardware
asset (like a laptop) when the ITAM system shows they did, it might result in
unnecessary additional procurements.
License Violations: Users might install unauthorized software and then deny
doing so. Without proper non-repudiation measures, tracking and proving such
installations becomes difficult, leading to potential licensing violations.
Security Implications: Malicious insiders or external attackers could exploit
the ITAM system to steal or damage assets and deny any wrongdoing. This could
pave the way for data breaches, theft of sensitive data, or even financial
fraud.
```

ChatGPT will then provide us with potential ways to mitigate these risks.

Listing 8.5   Possible remediation techniques for repudiation risks
---

```
Strong Authentication: Ensure that users accessing the ITAM system go through
rigorous authentication processes, ideally with multi-factor authentication
(MFA), to ensure that actions can be attributed to specific individuals.
Immutable Logging: Implement tamper-proof logging systems. Every action,
change, or transaction within the ITAM should be logged with a timestamp and
associated user details.
Digital Signatures: Crucial actions, especially those related to financial
transactions or significant asset changes, require a digital signature. This
offers an additional layer of verification and non-repudiation.
Role-Based Access Control (RBAC): Ensure users have specific roles and
permissions. Limiting access based on job roles can reduce the risk of
unauthorized actions and make it easier to trace back activities to
particular users.
Regular Audits: Periodically review and audit the logs and transactions
in the ITAM system to detect any discrepancies or potential repudiation
attempts.
```

User Training: Educate ITAM system users about the importance of accountability and the consequences of unauthorized actions. Making users aware can reduce inadvertent repudiation instances.
Whistleblower Policies: Encourage employees to report any suspicious activities without fear of retaliation.

As development practices evolve, so do the cyber threats we face. In this section, we explored the specific attributes of ChatGPT that make it a valuable asset in identifying and predicting potential cyber threats. With its ability to simulate conversations, analyze vast amounts of data swiftly, and provide insights based on patterns, ChatGPT emerges as a promising tool to enhance traditional threat modeling methodologies.

Finally, we briefly walked through a real-world application of ChatGPT in threat modeling. This case study underscores the practicality of using AI in real-life cybersecurity scenarios, highlighting the successes, challenges, and lessons learned from integrating ChatGPT into the threat modeling process.

Although modeling external threats using tools like ChatGPT can prove invaluable in limiting or preventing damage to organizations and their data, it is equally important to turn our focus toward the internals of our system and identify vulnerabilities therein. We will do this in the following section.

8.2   *Scrutinizing application design and identifying potential vulnerabilities*

The complexities of modern application design can sometimes conceal subtle flaws in both functionality and security. Using the analytical prowess of ChatGPT, we can dive deeper into these designs, transcending traditional human oversights and biases. With its vast knowledge and pattern-recognition capabilities, ChatGPT offers a unique vantage point that is capable of spotting common vulnerabilities and offering actionable feedback. In this section, we will explore how, by consulting with ChatGPT, we can critically assess application designs, ensuring that they are not only functional and user-friendly but also robust against potential threats.

8.2.1   *Evaluating design problems*

To start having ChatGPT evaluate our design, we can issue the following prompt:

 Please review this application design and pinpoint design issues. The design is in mermaid format

We then copy in the mermaid diagram from chapter 2. The following is an abridged list of some of the problems ChatGPT found in our design (interestingly, many of these suggestions were provided by ChatGPT in the first place).

> **Listing 8.6   Abridged list of design problems provided by ChatGPT**

The design described in the Mermaid class diagram is a comprehensive representation of multiple entities involved in an asset management system, with focus on the various assets and their depreciation strategies. Here are some points to consider about this design:

```
1. Inheritance vs Composition:
   - The strategies 'StraightLineDepreciationStrategy',
'DecliningBalanceDepreciationStrategy',
'DoubleDecliningDepreciationStrategy', and 'NoDepreciationStrategy' should
ideally inherit from 'DepreciationStrategy' to ensure they adhere to the same
interface.

2. DepreciatingAsset class:
   - 'DepreciatingAsset' appears to have a partial definition, perhaps it
should either inherit from 'Asset' or be more fleshed out.

3. Visitor Pattern:
   - The 'LineOfBusinessVisitor' class appears to be implementing the
visitor pattern. However, it's not clear if all the methods are necessary.
Do you expect every visitable object type ('Hardware', 'Software',
'DepreciatingAsset') to have distinct logic?
```

Far from an exhaustive list, this does give us a starting point to reflect on and sharpen our design.

8.2.2   *Recognizing common vulnerabilities*

In this section, we delve into how ChatGPT, with its extensive knowledge base and pattern-recognition capabilities, assists in uncovering hidden weaknesses and potential threats in software designs, marking a revolutionary advancement in proactive cybersecurity measures. We will ask it,

 Are there any vulnerabilities or exploits within this design?

It spits out a lengthy list from which the following few critical problems were pulled.

> **Listing 8.7   Abridged list of vulnerabilities and exploits found by ChatGPT**

```
1.  Password Security:
The User class stores a password field. It's essential that passwords are not
stored as plaintext for security reasons. Consider using a hashing mechanism
(e.g., bcrypt) to store password hashes rather than raw passwords.

2.  Role-Based Access Control (RBAC):
While the Role class seems to address RBAC by having a list of permissions,
ensure that the system implementing this design enforces these roles and
permissions appropriately. Be particularly careful about functions or methods
that modify user roles or permissions.
```

We can continue this interrogation by asking ChatGPT how to best implement its suggestions.

In the previous sections, we saw how ChatGPT can help find problems in software design. It's a powerful tool, but as has been previously articulated, it does not (and cannot) replace the need for skilled people. Think of it like this: ChatGPT is a handy helper, but humans are still in charge. When we use AI and human smarts together, we can make our online world safer. It's all about teaming up and using the best of both.

8.3   *Applying security best practices*

This section is your go-to guide for strong software security from start to finish. First we'll talk about the importance of having a security-focused mindset. Next, we'll cover the need for regular security tests to keep things tight. Then we'll discuss regular checkups or audits to ensure that everything's up-to-date. In short, we'll look at both the tools for security and the right ways to think about it.

8.3.1   *Setting the security mindset*

Security is not just about employing the right tools or adhering to the latest protocols; it's about fostering a mindset where security is intertwined with every action, decision, and strategy. This section will guide you through the foundational principles of establishing such a mindset, emphasizing the importance of vigilance, adaptability, and continuous learning in the face of modern cyber challenges.

ChatGPT can serve as a powerful tool for security training and awareness. You can use it as an interactive tool to teach your team the basics of cybersecurity, such as what cross-site scripting is and how it works. You can use it to plan incident responses: for example, asking it what your first steps should be if your server has been compromised.

You can also use ChatGPT to generate secure code guidelines and recommendations. For example, you may ask it to

 provide secure coding guidelines for Python

ChatGPT will then provide you with a lengthy list, including items such as input validation and securing your libraries, as well as suggestions for how to securely store your password and inject it at runtime.

We can also use ChatGPT to provide application-specific guidance. For example,

 Recommend steps for a secure deployment of a Flask web application.

Although there are any number of ways to secure our application, ChatGPT provides us with a curated list. A selection is provided in the following listing.

Listing 8.8   Abridged list of ChatGPT's top advice to secure Flask

```
Deploying a Flask web application securely requires a multifaceted approach
that covers everything from code-level security practices to server and
network configurations.

Here are the recommended steps:
1. Use the Latest Flask Version: Always use the most recent Flask version, as
it typically includes security patches for known vulnerabilities.

2. Avoid Debug Mode in Production: Never run a Flask application with app.
debug = True in a production environment. Debug mode can expose sensitive
information.
```

```
3. Use a Secure Web Server: Deploy your Flask application behind a
production-ready web server like Gunicorn, uWSGI, or mod_wsgi. These are
robust servers that can handle real-world traffic and have better security
mechanisms.

4. Implement HTTPS:
Use SSL/TLS to encrypt data between the server and client.
Use tools like Let's Encrypt to get a free SSL certificate.
```

With some understanding of how we can securely develop Python software, specifically Flask-based microservices, we can begin to test our application.

8.3.2   *Continuous security testing*

In this section, we explore how ChatGPT's vast knowledge base can help streamline the decision-making process, offer insights into tool capabilities, and provide guidance on effective tool usage for optimum application security. We will start by examining the differences between a static analysis tool and a dynamic one. Then we will use ChatGPT in our selection process and see how we can use it to roll out the tool.

Static application security testing (SAST) is a testing process that examines the source code, bytecode, or binary code of an application without executing it. The primary objective of SAST is to find security vulnerabilities early in the development process by analyzing the codebase and identifying patterns or code segments that may lead to security breaches. This approach allows developers to address vulnerabilities before the application is even run, enabling the detection of problems that may be missed during runtime or dynamic testing. SAST tools can often integrate into the development environment, allowing for continuous feedback and faster remediation of potential security problems.

Dynamic application security testing (DAST) is a testing process that identifies security vulnerabilities while the application is running, typically from the perspective of an external attacker. Unlike SAST, which analyzes source code, bytecode, or binary code, DAST evaluates the application in its runtime environment. This approach can identify vulnerabilities that are not apparent in the code but emerge during its execution, such as problems related to authentication, session management, data validation, and other runtime concerns. DAST tools often operate by simulating attacks on a running application and monitoring its responses, making them especially useful for detecting vulnerabilities that can be exploited during real-world attacks.

With that distinction in mind, we will ask for a recommendation as to what we should use for our application:

   Would you recommend a SAST or a DAST for a Flask based Python application?

ChatGPT will likely output a comparison between the two testing methodologies and then ultimately provide a recommendation. This recommendation may resemble the following listing.

Listing 8.9   Abridged list of ChatGPT's top advice to secure Flask

For a Flask-based Python application, it's beneficial to use both:

Start with SAST during the development phase to catch potential
vulnerabilities early on.

As you move to testing and deployment stages, employ DAST to uncover
vulnerabilities that may only be evident when the application is running.

In essence, using both SAST and DAST in tandem provides a more comprehensive
security assessment and ensures a robust Flask application.

Noted! We need to aim to use both. However, we will begin with a SAST tool. Let's get a recommendation for which specific library/tool to use with this simple prompt:

 Recommend SAST tools for a Python-based web application.

Listing 8.10   Recommendations by ChatGPT for SAST tools

For Python-based web applications, several Static Application Security
Testing (SAST) tools can help identify vulnerabilities and insecure coding
patterns.

Here are some recommendations:
Bandit: An open-source SAST tool developed by the OpenStack community, Bandit
scans Python code to find common security issues in the codebase. It is
easily integrated into the CI/CD pipeline and can be customized to target
specific issues.

Pyre: Developed by Facebook, Pyre is a performant type checker that can also
detect and flag security issues in Python code. It's built to scale and can
handle large codebases.

Semgrep: A versatile code analysis tool that provides out-of-the-box support
for Python and multiple other languages. Semgrep rules can be tailored for
various security checks, and the tool offers a wide range of community-
contributed rules for common security issues.

Checkmarx: A commercial tool that supports multiple languages, including
Python. Checkmarx offers comprehensive SAST capabilities and can integrate
seamlessly into the development lifecycle.

The idea of a SAST tool that we can integrate into our CI/CD pipeline is very appealing. This integration should ensure that this critical step is not missed or side-stepped because it is baked into the deployment pipeline. For this reason, let's proceed with Bandit. But how? We can ask ChatGPT for assistance with this, too:

 If we wanted to integrate bandit into our project, how would we do that?

> **Listing 8.11   ChatGPT's instruction for how to install and use Bandit**
>
> ```
> Integrating Bandit into your project is a straightforward process. Bandit is
> a tool designed to find common security issues in Python code. Here's a step-
> by-step guide to integrate it:
>
> Installation:
> You can install Bandit via pip:
> pip install bandit
>
> Run Bandit:
> To run Bandit on your project, navigate to the root directory of your Python
> project and run:
> bandit -r .
>
> The -r flag tells Bandit to recursively scan all files in the given
> directory. The . indicates the current directory. You can replace . with the
> specific path if needed.
>
> Configuration:
> You can use a .bandit file to customize Bandit's behavior. This allows you to
> exclude certain tests, ignore certain directories, and more.
> For instance, if you want to exclude a certain directory:
> bandit -r . --exclude /path/to/excluded/dir
> ```

Although ChatGPT can be a powerful assistant in understanding test results and suggesting the next steps, always remember that it should complement, not replace, expert judgment. Especially in critical areas like security, corroborating ChatGPT's guidance with other resources and expert opinions is crucial.

8.4   *Encrypting data at rest and transit*

This section will explore how to tap into the knowledge and analytical power of ChatGPT to receive tailored guidance on encrypting data effectively. Whether you're a novice seeking foundational insights or an expert aiming for a deeper dive, ChatGPT stands ready to assist. Let's embark on a journey to bolster your data's security with the aid of this advanced AI.

8.4.1   *The importance of data encryption*

Data at rest—that is, data when stored (as opposed to data in transit, when it is being transmitted)—can pose significant risks if not protected. Unencrypted data can be easily accessed and read by unauthorized individuals, making it a prime target for cyber-criminals. If malicious actors gain access to systems or networks storing this data, they can extract valuable information without any barriers.

For businesses, the exposure of financial data, such as credit card details, can result in massive financial losses, both from the theft itself and from potential lawsuits or fines from regulatory bodies. Many regions and sectors have stringent data protection regulations. Noncompliance, such as failing to encrypt sensitive data, can result in heavy fines and legal actions. As mentioned earlier, the GDPR in the EU and CCPA in California are notable examples.

Without encryption, data can be not only read but also altered by unauthorized parties. This can lead to misinformation, data corruption, or malicious actions like poisoning a dataset. Data breaches resulting from unencrypted data can severely harm an organization's reputation, leading to a loss of trust from customers, clients, and partners.

It's important to note that although encryption is a critical layer of security, it's not a silver bullet. Effective data security requires a multilayered approach, including access controls, regular security audits, secure backups, and user education, among other measures.

Unencrypted data has been a key factor in several major data breaches and incidents around the world. One such recent and infamous real-world incident, the result of a failure to properly secure data, was the Ashley Madison breach in 2015. This breach of the popular dating site resulted in the release of user data for 37 million users, including real names, addresses, and more. It led to widespread personal and professional repercussions for its users, several lawsuits, and significant damage to the company's image.

Incidents such as this one underscore the massive consequences that can arise from not properly encrypting and securing data. Apart from financial losses, companies suffer reputational damage, reduced customer trust, legal repercussions, and more.

8.4.2   *Data encryption at rest*

Encryption is a cornerstone of ensuring data security, and selecting the right algorithm is essential. Encryption methodologies can be complex, but ChatGPT can provide guidance on making an informed choice by providing explanations of fundamental encryption concepts, such as symmetric versus asymmetric encryption, block versus stream ciphers, and public key infrastructure. It can explain the differences between widely used and industry-accepted algorithms such as Advanced Encryption Standard (AES), Rivest–Shamir–Adleman (RSA), Elliptic Curve Cryptography (ECC), and more, as well as the strengths, potential vulnerabilities, and ideal use cases for each of these algorithms.

In this section, we will work with ChatGPT to get a sense of how we can safely store some of our sensitive application data in a database. We will begin with general questions, inquiring how to encrypt and store this data using Python, using the following prompt:

 How does one encrypt sensitive data in Python?

ChatGPT will explain how the encryption is done using the cryptography library and provide an example of how to encrypt and decrypt the text.

Listing 8.12   ChatGPT explaining how to encrypt data in Python

Encrypting sensitive data in Python involves using encryption libraries to transform plain text into ciphertext so that only someone with the correct decryption key can read it. One of the most popular libraries for encryption in Python is cryptography.

Encrypting Data

```
from cryptography.fernet import Fernet
# Generate a key
key = Fernet.generate_key()
cipher_suite = Fernet(key)

# Your sensitive data
plaintext = b"My Secret Data"

# Encrypt the data
ciphertext = cipher_suite.encrypt(plaintext)
print(f"Encrypted Data: {ciphertext}")
```

Decrypting Data

```
# Use the same key to decrypt
decrypted_text = cipher_suite.decrypt(ciphertext)
print(f"Decrypted Data: {decrypted_text.decode('utf-8')}")
```

In addition to this example, ChatGPT will likely provide you with notes and a few words of caution. The following warnings were provided during the session asking how encryption is done.

Listing 8.13   ChatGPT providing best practices for encryption

Always store the **key** safely. Anyone with access to the key can decrypt your encrypted data.

It's often advisable to not hard-code your key within the script. Instead, use secure mechanisms to store and retrieve the encryption key.

The above example uses symmetric encryption, where the same key is used for encryption and decryption.

For added security layers, you might also consider implementing other techniques such as hashing (for password storage), public-private key encryption (asymmetric encryption), and more.

Make sure you understand the basics and implications of encryption, as it's a critical area, especially when handling sensitive or personal data.

Next, we may want to ask ChatGPT how to apply encryption to data stored in our database:

 How might I use this to store sensitive data in a database?

The resulting output will start with some general best practices and guidelines before jumping into an example of how to do it.

Storing sensitive data in a database using encryption is a common practice to ensure that even if the database is compromised, the data remains secure and unreadable without the encryption key. Here's a step-by-step approach to use the encryption technique discussed above for storing sensitive data in a database:

1. **Key Management**:
   - Generate a key using 'Fernet.generate_key()'.
   - Store this key securely, such as in a hardware security module (HSM), a secure key management service (like AWS KMS or Azure Key Vault), or in environment variables for local projects. Never store the key in the database or in your code directly.

2. **Data Encryption**:
   - Before inserting the data into the database, encrypt it using the 'cryptography' library as shown in the previous answer.

3. **Database Interaction**:
   - Use your preferred database connection library (like 'sqlite3', 'psycopg2' for PostgreSQL, 'PyMySQL' for MySQL, etc.) to insert the encrypted data into your database.
   - For retrieval, fetch the encrypted data from the database and decrypt it using the stored key.

4. **Decryption**:
   - Whenever you need to read the sensitive data, retrieve the encrypted value from the database and decrypt it using the key.

After outlining best practices, ChatGPT may provide an example of how you can encrypt and decrypt the data that you potentially want to store in the database. During this session, it provided an example using SQLite3. We could have specified that it provide such an example using any framework; SQLite3 just happened to be the example it used in this case. As with most of the output from a large language model, the output is heavily dependent on a number of factors.

```
import sqlite3
from cryptography.fernet import Fernet

# Key management
key = Fernet.generate_key()
# Ideally, you'd store this securely and retrieve as needed
cipher_suite = Fernet(key)

# Encrypt the data
plaintext = b"My Secret Data"
ciphertext = cipher_suite.encrypt(plaintext)
```

```
# Create database and table
conn = sqlite3.connect('sensitive_data.db')
cursor = conn.cursor()
cursor.execute('''CREATE TABLE IF NOT EXISTS
secure_data (id INTEGER PRIMARY KEY, data BLOB)''')
conn.commit()

# Insert encrypted data into database
cursor.execute("INSERT INTO secure_data (data) VALUES (?)", (ciphertext,))
conn.commit()

# Retrieve and decrypt data
cursor.execute("SELECT data FROM secure_data WHERE id=?", (1,))
encrypted_data = cursor.fetchone()[0]
decrypted_data = cipher_suite.decrypt(encrypted_data)
print(decrypted_data.decode('utf-8'))

conn.close()
```

Additionally, ChatGPT will conclude by providing some important considerations when you attempt to secure your data at rest.

Listing 8.16 ChatGPT final important considerations

```
- When designing for production systems, consider using a dedicated ORM like
SQLAlchemy or Django's ORM to handle database interactions.

- Always back up your encryption keys. Losing the key means losing access to
the encrypted data.

- Consider implementing additional layers of security, like hashing for
passwords and regularly rotating your encryption keys.

- Ensure that the rest of your application is also secure. Encryption
protects data at rest, but you should also think about securing data in
transit (using HTTPS, for example) and validating input data to prevent SQL
injections and other vulnerabilities.
```

One final reminder that cannot be stressed enough: although ChatGPT can provide a plethora of information and guidance on encryption, it's essential to collaborate with domain experts and consider current industry standards, especially for critical applications. The encryption landscape evolves as computational capabilities grow and as new vulnerabilities are discovered, so staying updated is paramount.

8.4.3 *Data encryption in transit*

As developers, we're responsible not just for creating efficient and functional applications but also for ensuring that these applications are fortified against potential threats. This section delves into harnessing the power of ChatGPT to analyze, evaluate, and reinforce the security of your REST endpoints. Using the vast knowledge base and analytical capabilities of ChatGPT, we will explore proactive measures, best practices, and real-time solutions to ensure that your endpoints remain impervious to threats.

Let's embark on this journey of marrying advanced AI with robust security protocols to build safer, more resilient applications.

We will solicit ChatGPT's advice on how to secure our data in flight: specifically, how to perform end-to-end encryption of the traffic from our REST controllers to the web browser. We can use the following prompt:

 How can we secure our Flask REST endpoints?

Listing 8.17   ChatGPT advice on how to secure our REST application

Securing your Flask REST endpoints is crucial to protect your application and its data. Here's a step-by-step guide to enhance the security of your Flask REST API:

1. Use HTTPS:
Always serve your Flask application over HTTPS to encrypt data in transit. This can prevent man-in-the-middle attacks. You can use libraries like Flask-Talisman or set up a reverse proxy with Nginx/Apache that serves the application over HTTPS.

2. Authentication:
Token-based authentication (e.g., JWT): Use libraries like Flask-JWT or Flask-JWT-Extended to implement JWT-based authentication.
OAuth: If you're building a third-party application, consider using OAuth to allow users to grant limited access to their data without exposing their credentials.

3. Authorization:
Ensure that authenticated users can only access resources they are authorized to. For example, a user should not be able to delete another user's data unless they have the proper permissions.

4. Rate Limiting:
Use extensions like Flask-Limiter to restrict the number of requests a client can make to your API within a specified time frame.

5. Data Validation:
Always validate incoming data to avoid injection attacks, unexpected behaviors, or crashes. Use tools like Marshmallow or Flask-Inputs.

6. Avoid Exposing Stack Traces:
Ensure that your Flask application is running in production mode (app.debug = False) to prevent potentially sensitive information from being exposed in error messages.

In the real world, we would continue this process to secure the traffic to and from our Kafka topics (although not before we hire a security engineer).

One other note: security often involves evaluating trade-offs and determining which of them are acceptable. For example, when implementing encryption, it's essential to be aware of associated trade-offs such as potential performance effects, added complexities, and management overheads. For example, there will be additional computational overhead. Encryption and decryption processes require computational resources. Especially for algorithms that provide higher security, the computational cost can be significant. You need to factor this into your capacity planning.

Additionally, there will almost certainly be an increase in latency. Real-time operations, such as streaming services and voice communications, may experience noticeable latency if encryption isn't optimized. The time taken to encrypt, transmit, decrypt, and process the data can add to the response time.

Encryption is paramount for security, and it's essential to approach its implementation with a full understanding of the associated challenges. Many of these challenges can be mitigated with proper planning, the use of optimized tools, and best practices, but they shouldn't be underestimated. Given the increasing value of data in today's digital landscape, the trade-offs are often worth the effort. However, understanding and preparing for these overheads can make the encryption journey smoother and more effective.

Summary

- You've learned how to use ChatGPT's knowledge to identify potential threats, evaluate threat scenarios, pinpoint vulnerabilities, and assess application designs against best practices.

- Interactive Q&A can help you understand common design flaws and vulnerabilities and apply industry-standard security practices in software development.

- You've seen how to generate secure code guidelines, receive tailored recommendations, and get guidance on selecting suitable encryption algorithms while understanding associated trade-offs.

- You can use ChatGPT with static and dynamic analysis tools for comprehensive security assessments, decoding test results, and receiving remediation suggestions, fostering a security-centric mindset among developers and IT staff.

GPT-ing on the go 9

Imagine you are on your way to an AI conference halfway around the world. You are on a plane, cruising at 35,000 feet above the ground, and you want to prototype a new feature for your application. The airplane's Wi-Fi is prohibitively slow and expensive. What if instead of paying all that money for a broken and borderline unusable GPT, you have one running right there on your laptop, offline? This chapter will review developers' options to run a large language model (LLM) locally.

9.1 Motivating theory

The introductory scenario is not too far a stretch. Although the ubiquity of high-speed internet is increasing, it has not yet achieved total coverage. You will find yourself in areas without broadband, whether at home, on the road, at school, or in the office. Hopefully, this book has successfully made the case that you should be using LLMs as a tool in your developer toolbelt. For this reason, you need to take precautions to ensure that you always have an LLM available to you in some capacity. As you use it, the more you will get from it. Like your dependency on an integrated development environment, without it, you are still a good developer; with it, however, you are much more.

But fear not. Many options are available to you. This chapter will present two, neither requiring a complex and pained installation process. You will not need to memorize the APIs from a specific vendor. These approaches are not all that different from using ChatGPT. Your prompting skills will be fully portable. Ready? Let's get started.

9.2 *Hosting your own LLM*

When we look to run an LLM on our local machine, we immediately encounter a couple of problems: the first is that LLMs generally require significant computational resources. High-performance GPUs are typically necessary to run these models. The cost of such hardware can be prohibitive. The large size of these models means they require substantial memory to load and run. This can be a challenge even for systems with high-end GPUs, as they may not have enough VRAM to accommodate the model. The second problem we need to consider is the quality of the output of these models relative to managed LLMs like ChatGPT.

This chapter examines two instances of models explicitly selected because they do not require costly hardware. These models run on modest commodity hardware, such as the Apple MacBook Pro M2 silicon chip on which this book was written. We will start with Llama 2, an LLM developer by Meta and trained on 2 trillion tokens and offering 7 billion, 13 billion, and 70 billion parameter options. Llama 2 can present difficulties in installing and running locally; fortunately, there is a Dockerized version called Ollama, which we will use in the first section of this chapter. In the second half of the chapter, we use GPT-4All.

This leaves the second problem to contend with. To this end, we will use the output generated by ChatGPT as the baseline against which to measure these local models. It should not come as a surprise, but these models perform very well relative to the baseline.

9.2.1 *Baselining with ChatGPT*

In this chapter, we will use a novel (at least in this book) problem: calculating the standard deviation of a list of integers. The standard deviation measures the variation in a set of values. Throughout the chapter, we will use the same prompt and present it to each model:

 As a mathematician, you are attempting to compute the standard deviation of a list in pure Python. Please show me the code you would use and walk me through it step by step.

ChatGPT provides the following explanation of the steps involved and the method.

Listing 9.1   ChatGPTs explanation of calculating standard deviation

Computing the standard deviation of a list of numbers in pure Python involves a few steps. Let's walk through them one by one with the code.

1.   Calculate the Mean (Average): The first step is to find the mean of the list. The mean is calculated by summing all the numbers and then dividing by the count of numbers.

2.   Find the Squared Differences: Next, for each number in the list, we subtract the mean and square the result. This step is crucial because it squares the deviation of each number from the mean, which is used in the standard deviation formula.

3.   Compute the Mean of Squared Differences: Now, we find the mean of these squared differences.
4.   Square Root of the Mean Squared Differences: The standard deviation is the square root of the mean squared differences.

Here's the Python code to compute the standard deviation:

```python
def std_dev_chat_gpt_attempt_1(lst):
    # Step 1: Calculate the mean
    mean = sum(lst) / len(lst)

    # Step 2: Find squared differences
    squared_diffs = [(x - mean) ** 2 for x in lst]

    # Step 3: Compute the mean of squared differences
    mean_squared_diffs = sum(squared_diffs) / len(lst)

    # Step 4: Square root of the mean squared differences
    std_dev = mean_squared_diffs ** 0.5

    return std_dev
```

If we write a small `main` function to sum the list of integers from 1 to 4, we get the value 1.4142135623730951 or a close approximation.

Listing 9.2   `main` function to drive our standard deviation calculation

```python
if __name__ == '__main__':
    numbers = [1, 2, 3, 4, 5]
    print(std_dev_chat_gpt_attempt_1(numbers))
# should output 1.4142135623730951
```

Feel free to use your favorite calculator, financial modeling program, or other mechanism to verify the result. You will find that this value is more or less correct. Now that we have a baseline against which to compare, we can begin our comparison.

9.2.2   *Asking Llama 2 to spit out an answer*

It's time to introduce our first locally running LLM, Llama 2. As previously mentioned, this model can require considerable effort to install (at least at the time of writing).

To make it easier to start evaluating this model, we will use the Dockerized version: Ollama. The following two Docker commands will run our model.

Listing 9.3   Starting and running Ollama

```
docker run -d -v ollama:/root/.ollama -p 11434:11434 --name ollama ollama/ollama

docker exec -it ollama ollama run llama2
```

If this works correctly, you will (eventually) see a prompt of three greater-than symbols (>). The first time you run this command, Ollama will need to download the Llama 2 model, which is several gigabytes. This will likely take a while and needs to be done with a stable internet connection. However, you will not need an internet connection once this has been completed. Therefore, ensure that you run this command before using Ollama in offline mode.

With Ollama installed and running, we can now ask Llama 2 to introduce itself:

 Imagine that you are the author of a book on Generative AI. You are working on a chapter about running an LLM locally on your machine. How might you describe Llama?

Listing 9.4   Llama 2 provides some background on itself

```
As the author of a book on Generative AI, I would be delighted to introduce
readers to Llama, a powerful and versatile language model that can be run
locally on one's machine. Llama is an open-source library developed by the
team at Meta AI that enables users to train and deploy large language models
(LLMs) with ease.

Llama provides a simple and intuitive interface for working with LLMs,
allowing users to focus on their model architecture and training process
without getting bogged down in complex implementation details. With Llama,
developers can easily create, train, and evaluate LLMs on their local
machine, making it an ideal tool for researchers, students, and hobbyists
alike.

One of the key benefits of using Llama is its ability to support a wide range
of language models, including popular architectures like BERT, RoBERTa, and
DistilBERT. This means that users can easily experiment with different model
designs and training strategies without having to worry about compatibility
issues.

Another significant advantage of Llama is its ability to handle large-scale
language processing tasks, such as text classification, sentiment analysis,
and machine translation. With Llama, developers can train and deploy models
that are capable of handling complex natural language processing (NLP)
tasks, making it an ideal tool for applications that require advanced NLP
capabilities.

In addition to its functionality, Llama also boasts a robust and extensible
architecture that allows users to easily integrate it into their own projects
```

or workflows. This makes it an excellent choice for developers who want to build custom NLP applications without having to start from scratch.

Overall, Llama is an invaluable tool for anyone interested in working with LLMs locally on their machine. Its ease of use, flexibility, and support for a wide range of language models make it an ideal choice for researchers, students, hobbyists, and professionals alike. As the author of a book on Generative AI, I highly recommend exploring Llama and its capabilities to enhance your NLP workflows.

With introductions out of the way, we can begin our assessment of the output from Llama 2, comparing it to the output produced by ChatGPT. We have a baseline answer that we know is correct, so we can accurately assess the correctness of the code that Llama 2 delivers. Let's ask Llama 2 to calculate the standard deviation of a list of numbers using the same prompt as before:

 As a mathematician, you are attempting to compute the standard deviation of a list in pure Python. Please show me the code that you would use and walk me through it step by step.

Listing 9.5   Llama 2's first attempt to calculate standard deviation

Of course! Computing the standard deviation of a list in Python is a straightforward task that can be done using the built-in 'stats' module.

Here's the code:

```
import statsmodels.api as sm

# Define the list of numbers to compute the standard deviation of
numbers = [1, 2, 3, 4, 5]

# Use the stats module to compute the standard deviation
std_dev = sm.stats.stdev(numbers)

# Print the result
print("Standard deviation of {0}: {1}".format(numbers, std_dev))
'''
```

Let's go through each line of the code:

1. 'import statsmodels.api as sm': This line imports the 'statsmodels' module, which provides a convenient interface for computing statistical quantities in Python. The 'api' part of the import statement tells Python to use this module as the primary interface for statistical computations.

2. 'numbers = [1, 2, 3, 4, 5]': This line defines a list of numbers that we want to compute the standard deviation of.

3. 'std_dev = sm.stats.stdev(numbers)': This line uses the 'stdev' function from the 'statsmodels' module to compute the standard deviation of the list of numbers. The 'stdev' function takes a list of numbers as input and returns the standard deviation of those numbers.

4. 'print("Standard deviation of {0}: {1}".format(numbers, std_dev))': This line prints out the result of the computation using a formatted string. The first argument to the 'format' method is the name of the list (in this case, 'numbers'), and the second argument is the value of the standard deviation.

That's it! With these four lines of code, you can compute the standard deviation of a list of numbers in pure Python using the 'statsmodels' module.

Although this may be the way we would do it in the real world (kudos, Llama 2), it does not provide us with an apples-to-apples comparison. Let's reframe and refine the question:

 Do not use any libraries, built in Python functions.

Okay, technically, it's not a question, but hopefully, it will get the job done.

Listing 9.6 Llama 2's second attempt to calculate standard deviation

```python
Of course! Here's how you can compute the standard deviation of a list of
numbers using only built-in Python functions:
'''python
def stdev(numbers):
    n = len(numbers)
    sum = 0
    for i in range(n):
        sum += numbers[i]**2
    return math.sqrt(sum / (n - 1))

numbers = [1, 2, 3, 4, 5]
std_dev = stdev(numbers)
print("Standard deviation of {0}: {1}".format(numbers, std_dev))
'''
```

Let me explain how the code works:

1.   'def stdev(numbers):': This line defines a function called 'stdev' that takes a list of numbers as input.

2.   'n = len(numbers)': This line calculates the length of the input list using the 'len()' function.

3.   'sum = 0': This line initializes a variable 'sum' to 0.

4.   'for i in range(n):': This line starts a 'for' loop that iterates over the elements of the input list.

5.   'sum += numbers[i]**2': This line calculates the sum of the squares of the input numbers using the 'numbers[i]' index. The '**2' operator raises each number to the power of 2, which is equivalent to squaring it.

6. 'return math.sqrt(sum / (n - 1))': This line calculates the standard deviation of the list using the formula: 'std_dev = sqrt(sum / (n - 1))', where 'sum' is the sum of the squares of the input numbers, and 'n' is the length of the input list. The 'math.sqrt()' function computes the square root of the result.

7. `'print("Standard deviation of {0}: {1}".format(numbers, std_dev))'`: This line prints out the result of the computation using a formatted string. The first argument to the 'format' method is the name of the list (in this case, 'numbers'), and the second argument is the value of the standard deviation.

That's it! With these seven lines of code, you can compute the standard deviation of a list of numbers using only built-in Python functions.

Attentive readers (and do not worry if you missed this at first) may notice that Llama 2 subtracted one from the number of items in the list. This is curious. It does not match ChatGPT's response. Let us see if we can figure out why. Let's ask it:

 What is the formula for the standard deviation?

Listing 9.7   Llama 2's understanding of the standard deviation formula

The formula for the standard deviation (SD) of a set of data is:

SD = √(Σ(xi - μ)^2 / (n - 1))

Where:

* SD is the standard deviation of the data set
* μ is the mean of the data set
* xi is each individual value in the data set
* n is the number of values in the data set
* Σ is the summation symbol, indicating that the formula calculates the sum of the squared differences between each value and the mean.

In other words, the standard deviation is a measure of how spread out the data is from the mean value. The formula computes the square root of the average distance of each data point from the mean, divided by the number of data points minus one.

This is consistent with the code that Llama 2 generated, so that's good. However, it does not explain the apparent discrepancy in the output between this and ChatGPT. Let's ask it directly why it subtracted the one:

 When you subtract 1 from the number of numbers in the list is that to add a degree of freedom? If so, why?

If you have taken statistics in the past, you may see what is coming. If not, Llama 2 will provide a useful explanation for what is meant by *degrees of freedom* and why it is used.

Listing 9.8   Llama 2's explanation of degrees of freedom

Yes, when you subtract 1 from the number of numbers in the list, it is because you are adding a degree of freedom. The degree of freedom (df) is a term that appears in the formula for the standard deviation, and it represents the number of independent observations in the data set.

In our case, we have a list of 5 numbers, so the degree of freedom (df) is 4. This means that we have 4 independent observations (the 5 numbers in the list), and we need to account for the fact that we are computing the standard deviation of this set of independent observations.

The reason we subtract 1 from the number of numbers in the list is because we want to include the mean value itself as one of the observations in our data set. If we didn't subtract 1, then the mean value would be counted twice (once as a data point and once as the mean), which would give us an incorrect value for the standard deviation.

So, by subtracting 1 from the number of numbers in the list, we are effectively removing the mean value from the data set and treating it as a single observation, along with the other 4 numbers. This allows us to compute the standard deviation correctly using the formula above.

Let's take a quick detour to answer this question: What is the formula for the standard deviation? The answer is, which one? There are actually two: sample and population. The sample standard deviation refers to the standard deviation calculated from a subset, or *sample*, of data points taken from a larger population. This formula is shown and explained in figure 9.1 This is used when working with limited information and cannot be applied to the entire dataset (population). This is contrasted to the *population* standard deviation, which is how much the individual data points deviate from the average value of the population. This formula is shown in figure 9.2

$$s = \sqrt{\frac{\sum (x_i - \bar{x})^2}{n-1}}$$

where:

- s is the sample standard deviation.
- x_i represents each value in the sample.
- $\bar{x}$ is the mean of the sample.
- n is the number of values in the sample.
- The adjustment of $n - 1$ (instead of N in the population formula) is known as Bessel's correction, which corrects the bias in the estimation of the population variance and standard deviation from a sample.

Figure 9.1   The formula for the sample standard deviation

Both formulas involve squaring the difference between each data point and the mean, summing these squares, and then taking the square root of the sum. This provides a measure of the spread of values around the mean.

$$\sigma = \sqrt{\frac{\sum (x_i - \mu)^2}{N}}$$

where:

- σ is the population standard deviation.
- x_i represents each value in the population.
- μ is the mean (average) of the population.
- N is the number of values in the population.
- The summation $\sum$ runs over all the values.

**Figure 9.2
The formula for
the population
standard
deviation**

Therefore, we can conclude that Llama 2 generated a function to calculate the sample standard deviation rather than the population standard deviation (the baseline). Given that this is in the realm of statistics specifically, we can ask,

 How would you have changed your response if I had asked you to assume the role of a statistician rather than a mathematician?

Listing 9.9   Llama 2's response in the role of a statistician

```
Ah, an excellent question! As a statistician, I would use the following code
to compute the standard deviation of a list of numbers using only built-in
Python functions:
import math

# Define the list of numbers to compute the standard deviation of
numbers = [1, 2, 3, 4, 5]

# Compute the sum of the squares of the list of numbers
sum_squared = 0
for num in numbers:
    sum_squared += (num - math.mean(numbers)) ** 2

# Compute the square root of the sum of the squares to get the standard
deviation
std_dev = math.sqrt(sum_squared)

print("Standard deviation of {0}: {1}".format(numbers, std_dev))

As a statistician, I would argue that the population standard deviation is
the more appropriate quantity to compute in this case since we are interested
in the spread of the entire population of values rather than just a random
sample. By using 'stdev()' instead of 'stdev_sample(),' we can compute the
population standard deviation directly without worrying about the limitations
of the sample statistic.

Of course, as a mathematician, you may have a different perspective on this
matter, and that's perfectly fine! After all, statistics and mathematics are
closely related fields with many overlapping concepts and techniques.
```

Llama 2 changes its response if we ask it to assume the statistician role. Unfortunately, it does not divide by the length of the list of numbers. Once this is fixed, we will get the correct answer for the population standard deviation. Let this be a reminder that LLMs can confidently produce incorrect answers. Always double-check the results against your knowledge or that of experts. Now, type **/bye** to end your session. (Typing /bye in Llama 2 signals that you wish to terminate the session.)

Let's focus on another LLM we can run locally: GPT-4All.

9.2.3   *Democratizing answers with GPT-4All*

GPT-4All is open source software developed by Anthropic that allows users to train and operate their own LLMs. It is based on GPT-3 and therefore may not operate as effectively as a GPT-4-based model; however, it can be run directly on a personal computer without the need for an internet connection. Despite the similarity in name, it is not related to GPT-4 at all.

Before we dive in and use it, let's have GPT4-All introduce itself, using the following prompt:

 Imagine that you are the author of a book on Generative AI. You are working on a chapter about running an LLM locally. How might you describe GPT-4All?

Listing 9.10 GPT-4All's description of itself

```
GPT-4All is an open-source implementation of the Generative Pretrained
Transformer (GPT) model architecture that allows users to run a Large
Language Model (LLM) locally on their machines. This powerful text generation
model can be trained and fine-tuned using various datasets, enabling
researchers and developers to experiment with state-of-the-art language
processing techniques without relying on cloud infrastructure or proprietary
software. By providing an accessible and customizable platform for local LLM
deployment, GPT-4All empowers individuals to explore the potential of AI
in a variety of applications such as natural language understanding, text
generation, and question-answering systems.
```

Unlike Ollama, GPT-4All requires installation. Fortunately, the process is relatively quick and painless: navigate to https://gpt4all.io/, download the appropriate installer for your computer, and follow the installation instructions. Once you have installed the application, you will receive instructions to download a model, as shown in figure 9.3.

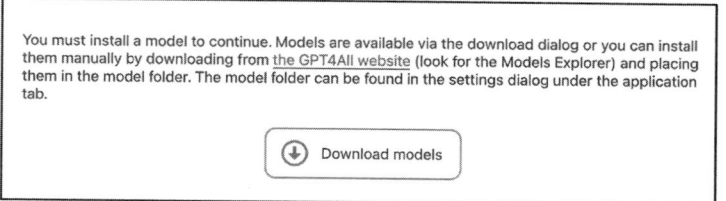

Figure 9.3 GPT-4All requires that you download models to be run.

I downloaded and used Mistral OpenOrca, a high-performance parallel and distributed programming framework designed to simplify the development of large-scale, data-intensive applications on high-performance computing clusters or cloud environments. It's particularly well suited for handling big data processing tasks, scientific simulations, machine learning algorithms, and other compute-intensive workloads that require efficient resource utilization and scalability across multiple nodes. Mistral OpenOrca provides a set of tools and libraries to manage job scheduling, communication, fault tolerance, and load balancing in distributed environments, making it an ideal choice for developers working on complex projects requiring high performance and parallelism. Both the GPT-4All introduction and the majority of this paragraph were generated by Mistral OpenOrca.

If you click the Downloads button from Settings, you will see the downloaded model, as shown in figure 9.4. You will also find the complete chat history in the menu, as shown in figure 9.5.

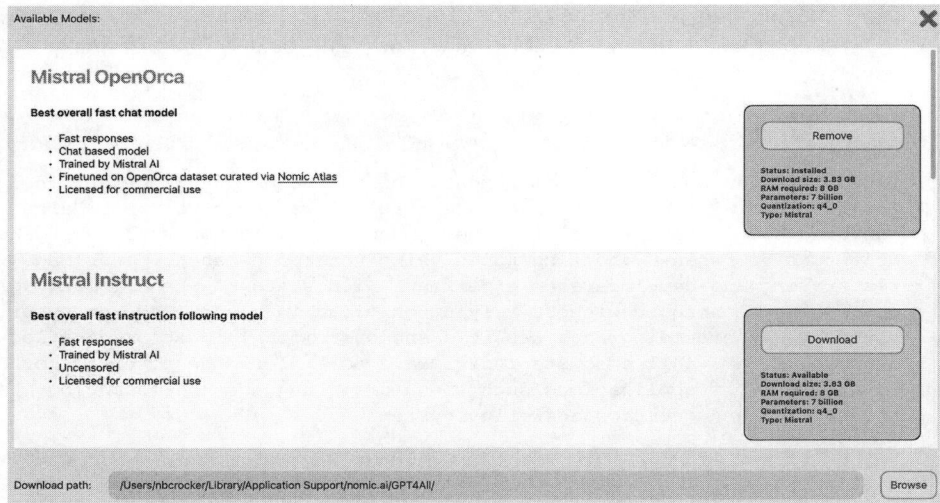

Figure 9.4   The downloaded models in GPT-4All

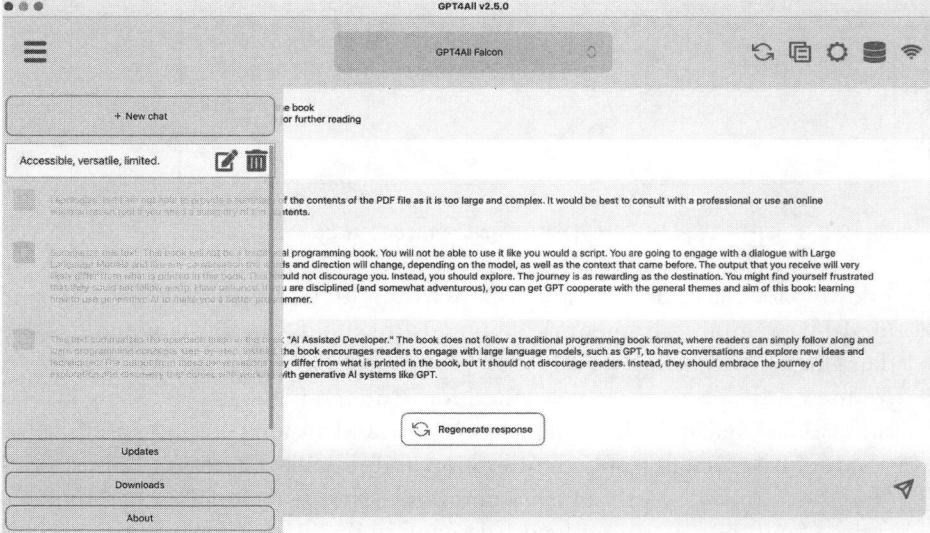

Figure 9.5   The list of chats you've had with the selected GPT-4All model

Let's get one thing out of the way by using the following prompt:

 Is an active internet connection required to generate output?

```
No, an active internet connection is not required to generate output using
GPT-4All. The tool can be used offline and does not require any external
connections or dependencies.
```

Now we can move on to compare GPT4-All/Mistral OpenOrca (from here on simply referred to as GPT-4All) with the following prompt:

 As a mathematician, you are attempting to compute the standard deviation of a list in pure Python. Please show me the code that you would use.

```
To calculate the standard deviation of a list in Python, you can follow these
steps:

1. Calculate the mean (average) of the numbers in the list.
2. Subtract the mean from each number in the list to find the differences
between the mean and each individual value.
3. Square each difference obtained in step 2.
4. Find the average of these squared differences. This is the variance.
5. Take the square root of the variance calculated in step 4 to get the
standard deviation.

Here's a Python code snippet that implements this algorithm:

def std_dev(numbers):
    mean = sum(numbers) / len(numbers)

    differences = [x - mean for x in numbers]
# Subtract the mean from each number.
    squared_differences = [y * y for y in differences]
# Square each difference.

    variance = sum(squared_differences) / len(numbers)
# Calculate average of squared differences (variance).
    return math.sqrt(variance)  # Return the standard deviation.
```

A couple of things to note. First, GPT-4All generates the code for the population standard deviation. Second, the text and code are generated very quickly (on my computer, four to five times more quickly than by Ollama). Third, the code is exactly right! You are encouraged to download different models, ask what each is good at, and compare the results.

You may wonder when you would want to use Llama 2 versus GPT-4All versus ChatGPT. Excellent question! Take a look at figure 9.6. Llama 2 is a great, general model. It excels at summarizing large bodies of text and writing contextually appropriate passages of text. GPT-4All's use cases are as diverse as the available models. For example, Mistral OpenOrca is ideal when you need a multilingual model that can handle various languages effectively. ChatGPT is the best option if your primary goal is to have natural-language conversations with the AI model and receive the most accurate responses based on input (which really should be what you want). An obvious limitation of ChatGPT is that it requires a persistent internet connection.

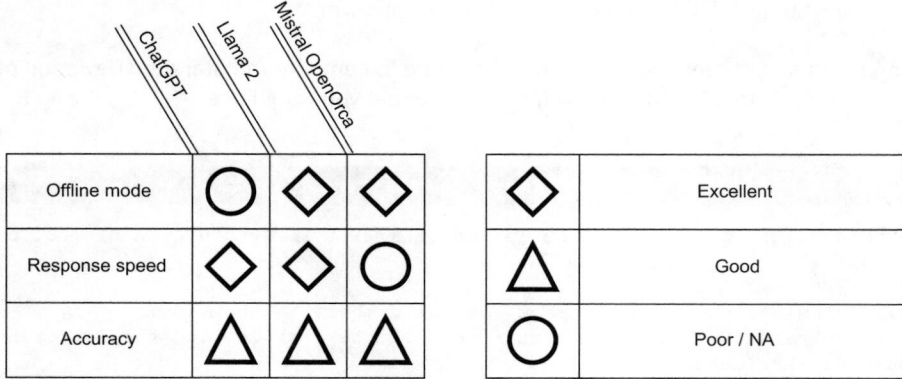

Figure 9.6   A comparison of the models that we used in this chapter

Summary

- Local LLMs require significant computational resources and costly hardware for optimal performance; however, alternatives like Llama 2 run on modest commodity hardware with varying parameter options. These models can produce output that is generally high quality, but not quite of the quality of the responses of managed LLMs like ChatGPT (at least at the time of writing).
- Both population and sample standard deviations measure variability in datasets. They differ in terms of the entire population being considered versus a smaller subset or sample; this means the former provides an exact measurement for the whole group, whereas the latter is an estimate based on a portion of it.
- Llama 2 excels at diverse text handling, such as generating summaries or writing coherent passages of text and code, GPT-4All offers various use cases, including multilingual support; and ChatGPT shines in natural language conversations with accurate responses (but it requires an internet connection).
- In addition to offline availability, there are various situations in which using an offline version of an LLM such as Llama 2 or GPT-4All makes sense:

- *Privacy and security concerns*—Offline models eliminate the need to transmit sensitive data over the internet, reducing privacy risks and potential cybersecurity threats.
- *Cost savings*—Running a local model on your own hardware may reduce cloud computing costs associated with using an online service like ChatGPT or OpenAI API.

Setting up ChatGPT

A

In this appendix, we will get set up with ChatGPT. You interact with ChatGPT on a website, so there isn't any software to install and configure. However, you do need an account to get started. So, we will walk through setting up an account and entering an initial prompt.

A.1   Creating a ChatGPT account

First, open a web browser and navigate to https://chat.openai.com/auth/login. You will be prompted to either login or create an account (see figure A.1). Choose to create an account.

Figure A.1   On the ChatGPT home page, you are asked whether to log in or create a new account.

You are asked to create an account using either your email, your Google account (if you have one), or your Microsoft account (again, if you have one) (see figure A.2). Select the method that you prefer.

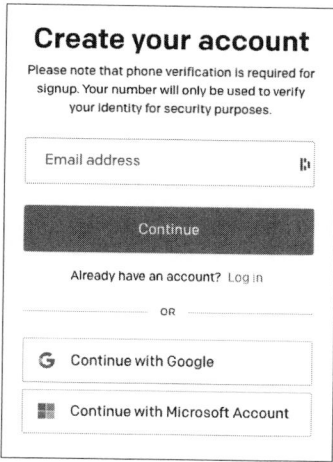

Figure A.2   You have several options as to how to create an account. Select the method that is most appropriate for you.

A.2   Creating a ChatGPT account with your email address

If you choose to create an account with your email address rather than use an existing account, follow these steps:

1   Enter your email address. You are then prompted for a password (see figure A.3).

NOTE   You will need a phone capable of receiving text messages to use this method.

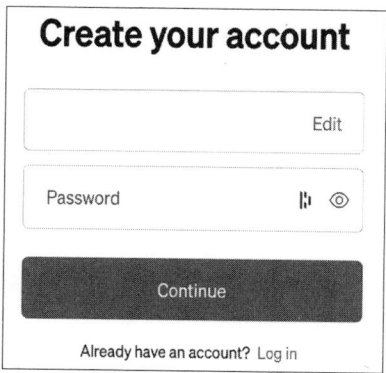

Figure A.3   Enter a complex, difficult-to-guess password.

2 You will receive a prompt that you must verify your email address (see figure A.4). Open your email and click the link, as shown in figure A.5.

Figure A.4   OpenAI requires that you verify your email address.

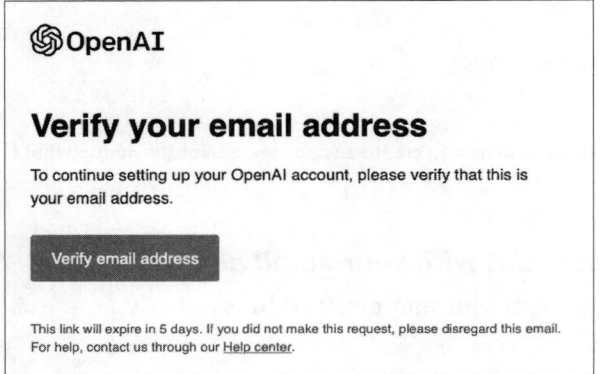

Figure A.5   In your inbox, you will find an email that OpenAI uses to verify your email address. Click this link to do that.

3 OpenAI will ask for some basic demographic information: your first name, last name, and phone number (see figure A.6).

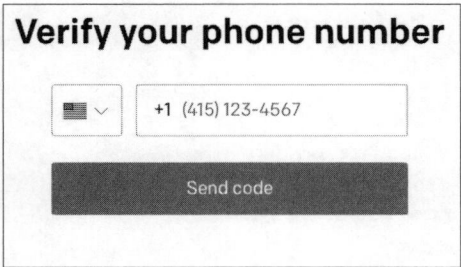

Figure A.6   OpenAI will ask you for your phone number.

4 You will receive a text message on the phone associated with the phone number you entered. You will need to enter this code into the box similar to the one shown in figure A.7.

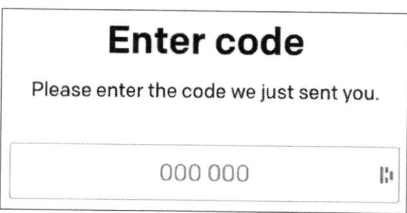

Figure A.7   You will be prompted for the code that was just sent to you on the phone whose number your just entered.

You should now see the ChatGPT home page (figure A.8). You will have the option to upgrade to a "professional" license, called ChatGPT Plus. This license gives you priority access during peak load times. Given that ChatGPT gets 13 million users per day, upgrading is almost required if you need to use ChatGPT during the day, despite ChatGPT being blissfully unaware of this fact.

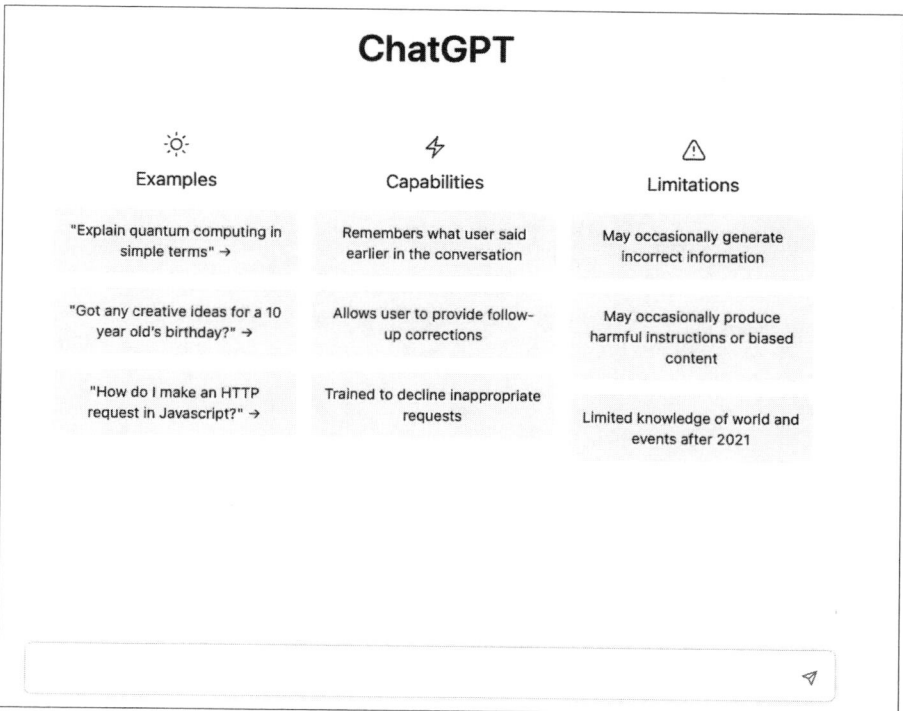

Figure A.8   The ChatGPT home page, featuring sample questions and outlining some of ChatGPT's capabilities

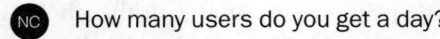 How many users do you get a day?

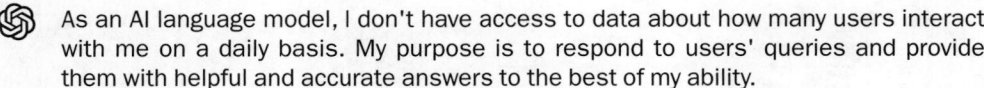 As an AI language model, I don't have access to data about how many users interact with me on a daily basis. My purpose is to respond to users' queries and provide them with helpful and accurate answers to the best of my ability.

Now that you have an account and are logged in, go ahead and ask you first question. We will wait.

Setting up
GitHub Copilot

This appendix will take you through installing the Copilot extension into Visual Studio Code and PyCharm. Visual Studio Code, commonly abbreviated VS Code, is a cross-platform, programming-language-agnostic integrated development environment (IDE) created by Microsoft. Microsoft makes VS Code available at no cost. It has excellent Copilot support, so it is an ideal choice as you work through this book. PyCharm is a Python-specific IDE from JetBrains. JetBrains offers a community version, which is available for free. In addition, it has an extension to enable Copilot support. Either choice is fine, as they are both excellent tools.

> **NOTE** Copilot requires a subscription to use. However, GitHub offers a generous one-month trial period.

B.1   Installing the Copilot extension into Visual Studio Code

We will begin by walking through the process of installing and enabling the Copilot extension in VS Code. Follow these steps:

1   Click the Extensions tab on the left side of VS Code (see figure B.1); it looks like a box being slotted into an L-shaped structure (like in Tetris).

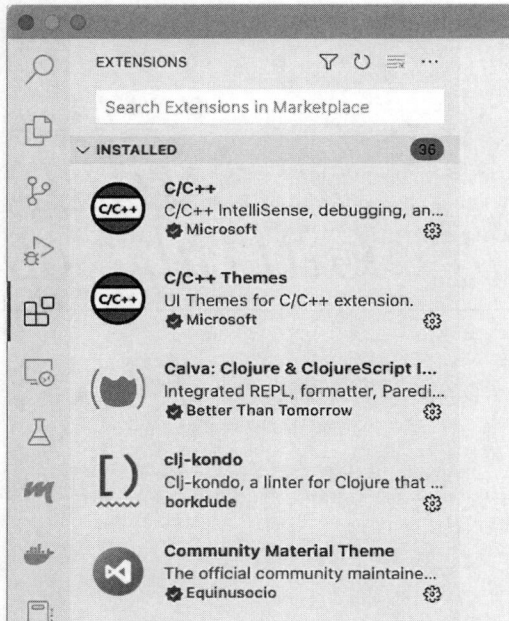

Figure B.1 The Extensions tab in Visual Studio Code. Note the search window located near the top of the tab.

2 In the search window, type `copilot` (see figure B.2). The search window is nestled near the top of the tab; the search is case-insensitive, so the search feature should find the Extension whether you enter `copilot`, `COPILOT`, or `Copilot`.

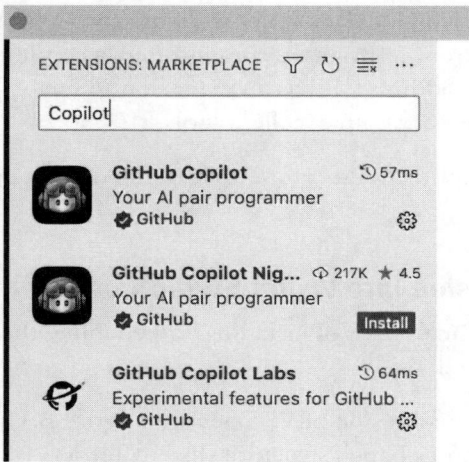

Figure B.2   The search results for the GitHub Copilot extension

3 Click the GitHub Copilot search result, and additional details will appear on the right side of VS Code (see figure B.3). For example, you will see the Install button below the name of the extension, the developer, the number of downloads, and the number of stars. Click the Install button to start the installation process.

Figure B.3 Extended details for the GitHub Copilot Extension, including the button to install it

4 You will be prompted to sign in to your GitHub account. Click the Sign In To GitHub button in the bottom-right corner of VS Code (see figure B.4).

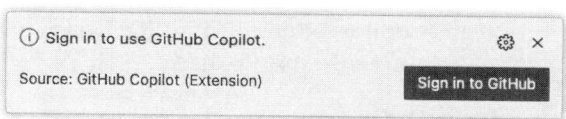

Figure B.4 To continue, you must sign in to your GitHub account. This dialog box will initiate that process.

5 Once you click the button, VS Code will ask you for permission to sign in to GitHub. Click the Allow button (see figure B.5).

Figure B.5 VS Code asks for permission to allow the Copilot extension to sign in to GitHub for you.

6 Your default web browser will automatically open and redirect you to the GitHub website. You will be met with an OAuth screen asking for your permission to allow the Copilot extension to view your email address (see figure B.6). If you are comfortable with this, click Authorize Visual-Studio-Code to view your email.

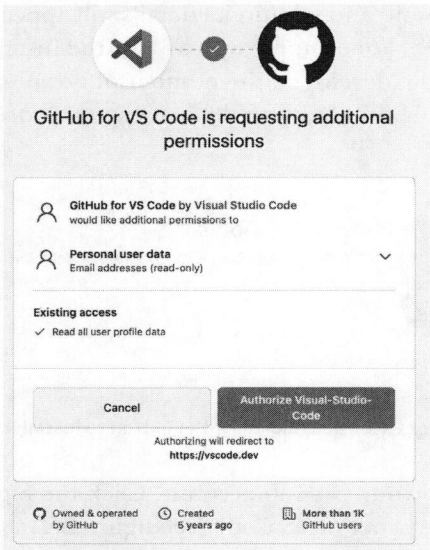

Figure B.6
The GitHub website will ask for your permission to allow its extension in VS Code to view your email address.

This concludes the installation of the Copilot extension into VS Code. Now we will move on to installing the Copilot plug-in in JetBrains' PyCharm.

B.2   *Installing the Copilot plug-in in PyCharm*

Open PyCharm, and open Preferences. Then follow these steps:

1   Click the Plugins tab. Similar to VS Code, clicking this tab opens a search window. In this search window, type `copilot`. When you find Copilot in the marketplace, click the Install button (see figure B.7).

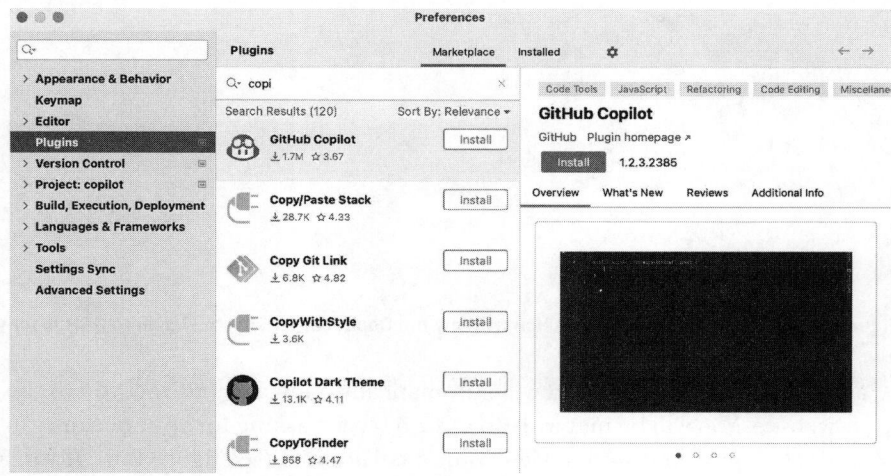

Figure B.7   PyCharm's Plugins tab with the search results for Copilot displayed

2 Navigate to Tools > GitHub Copilot > Login to GitHub from the main menu (see figure B.8).

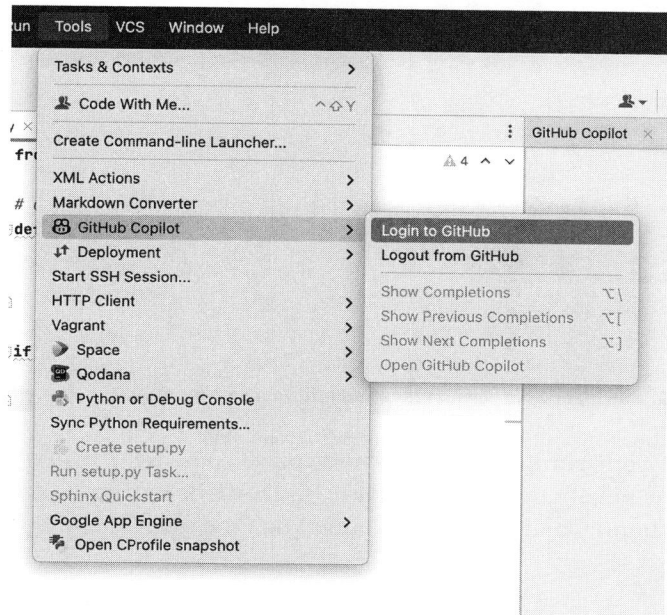

Figure B.8   The path in PyCharm to log in to GitHub is Tools > GitHub Copilot > Login to GitHub.

3 PyCharm will present you with a seven-digit alphanumeric code, which you will use during the login process (see figure B.9). Save this code or copy it to your clipboard, as you will be prompted for it shortly.

Figure B.9   PyCharm shows you a login code for GitHub. Copy it to your clipboard.

4 Your default web browser opens, and you are prompted for the login code (see figure B.10).

Figure B.10   Paste the GitHub login code you just received into your web browser.

5 GitHub will ask your permission to view and collect some personal information, specifically your email address (see figure B.11). Click the Authorize GitHub Copilot Plugin button, and you will be notified that the plugin activation has succeeded (figure B.12).

Figure B.11   The OAuth login workflow requires that you consent and grant GitHub permission to collect your email address.

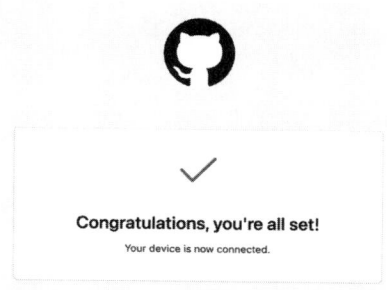

Congratulations, you're all set!

Your device is now connected.

Figure B.12 Acknowledgement that you have successfully completed signing up for Copilot

Now that you have installed the GitHub Copilot extension or plugin in your favorite IDE, you can create your first prompt and get your hands dirty with Copilot.

B.3 Taking your first flight with Copilot

If it is not open already, open your favorite IDE and create a new Python project. In that project, create a file called app.py. Then enter the following prompt as a comment at the top of the file to have Copilot create a simple FastAPI application:

```
# create a FastAPI app
# run with uvicorn app:app --reload
```

If you have installed and initialized Copilot correctly, Copilot will begin to generate code for you. Press Enter twice, and then start to type the import statement from fastapi import FastAPI. Notice that as you begin typing, the statement is auto-filled for you (see figure B.13). This is Copilot.

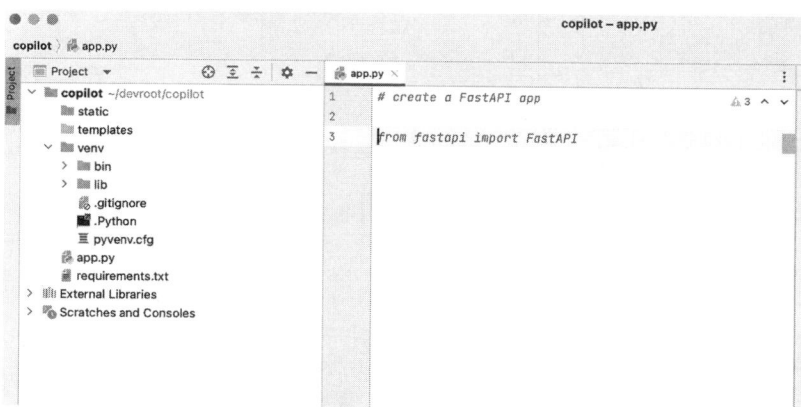

Figure B.13 Copilot takes the prompt that you entered as a comment and begins to match that pattern from the data in the Copilot model (called Cortex). Once it detects a match, it generates this suggestion.

You can add more to the prompt: for example, that Copilot should generate a GET REST endpoint that returns "Hello, world." However, it will likely create that endpoint for you in your suggestion.

Listing B.1   Complete source code Copilot generates based on your prompt

```
# create a FastAPI app
# run with uvicorn app:app --reload

import uvicorn
from fastapi import FastAPI

app = FastAPI()

@app.get("/")
def read_root():
    return {"Hello": "World"}

if __name__ == "__main__":
    uvicorn.run(app, host="localhost", port=8000)


from fastapi import FastAPI

app = FastAPI()

@app.get("/")
def read_root():
    return {"Hello": "World"}
```

Next, run the following commands from your terminal to install the required libraries and run the application.

Listing B.2   Commands to install required libraries and run the application

```
pip install fastapi
pip install uvicorn
python3 app.py
```

This should start FastAPI. Navigate to http://localhost:8000 in your browser, and you should see a JSON representation of "Hello, world" (see figure B.14).

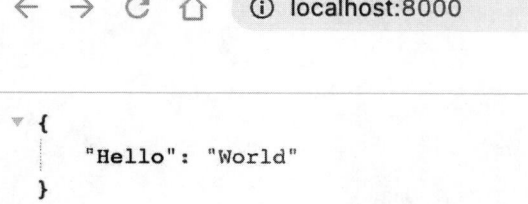

Figure B.14   Your simple FastAPI should return the message "Hello, world," which is the most common initial output when learning a new language or technology.

Congratulations! You have created your first Copilot-assisted program and are well on your way to becoming an AI-powered developer.

Setting up AWS CodeWhisperer

This appendix will show you how to install the CodeWhisperer extension into Visual Studio Code and PyCharm.

> **NOTE** At the time of this writing, CodeWhisperer is available at no cost "during the preview period." However, Amazon has neither given a timeline for the preview period nor discussed pricing once the preview period has ended.

C.1 Installing the CodeWhisperer extension into VS Code

Installing the CodeWhisperer Extension into VS Code is similar to installing the Copilot extension. This approach is uniform, which is the nature of extensions. Here are the steps:

1 Click the Extension tab, and search for AWS Toolkit. Once you have located the correct extension, click Install (see figure C.1).

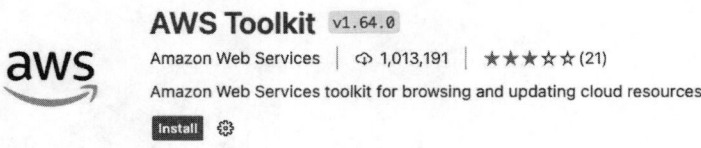

AWS Toolkit `v1.64.0`

Amazon Web Services | ⓓ 1,013,191 | ★ ★ ★ ☆ (21)

Amazon Web Services toolkit for browsing and updating cloud resources

Install ⚙

Figure C.1   The details of the AWS Toolkit with the Install button

2 Once the extension is installed, click the AWS tab on the left side of VS Code to display the Developer Tools menu. Click the Select a Connection option (see figure C.2).

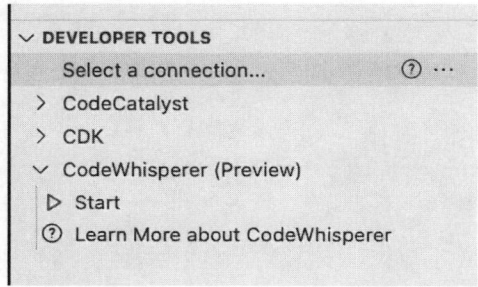

Figure C.2   The Developer Tools menu of the AWS Toolkit tab. Note that in addition to the Select a Connection option, there is an option for CodeWhisperer.

3 Choosing Select a Connection for the first time opens a dropdown in the center-top of VS Code. Select "Use a personal email to sign up and sign in with AWS Builder ID" (see figure C.3).

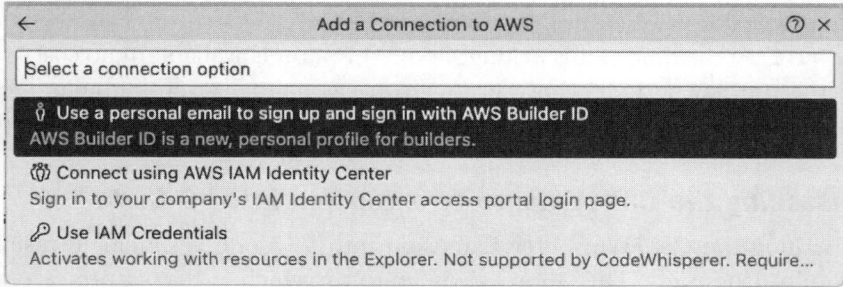

Figure C.3   The dropdown to select how you will connect to the AWS CodeWhisperer service

4 A dialog box appears with an access code (see figure C.4). Copy this code, and then click the Copy Code and Proceed button.

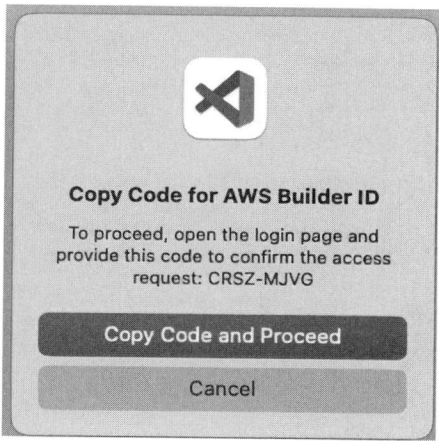

Figure C.4   **You need a personalized access code to register your VS Code instance with AWS and CodeWhisperer.**

5 VS Code will ask your permission to open the Amazon AWS website. Click Open (see figure C.5).

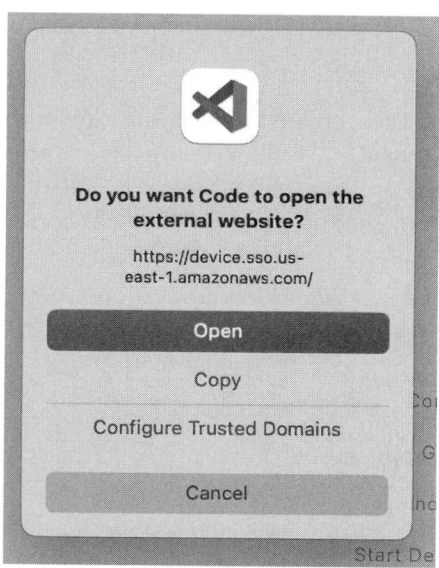

Figure C.5   **VS Code requires explicit permission to proceed to the AWS website.**

6 Once VS Code has your permission, your default web browser will open to the AWS website. AWS will ask you to enter your email address (it recommends using your personal email address; see figure C.6).

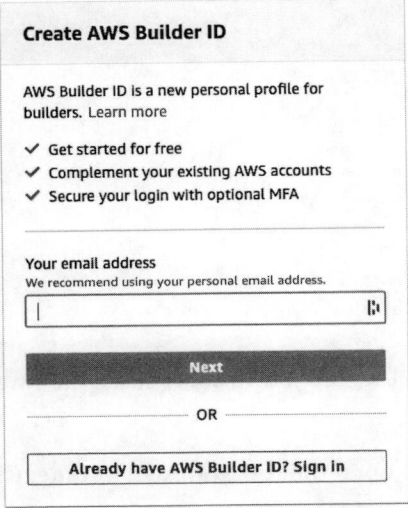

Figure C.6   Once you have your personalized access code and navigate to the AWS website, you will be asked to create an account or log in.

7 When you have successfully logged in or created an account, AWS will prompt you to allow permission to access your data. You are expressly granting permission to build context from the code in your IDE editor. Without this context, CodeWhisperer cannot perform its magic. You should click the Allow button (see figure C.7).

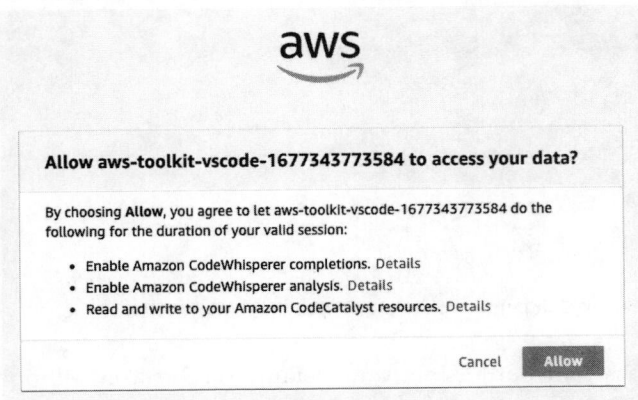

Figure C.7   CodeWhisperer needs your permission to access the code in your editor. Once it has that permission, it can make code suggestions.

8 With your permission, CodeWhisperer is now ready to go. You will receive a confirmation (see figure C.8).

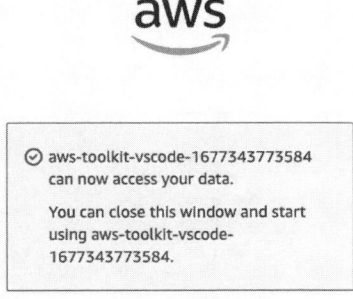

Figure C.8   AWS has registered your account, and you are ready to continue.

9 You must review and affirm the Amazon CodeWhisperer Terms of Service (see figure C.9). If you agree to these terms, click the Accept and Turn On Code-Whisperer button.

Figure C.9   Review the terms of service carefully. Then, if you agree, click the button affirming that you agree.

CodeWhisperer is now ready to use in VS Code.

C.2   *Installing the CodeWhisperer plug-in in PyCharm*

The process of installing the CodeWhisperer Plugin in PyCharm is very similar to the process of installing the extension in VS Code. The steps are the same, but the menus differ slightly. If you read the last section, you are well-armed to tackle this section. Even if you did not read the previous section, we will walk through the process, making it straightforward and painless. Follow these steps:

1   Open Preferences (on a Mac) or Options (on Windows), and click the Plugins tab. Search for "AWS Toolkit," and when you have found it, click the Install button (see figure C.10).

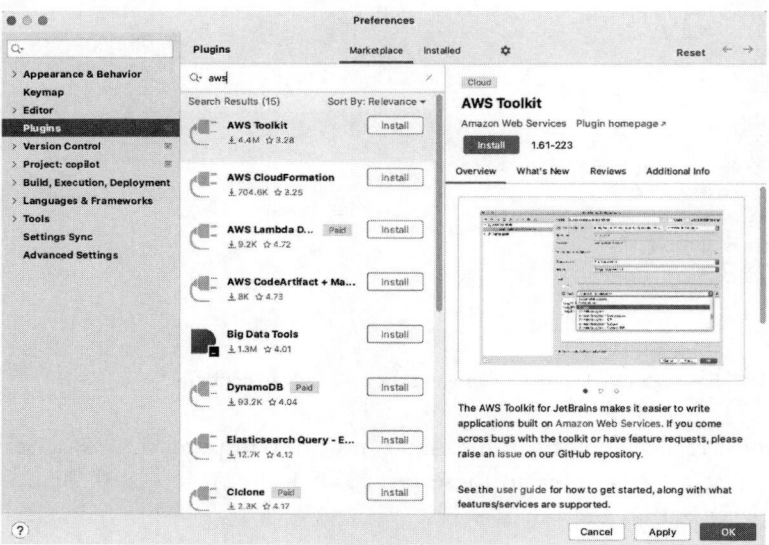

Figure C.10   The Plugins tab after we searched for and found AWS Toolkit

2   After you complete the plug-in installation, click the AWS Toolkit tab in the bottom-left quadrant of PyCharm (see figure C.11). This will bring up the developer tools and allow you to create a new connection to AWS.

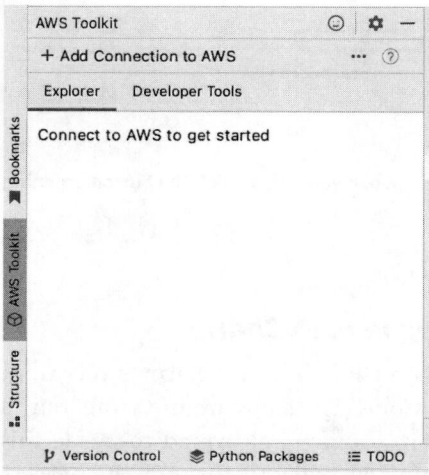

Figure C.11   The AWS Toolkit tab allows you to connect to AWS and start and pause CodeWhisperer.

3 Click + Add Connection to AWS. Doing so launches a dialog box asking you to select how to connect to AWS and which credentials to use. Choose "Use a personal email to sign up and sign in with AWS Builder ID" and click Connect (see figure C.12).

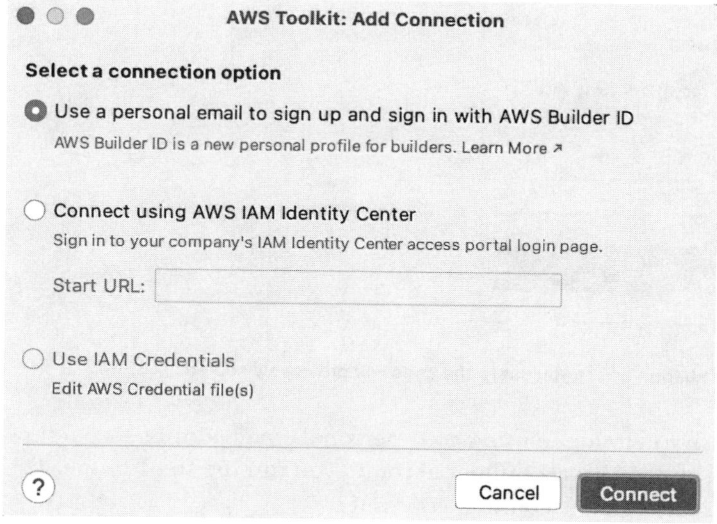

Figure C.12 **Dialog asking you to select how you will connect to AWS**

4 PyCharm will launch another dialog containing a personal access code (see figure C.13). You need to copy this code, because you must authorize AWS to access the data in your PyCharm editor. Click Open and Copy Code.

Figure C.13 **This dialog contains your personalized code and the button to continue.**

5 Your default browser will open and navigate to the AWS website, where there is a window to paste your access code (see figure C.14). Enter this code, and click Next.

Figure C.14   The web form where you paste the code you previously copied

6   AWS will ask you to log in using your personal email address (see figure C.15). If you do not already have a Builder account, you can register for one. Then, either log in or create a new account to continue.

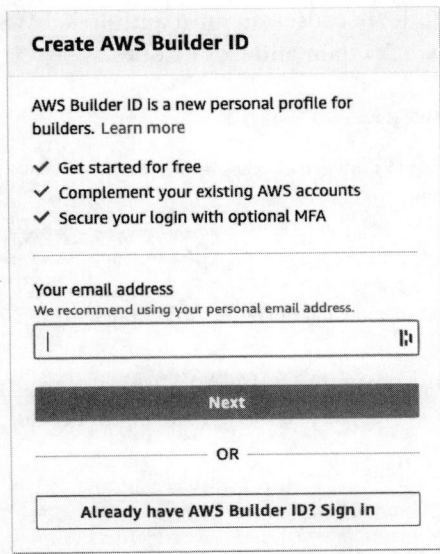

Figure C.15   You can log in to an existing Builder account or register for a new one.

7 We are nearing the end of this process and will be using CodeWhisperer before you know it. You will find that the effort is well worth it. All that is left is to authorize AWS to collect specific (and limited) personal data: your email address and the context of your editor (see figure C.16). Then, click Allow to continue.

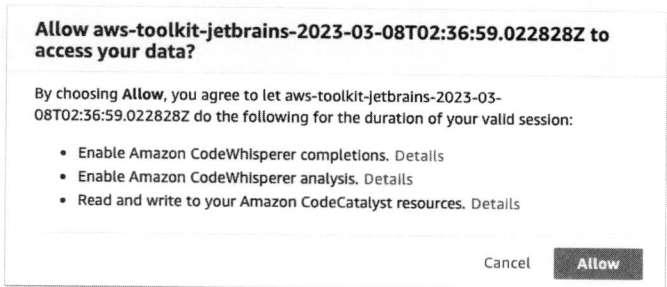

Figure C.16   AWS needs your permission to collect information so that CodeWhisperer can provide suggestions.

8 You will receive confirmation that the AWS Toolkit, which includes CodeWhisperer, has been authorized for use in PyCharm (see figure C.17).

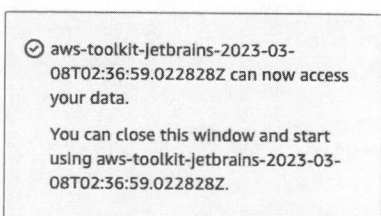

Figure C.17   AWS confirms that CodeWhisperer is ready to go.

Now you can begin to use the tool. First you need to start the CodeWhisperer's code suggestion engine. Go back to the AWS Toolkit tab (bottom-left by default), click Developer Tools, expand CodeWhisperer, and click Start (see figure C.18).

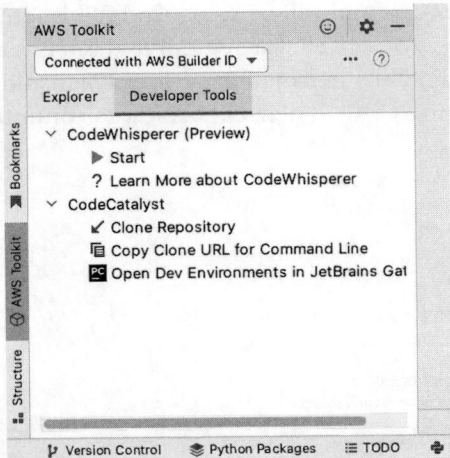

Figure C.18 The AWS Toolkit widget from which you can start (and stop) CodeWhisperer's code suggestion engine

Once you have started CodeWhisperer, the AWS Toolkit plug-in will present you with the Amazon CodeWhisperer Terms of Service to review and accept (or reject) (see figure C.19). To use CodeWhisperer, you must accept these terms, but you should still read them carefully. If you accept, click the Accept and Turn On CodeWhisperer button.

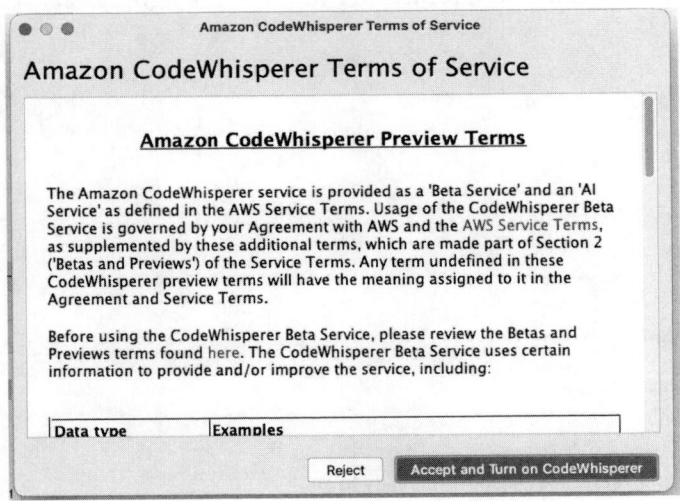

Figure C.19 The Amazon CodeWhisperer Terms of Service. You must accept these terms to use CodeWhisperer.

Now, let's get hacking.

C.3   *Uttering your first words with CodeWhisperer*

With the setup and preliminaries out of the way, let's build a basic Flask application. In your preferred IDE, create a file called app.py. Next, add the following prompt as a comment in the file. Just like Copilot, CodeWhisperer accepts prompts as comments:

```
# create a Flask application that has a route to /
# which returns the text "Hello World."
```

When you press Enter after this prompt, CodeWhisperer will suggest an `import` statement (see figure C.20).

Figure C.20   Your first CodeWhisperer suggestion: in this case, an `import` statement

Continue to press Enter and marvel as CodeWhisperer auto-completes the program line by line. You might consider reformatting the code to make it more readable, but it should work without significant issues. You may need to use pip to install Flask: `pip install flask`.

Listing C.1   Complete source code listing (formatted for readability)

```python
# create a Flask application that has a route to /
# which returns the text "Hello World."
from flask import Flask

app = Flask(__name__)


@app.route('/')
def hello_world():
    return 'Hello World

if __name__ == '__main__':
    app.run()
```

Run this application. Your application should be bound to the default port: 5000 (see figure C.21).

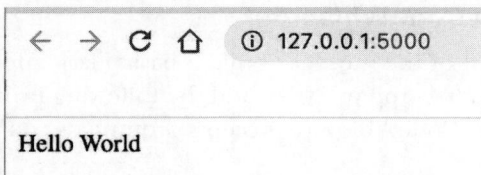

Figure C.21   Your first CodeWhisperer-assisted application, running on the default port

Congratulations! You now have another tool in your AI-assisted toolbelt. You are ready to continue your journey into high(er) productivity.

index